EGYPTIAN DECORATIVE ART

W. M. FLINDERS PETRIE

DOVER PUBLICATIONS, INC.
Mineola, New York

Published in Canada by General Publishing Company, Ltd., 30 Lesmill Road, Don Mills, Toronto, Ontario.

Bibliographical Note

This Dover edition, first published in 1999, is an unabridged and unaltered republication of the work first published in 1895 by G. P. Putnam's Sons, New York.

Library of Congress Cataloging-in-Publication Data

Petrie, W. M. Flinders (William Matthew Flinders), Sir, 1853–1942.
    Egyptian decorative art / W. M. Flinders Petrie.
        p. cm.
    Originally published: New York : G. P. Putnam's Sons, 1895.
    Includes index.
    ISBN 0-486-40907-4 (pbk.)
      1. Decoration and ornament—Egypt. I. Title.

NK1190.P5 1999
745.4'4932 21—dc21   99-042980

Manufactured in the United States of America
Dover Publications, Inc., 31 East 2nd Street, Mineola, N.Y. 11501

CONTENTS

—◆◇◆—

CHAPTER I

SOURCES OF DECORATION

CHAPTER II

GEOMETRICAL DECORATION

v

116889

CHAPTER III

NATURAL DECORATION

CONTENTS

CHAPTER IV

STRUCTURAL DECORATION

CONTENTS

CHAPTER V

SYMBOLIC DECORATION

ABBREVIATIONS

C. M.   Champollion, Monuments.
Duem.   Duemichen Hist. Inschr.
F. P. coll.   Flinders Petrie collection.
Goodyear.   Grammar of the lotus.
H. S.   Historical Scarabs (Petrie).
I.   Illahun (Petrie).
K.   Kahun (Petrie).
L. D.   Lepsius Denkmaler.
P. and C.   Perrot and Chipiez, Egypt.
P. and C. Ass.   Perrot and Chipiez, Assyria.
P. I.   Petrie, Illahun.
P. M.   Petrie, Medum.
P.   (Prisse, Art ; numbers refer to numbering in Edwards
Prisse. (Library copy, plates being issued unnumbered.
P. Mon.   Prisse, Monuments.
R. C.   Rosellini, Mon. Civili.
R. S.   Rosellini, Mon. Storici.
Schuck.   Schuckhardt's, Schliemann.
T. A.   Tell el Amarna (Petrie).
Tanis.   Tanis (Petrie).
W. M. C.   Wilkinson, Manners and Customs.

The shading of the figures is according to heraldic colours :
‖ red, = blue, \ green, ∥ purple, ▦ yellow.

CHAPTER I

THE SOURCES OF DECORATION

IN dealing with the subject of decorative art in Egypt, it is needful to begin by setting some bounds to a study which might be made to embrace almost every example of ancient work known to us in that land. The Egyptian treatment of everything great and small was so strongly decorative that it is hard to exclude an overwhelming variety of considerations. But here it is proposed to limit our view to the historical development of the various motives or elements of decoration. The larger questions of the æsthetic scheme of design, of the meaning of ornament—symbolic or religious, of the value and effect of colour, of the relations of parts, we can but glance at occasionally in passing ; in another branch, the historical connection of Egyptian design with that of other countries, the prospect is so tempting and so valuable, that we may linger a little at each of these bye-ways to note where the turning occurs and to what it leads. As I have said, all Egyptian design was strongly decorative. The love of form and of drawing was perhaps a greater force with the Egyptians than with any other people. The early Babylonians and the Chinese had, like the Egyptians, a pictorial writing ; but step by step they soon dropped the picture altogether in favour of the easier abbreviation of it. The Egyptian, on the contrary, never lost sight of his original picture ; and however much his current hand altered, yet for four or five thousand years he still maintained his

true hieroglyphic pictures. They were modified by taste and fashion, even in some cases
their origin was forgotten, yet the artistic
form was there to the very end.

But the hieroglyphs were not only a
writing, they were a decoration in them-
selves. Their position was ruled by their
effect as a frieze, like the beautiful tile
borders of Cufic inscription on Arab architecture; and we never see in Egypt the
barbarous cutting of an inscription across
figure sculptures as is so common in Assyria.
The arrangement of the groups of hieroglyphs was also ruled by their decorative
effect. Signs were often transposed in order
to group them more harmoniously together
in a graceful scheme ; and many sounds had
two different signs, one tall, another wide,
which could be used indifferently (at least in
later times) so as to combine better with the
forms which adjoined them. In short, the

Egyptian with true decorative instinct clung to his pictorial writing, modified it to adapt it to his designs, and was rewarded by having the most beautiful writing that ever existed, and one which excited and gave scope to his artistic tastes on every monument. This is but one illustration of the inherent power for design and decoration which made the Egyptian the father of the world's ornament.

In other directions we see the same ability. In the adaptation of the scenes of peace or of war to the gigantic wall surfaces of the pylons and temples; in the grand situations chosen for the buildings, from the platform of cliffs for the pyramids at Gizeh, to the graceful island of Philæ; in the profusion of ornament on the small objects of daily life, which yet never appear inappropriate until a debased period;—in all these different manners the Egyptian showed a variety of capacity in design and decoration which has not been exceeded by any other people.

The question of the origination of patterns at one or more centres has been as disputed as the origination of man himself from one or more stocks. Probably some patterns may have been re-invented in different ages and countries ; but, as yet, we have far less evidence of re-invention than we have of copying. It is easy to pre-suppose a repeated invention of designs, but we are concerned with what has been, and not with what might have been. Practically it is very difficult, or almost impossible, to point out decoration which is proved to have originated independently, and not to have been copied from the Egyptian stock. The influences of the modes of work in weaving and basket-work have had much to do with the uniformity of patterns in different countries ; apparently starting from different motives, the patterns when subject to the same structural influences have resulted in very similar ornaments. This complicates the question undoubtedly ; and until we have much more research on the history of design, and an abundance of dated examples, it will be unsafe to dogmatise one way or the other. So far, however, as evidence at present goes, it may be said that—in the Old World at least—there is a presumption that all the ornament of the types of Egyptian designs is lineally descended from those designs. Mr. Goodyear has brought so much evidence for this, that—whether we agree with all his views or not—his facts are reasonably convincing on the general descent of classic ornament from Egyptian, and of Indian and

Mohammedan from the classical, and even of Eastern Asian design from the Mohammedan sources. A good illustration of the penetrating effect of design is seen in a most interesting work on the prehistoric bronzes of Minusinsk in Central Asia, near the sources of the Yenesei river, and equidistant from Russia and from China, from the Arctic Ocean and from the Bay of Bengal. Here in the very heart of Asia we might look for some original design. But yet it is easy to see the mingled influences of the surrounding lands, and to lay one's finger on one thing that might be Norse, on another that might be Chinese, or another Persian. If, then, the tastes of countries distant one or two thousand miles in different directions can be seen moulding an art across half a continent, how much more readily can we credit the descent of design along the well-known historical lines of intercourse. The same thing on a

lesser scale is seen in the recent publication
of the prehistoric bronzes of Upper Bavaria ;
in these the designs are partly Italic, partly
Mykenaean. If forms were readily re-invented again and again independently, why
should we not find in Bavaria some of the
Persian or Chinese types ? Nothing of the
kind is seen, but the forms and decoration
are distinctly those of the two countries from
which the ancient makers presumably obtained
their arts and civilisation. Yet again, to come
to historical times, the elegant use of the
angle of a third of a right angle so generally
in Arab art, is very distinct and characteristic.
Yet if patterns were continually re-invented,
how is it that no one else hit on this simple
element for thousands of years ? The very
fact that the locality and date of an object of
unknown origin can be so closely predicted
by its style and feeling in design, is the best
proof how continuous is the history and evo-

lution of ornament, and how little new invention has to do with it—in short, how difficult
it is to man to be really original.

Now we can see a source for most of our
familiar elements of design in the decoration
which was used in Egypt long before any
example that is known to us outside of that
land. And it is to Egypt then that we are
logically bound to look as the origin of these
motives. If, then, we seek the source of
most of the various elements of the decoration
which covers our walls, our floors, our dishes,
our book-covers, and even our railway stations,
we must begin by studying Egypt.

As our object is the history and evolution
of the various elements of decoration, we
may classify these elements under four divi-
sions. There is the simplest geometrical
ornament of lines and spirals and curves, and

of surfaces divided by these into squares and circles. There is the natural ornament of copying feathers, flowers, plants, and animals, There is structural ornament which results from the structural necessities of building and of manufacture : these often result in the perpetuation of defects or copies of defects, like the circle stamped in the plain end of meat tins which is made to imitate the circular patch soldered on to the other end, so trying to establish a balance of appearance. Many architectural devices and difficulties are perpetuated for us in this way long after the original purpose has passed away ; such as the cylindrical bosses projecting from the walls in Moslem architecture, which imitate the projecting ends of pillars torn from ruins and built into the wall, though rather too long for the position. The origin and the imitation can be seen side by side at Jeru-salem. Structural ornament is therefore often of the greatest historical value as pointing to a condition of things that has since vanished.

Lastly, there is symbolic ornament. Some now claim most decoration as having some symbolic or religious meaning; of that I shall say nothing, as it is but an hypothesis. But there is no question of the symbolical intention of many constantly repeated ornaments in Egyptian work, as the globe and wings, the scarab, or the various hieroglyphs with well-known meanings which are interwoven into many designs.

CHAPTER II

GEOMETRICAL DECORATION

The Line.

ONE of the simplest and the earliest
kinds of ornament that we find is the
zigzag line, which occurs on the oldest
tombs, 4000 B.C. So simple is this, that
it might be supposed that every possible
variety of it would be soon played out.
Yet, strange to say, two of the simplest
modifications are not found till a couple
of thousand years after the plain zigzag
had been used. The wavy line in curves
instead of angular waves is not found till
the XVIIIth dynasty, or about 1500 B.C. ;
while the zigzag with spots in the spaces

is equally late, and is generally foreign to
Egypt.

The plain repeated
zigzag line is used

1.—VI. dyn., L.D., II. 98.

down to late times, but generally with
variety in colour to give it interest. From
the earliest times this was symmetrically
doubled, so as to give a row of squares
with parallel borders ;
or with repeated zig-
zag borders in alter-

2.—IV. dyn., Mery, Louvre.

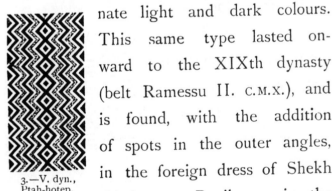

nate light and dark colours.
This same type lasted on-
ward to the XIXth dynasty
(belt Ramessu II. c.m.x.), and
is found, with the addition
of spots in the outer angles,
in the foreign dress of Shekh

3.—V. dyn.,
Ptah-hotep,
Perrot XIII.

Absha, at Benihasan, in the

XIIth dynasty.

A later stage was to repeat the squares

with varieties of colour;
and also to introduce
details into the squares,
and so make them com-
pound patterns, as in
the XVIIth dynasty at
El Kab, where the

4.—Prisse, Art. 84.

sequence of the blue, green, and red lines
makes a brilliant effect from these simple
elements.   Not only a square, but also a
hexagon, was worked into the same design.
This, from the nature of it, suggests a
rush-work screen, and
probably it was plaited
with rushes in three
directions, and hence
the production of this
particular angle. The
previous zigzag pat-

5.—L.D., 11. 130.

terns all suggest weaving; and in some in
Ptah-hotep's tomb (Vth dyn.) closely woven

and complex zigzag patterns are shown
which are evidently copied from textiles,
as we shall see further on in the chequer
patterns.

The use of spots for filling in corners was
foreign to the Egyptian. We first find it in the
garments of the Amu, or people of northern
Arabia, in the XIIth dynasty. Till then a spot
is never seen, except for the centre of a square;
but the Amu dresses
are covered with spots
in every space, and
even along the bars

6. – XII. dyn. Amu dress.

and stripes of colour. The same is seen on
the later dresses of the Amu in the XIXth
dynasty, and also in the
dress of the Phœnicians,

7.—XVIII., Keft dress.
C.M. excl.

or Keft people. It re-
curs on the foreign vases

8.—XX. Vase, C.M. cclix.

probably brought in from the Ægean ; and
it is only found in Egyptian products

during the XVIIIth dynasty, when foreign
fashions prevailed, though it is but rare
then. Hence we may fairly set aside
this use of spots as a foreign or Asiatic
element, akin to the filling in of spaces on
early Greek vases with rosettes and other
small ornaments.

The zigzag line only became changed into
a rounded wavy line in the later time of
the XVIIIth dynasty.

9.—XVIII., P. i. xvii. 7.

This probably results
from the earlier patterns being all direct
copies of textiles which maintained recti-
linear patterns ; but when the same came
to be used on pottery (as above), or on
metal work (shield border, L.D. iii. 64),
then curves were readily
introduced. On a golden
bowl repeated waves are

10.—XVIII. Vase,
R.C. lvii.

shown, deepened so as to receive further
figures.

The Spiral.

The spiral, or scroll, is one of the greatest elements of Egyptian decoration; it is only second to the lotus in importance, and shares with that the origination of a great part of the ornament of the world. The source of the spiral and its meaning are alike uncertain. It has been attributed to a development of the lotus pattern; but it is known in every variety of treatment without any trace of connection with the lotus. It has been said to represent the wanderings of the soul; why, or how, is not specified; nor why some souls should wander in circular spirals, others in oval spirals, some in spirals with ends, others in spirals that are endless. And what a soul was supposed to do when on the track of a triple diverging spiral, how it could go two ways at once, or which line it was to take — all these difficulties suggest that the theorist's soul was on a remarkable spiral.

The subject of spirals fall into two groups. The older group by far are the scarabs, which contain spirals on a limited and small field ; the other group are those continuous patterns on ceilings, furniture, &c., which are capable of indefinite extension by repetition. As the scarabs are far the older examples, there is a presumption that spirals may have even originated on scarab designs ; and the hesitating and simple manner of the oldest instances on scarabs indeed seems as if the engravers were merely filling a

 space, and not copying any well-known pattern. The earliest that can be certainly dated is one of

11.—F.P. coll.

Assa, of the Vth dynasty, on which a
bordering line is interrupted at the ends
and turned in to fill the space on either
side of the name. From the cramped way
in which this is done, and the want of uniformity in the spirals, it seems as if no
regular pattern were in view, but only the
need of avoiding an unsightly gap in the
design. We next see spirals
used in the same way to fill
up at the sides of the inscription on the scarabs of Pepy,
without any attempt to connect

12.—F.P.
them into a continuous pattern ;
and on the scarabs of Ma·abra,
probably soon after, the same
loose spirals are seen thrown
in to fill up. In none of these
13.—F.P.
cases is the ornament anything but the
means of supplementing the required inscription ; nothing is arranged for the sake

of it, and it is treated as a mere after-thought. Nor is it until the XIIth dynasty that any continuous spiral design can be dated. For over a thousand years, then, the spiral is only to be found as an accessory on scarabs, a fact which strongly suggests that it originated in this manner.

Before describing spirals further, it is needful to settle some definite names for their varieties. Where the lines are coiled closely in a circular curve, as in Assa's scarab, they may be termed *coils;* where lengthened out, as in Pepy's, we may term them *hooks;* where lengthy in the body between the turns, as in Ma·abra's, they are rather *links*. Where the line is broken at each spiral, as in all the above, it is a *chain* of spirals ; but where the same line is maintained unbroken throughout it is a *continuous* spiral, and these are found in all varieties of coils, hooks, or links.

Sometimes the continuous line has separate ends, but more usually it is *endless*, returning into itself.   These terms will suffice to distinguish the varieties, and enable us to speak of a spiral with definiteness.

These detached spirals continued in use in the XIIth dynasty, generally as loose links, often not hooking together, as in this of Usertesen II.   In the XVIIIth dynasty this is still found as a

14.—Louvre.

general surface ornament on the boat covers of Hatshepsut at Deir al Bahri, and on the base of a Kohl vase in the Ghizeh Museum.

15.—Ghizeh.

But the spiral was developed, apparently under Usertesen I., into a chain of coils, which are drawn with great beauty

Fig. 16.   F.P coll.   Fig. 17.

and regularity. Such care indicates that the design was a novelty, which was not yet stereotyped and reproduced as a matter of course. In no later reign were spirals ever so beautifully and perfectly executed. This type was revived under Amenhotep II. (H. S. 1097). In about the XIIth dynasty it was combined with the lotus in

18.—Turin.

perhaps the most perfect design that remains on any scarab—a continuous coil with flowers and buds in the spaces. But it was felt that the spirals all round occupied too much of the field, so the top and bottom were left free for inscribing, and the ornament was limited to the sides, as in this chain of hook pattern of Usertesen I. This design, with the line continued around the top as well as the base, was the staple

19.—F.P.

decoration of the private scarabs of the XIIth–XIIIth dynasties, many of which
are of great beauty.
Both types are found,
but the hook pattern

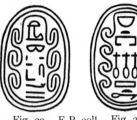

Fig. 20.   F.P. coll.   Fig. 21.

is more usual than the coils.

In the finest work, however, the line
is made endless, a
single continuous
line forming the
whole pattern, as
in the endless hook

Fig. 22.   F.P. coll.   Fig. 23.

pattern of Setmes, and the endless coil
pattern of Ptaherduen.

In the few spiral
scarabs of later
times the pattern is
not only placed at
the sides, but is

24.—Paris.   25.—F.P,

carried all round, as we see in that of

Amenhotep I. and one of Ramessu II., which latter is the latest spiral pattern known on scarabs.

The long links were seldom used in

26.—F.P. coll.

continuous patterns around scarabs, as in this, but were more usually employed for independent spiral patterns without any inscriptions.

After serving as adjuncts to inscriptions,

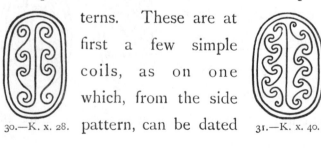

27.—F.P. coll.　　28.—K. x. 50.　　29.—I. viii. 69.

the spirals became elaborated as sole pat-

terns. These are at first a few simple coils, as on one which, from the side pattern, can be dated

30.—K. x. 28.　　　　　　　31.—K. x. 40.

to about the VIIIth dynasty. These, when elaborated with more coils or links, sometimes developed to great length.

Such patterns required but little ingenuity, and it is rather in the design of continuous spirals that the Egyptian showed his skill. The problem was how to arrange a number of coils in a sym-

32.—K. x. 17.

metrical system uniformly covering the surface of the scarab, and yet to connect them in a true series. This was done in various ways, usually by introducing long loop lines around the edge. One of the simplest type is— In another a cross pattern is formed which is entirely of

33.—F.P.

C coils, like frequent patterns

34.—I. x. 176.   at Mykenæ.

Others fill up by establishing a repeat-

ing pattern, which might be indefinitely multiplied, as —
and the difficulty is avoided on a large silver scarab of early date by

35.—F.P.

36.—F.P.

37.—F.P.

shortening the links to allow of the connecting line passing the ends.

This difficulty of designing good covering patterns out of true continous lines probably led to the evasion of introducing false links. Thus what would otherwise have been an opening in the middle was barred across.

38.—I. x. 158.

39.—K. x 27.

40.—K. x. 48.

Some beautiful effects were obtained by

this false barring, which does not, at first sight, catch the eye, as in these two examples.

41.—F.P.   42.—F.P.

In the latter, two complete lop-sided spiral groups are joined by long false links around the outside. Another favourite device which often occurs is also compounded of lop-sided groups, or rather of a cross group, like Fig. 43, with four false links joining in the middle.

43.—F.P.

Some other devices did not profess to cover the whole field, as in Figs. 44 and 45; and sometimes two separate

44.—I. x. 144.

45.—I. x. 155.   46.—F.P.   47.—Turin.

lines of design were superposed, a single element of the same design being found as late as Tahutmes III.

The spiral had thus been greatly developed as a detached ornament for a small surface ; but in architecture and furniture it was required as a continuous decoration on borders and on large surfaces. Hence its development was in many ways different, and—so far as we know—later by a whole cycle of history than the development on the scarabs. On those small objects it started in the Vth dynasty, became fully elaborated in the XIIth, is common in the XIIIth, and only very occasionally found in the XVIIIth, disappearing altogether in the XIXth. On walls and furniture it is rare in the XIIth dynasty, becomes usual in the XVIIIth, flourishes in the XIXth and XXth, and is decadent in the XXVIth.

The simplest form in which it is found is as a chequered pattern series of S spirals, apparently on cloths thrown over boat cabins. On Hat-shepsut's boat the spirals are close together (Duem. XXI.) ; but rather later, on the

Fig. 48.

boat of Neferhetep, they are spread with chequers of red and blue between them (W.M.C. lxvii.).

About the same period they appear as a continuous coil pattern in relief on the columns of the *harim* well at Tell el Amarna. The spiral in relief being in yellow, it pro-

Fig. 49.

bably was copied from a jewellery pattern in which a strip of gold was twisted into spirals, and the spaces filled with squares of coloured stones or pastes, judging from the analogy of the inlaid capitals. This example being earlier than most of the spiral decorations of surfaces may thus open our eyes to the meaning of some such designs ; and, in general, a close continuous coil returning on itself may well be a copy of a strip of sheet metal, doubled, and rolled up.

The next stage is where continuous lines

of spiral patterns are placed side by side, and other patterns developed in the spaces between them. Sometimes the intervening

50.— P. 85. 1.

patterns become so complex as to overshadow the mere spirals, as in the splendid ceiling of Neferhotep, in the XVIIIth dynasty. And in this the far more complex quadruple spiral begins to appear, as we shall see presently.

The lines of spirals were not only placed parallel, but were also crossed. For some reason this type was never well developed, but remained one of the coldest and most mechanical of all, look-

51.—P. 85.

ing in the later stage of the XXVIth dynasty like a most debased wall paper.

But the glory of Egyptian line decoration was in the quadruple spiral, of which the most elementary

52.—C.M. cclv.

example is on a boat cover as late as the

XXth dynasty (Ramessu IV.); though it has passed through this stage long before that time—if indeed this may not be re-garded as a degraded simplification of it. It is also sometimes rhombic in plan.

53.—P. 86.

From this was developed a peculiar pattern by the omission of the lines which define the spirals, thus reducing it to a system of rows of hollow-sided quadrangles without any apparent connection. The main development of the quadruple spiral was with

54.—XIIth dyn. R.C. lxxii.

rosettes or lotus filling the hollow squares.

This became a stock subject with the

Egyptian, and from thence a main pattern
in other lands. The fill-
ing in was either a flower
pattern or a rosette, which
might be either a flower
or a leather pattern, as we
shall notice further on.

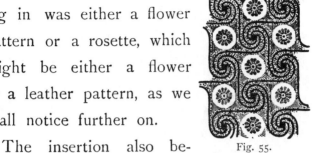

Fig. 55.

The insertion also be-
came more complex, four lotus flowers being
placed in each angle of the hollow square;
and the spirals being
more heavily developed,
in order to gain enough
space for complexity in
the squares between
them. Such a system
could hardly be carried

56.—P. 86.

further, but reached its limits; like the
limit of size in the Great Hall of Karnak,
where the columns occupy too large an
area in proportion to the clear space.

In another direction, however, the spiral

57.—P. 80.

blossomed further, in the parallel lines of spiral pattern. These became developed by introducing link lines so as to form a quintuple spiral, which was further complicated by lotus flowers and buds in the hollows and recesses.

In this direction, again, the Egyptians had reached the limit beyond which more detail would be merely confusing. By careful use of colour to separate the various parts, these complex patterns remain clear and pleasing in spite of their richness of detail.

The quadruple spiral had, however, another development, of C links, which is rather too formal to be beautiful, and lacks the flamboyant grace of the chains of

spirals.   Still   it   has   a   simple   dignity,
related   to   the   scarab
spirals   rather   than   the
flowing   surface   patterns.
This   became   formalised
into   a   torturing   kind   of
design,   which   can   only
be   described   as   "cur-

58.—P. 85.

sedly   ingenious."   By   simplifying   the   previous   pattern,   a   wave
was   invented   which
was   equal   in   each
direction,   and   four   of
these   were   crossed   in
a   manner   which   nothing   but   bold   colouring
could   make   intelligible.

59.—P. 83.

The   fret   patterns   are   all   modifications   of
corresponding   spirals.   The   cause   of   such

change is obviously the influence of weav-

60.—L.D. II. 57.

ing. As early as the Vth dynasty we find a fret of rhombic form in basket-work in the screen behind the figure of Ptah·bau·nefer, at Gizeh. The angles show that the plaiting was in three direc- tions, as we saw in the basket-work pat- tern at Benihasan (Fig. 3). But frets in general are very rare until a late period, and they doubtless depend on the adapta- tion of spirals to textiles. We see no trace of the fret in the Mykenaean art, the spiral there being figured on stone or metal, while the women wore flounced dresses with scale pattern. But in the pre-Persian age fret pattern weaving in borders was the standard design, as we see on the coloured robes of the Parthenon statues; and immediately after that the stiffest of square frets swarms over Greek art, to the exclusion of the graceful spirals and scroll borders.

The chains of links were copied in the

61.—P. 82.

62.—P. 83.

fret pattern with no difference except in squaring up the curves. The same is true of the quad- ruple spirals, which appear likewise modi- fied; and this change seems to have led to

63.—P. 83.

another simplified form, which is on the

same idea as the torturing design (Fig. 59), but which is less ingenious, and is still possible as an ornament.

So far we have viewed only the course of Egyptian design, nor can we travel far outside of it within these pages. Moreover, as it is dated before any other such decoration in other countries, it is well to view its course as a whole without confusing it with the various fragments borrowed from it by other lands. Yet we may well turn now to see the beginning of the course of European decoration at Mykenae,

64.—Schuck. 256.

and observe its close contact with that of Egypt. The spiral is the main element of pre-historic decoration in Greece; the parallel chains of links occur almost exactly as we have already seen them in the pattern of Neferhotep, but omitting the inner details added in the spaces.

The quadruple spiral is splendidly shown in the ceiling of Orchomenos, with a lotus flower in each space; also as a simpler form without any filling in of the squares on the grave stele (Schuck. 146). While even the ox head

65.—Schuck. 290.

with a rosette between the horns, in the grand quintuple spiral pattern (Fig. 57), is strangely paralleled by an ox head of silver with a large rosette on the forehead found at Mykenae (Schuck. 248).

In observing these equivalents it must be noted that whole patterns with their detail are taken over complete from Egypt. There are none of the series of intermediate steps which we have traced in the mother country ; and where a simpler form occurs it is known to be later, the grave steles being after the age of the great ceiling.   Thus there is the surest sign of a borrowed art, apart from the facts of the exact resemblances we have noted.   Of course the Mykenaean designs are mostly influenced by the taste of the race.   Many of them are strongly European, and might be of Celtic or Norse work, as has been shown by Mr. Arthur Evans ; but the source of the designs lies in the two thousand years' start which Egypt had before Europe awoke.

A separate form of the spiral pattern is that used for borders, otherwise called the wave or maeander, which merged into the guilloche.   Although the chain of coils on the scarab borders in the XIIth dynasty may be regarded as a wave border, yet no example is known of this border on other objects until the XVIIIth dynasty. At that time it appears as often on foreign objects as on Egyptian, and the only instance of the guilloche is on foreign dress. Hence this development of the spiral idea may well be due more to the Aegean civilisation than to that of Egypt. This will agree with the occurrence of the guilloche on black pottery

Fig. 66.

from Kahun, which class, wherever it can be dated, is found to belong to the XIIth–XIIIth dynasty. The metal vases shown on the monuments of the XVIIIth–XXth dynasties are mostly foreign tributes, and on them the wave border is

67.—R.C. lvii.

68.—P. 97. 105.

69.—R.C. lxii.

common, merging into a twisted rope bor-

70.—R.C. lvii.

der, which is also found — though rarely —on scarabs of the Middle Kingdom.

In Egyptian use this border is seldom found. A box in the Louvre had a line of long links; and a scroll edge appears to

Fig. 71.

Fig. 72.

the standard of Ramessu II. But more usually the scroll is associated with the lotus, as in these—

73.—P. 89.

74.—P. 89.

The innumerable adaptations of this in Greek and later designs are familiar enough to us.

The influence of weaving has been very great upon these wave borders. As I have before noticed, the woven borders, reducing the pattern to a fret, are shown on the pre-Persian statuary at Athens, and precede the most common and oft-repeated use of the fret or key pattern borders in Greece, and thence in all classical, medi-æval, and modern times.

Another type of border, which may be connected with this, is found in the Ramesside age. As it occurs as stitching on leather, and is well  adapted to quilting or

75.—R.C. cxxi.

sewing bands together, it may well have been derived from that; but it is also found on metal work, with which it does not seem to be connected by origin.

76.—R.C. lxi.

77.—P. 103.

The source of chequer patterns is unmistakably in plaiting and weaving. On the oldest monuments the basket sign, *neb*, is chequered in different colours; so are also the baskets of farm produce carried by the servants, as shown in the tombs. The modern Nubian basket-work is well known for the many patterns which it bears like the ancient Egyptian. The chequer pattern is found in every period in Egypt, and is perhaps most common in the latest forms on the sides of thrones in the Ptolemaic age. In the Old Kingdom many varieties were in use. The plain chequers of red or black with white, the squares filled with black and red crosses on a green and yellow chequer; or diagonal square patterns

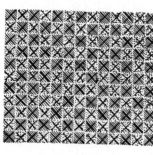

78.—P. and C. xiii.

developed by lines of
chequers, which are often
not square but elongated,
thus forming general and
wide-spread patterns

79.—P. and C. xiii.

which attract the eye on large
surfaces. These are best seen
in the tomb of Ptahhotep
(P. and C. xiii.) and in that
of Peheniuka (L.D. i. 41),
both of the Vth dynasty, at
Sakkara.

80 —L.D. i. 41.

In the Middle Kingdom we find chequers
covered with bars of
colour, red and green,
at Benihasan.

81.—L.D. ii. 130.

Under the empire
chequers are less
common owing to
the greater develop-
ment of more elabo-

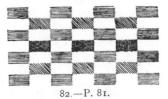

82.—P. 81.

rate decoration. A pleasing variety was formed by lengthening the squares, a change doubtless copied from weaving, where oblong squares serve to break the monotony of the pattern.

In later ages of the Saitic and Greek times the chequer is a common resource,

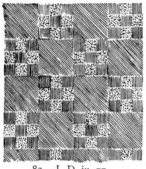

but is seldom treated with originality or grace, and we do not find any new depar- ture or advance in the mechanical execu- tion of the later ex-

83.—L. D. iv. 77.

amples. One slight novelty was the alternation of whole and divided squares of colour, under Claudius.

Somewhat analogous are the net-work patterns. They seem to be probably derived from stitch-pattern over dresses. Though found in the XIIth dynasty they are not usual until the XVIIIth dynasty, and they are generally on the dresses of goddesses. A simple example is on a horse-cloth of Ramesside age, which

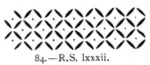

84.—R.S. lxxxii.

shows that these can hardly represent long beads, but rather stitching or quilting. A more elaborate form

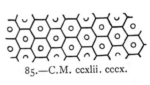

85.—C.M. ccxlii. cccx.

is on the dress of Bast in the tomb of Seti I., in hexagons.

But this design rose to importance when it was introduced as an architectural element in the decora-

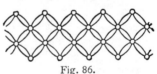

Fig. 86.

tion of columns at Tell el Amarna. There it is coloured yellow, and the spaces are alternate red and blue.

The Egyptians never used circles freely in decoration; no examples are known before the XVIIIth dynasty, and but few then.

The intersecting circles, forming a kind

87.-- P. 79.

of net-work, are found in the XVIIIth dynasty in blue on a yellow ground; and the same occurs in black on blue and red ground, in later times (L.D. I. 41). Besides the rosettes other patterns were introduced into the

88.—P. 84.

89.—P. 86.

spaces, which were coloured red and green alternately. But the most beautiful type was with contiguous circles not intersecting, and each containing four lotus flowers.

The circle, however, never became of importance, probably because it was too stiff and mechanical for the Egyptian, who delighted in the waving spiral patterns and the unlimited variety of lotus developments. It is remarkable that there is not a single example of the circle divided into six, or with six segmental arms, which is so common a motive in Assyria and Syria, and which results so readily from stepping the radius around the circle. This seems to show that the Egyptian did not use compasses at any time, but always worked with a string and points. The absence of a simple and self-evident motive like the sixth of the circle is almost more striking than a peculiar motive being present.

CHAPTER III

NATURAL DECORATION

THOUGH it might be supposed that the imitation of natural forms would be the earliest form of decoration, yet this is not the case. On the contrary, we find the geometrical forms of wave lines, and chequers copied from weaving, and the varieties of the spiral, were the first ornaments of importance in Egypt; while the natural forms of feathers and flowers were not generally imitated till a later time.

One source of simple pattern that has been little noticed is the feather, and the variety of its forms. Fortunately we have

these different forms shown unmistakably
as feathers on the coffins of the Antefs in
the XIth dynasty, before we find them in
common use elsewhere.   Hence we can
have little doubt as to their real origin.
On these coffins the royal mummies are
figured as swathed around in protecting
wings, representing those of Isis at the
sides and of the vulture of Mut on the
head.   The feathers have different forms
according to the part of the wing which
they occupy.   Thus on one coffin we find
all of the following types of feathers :—

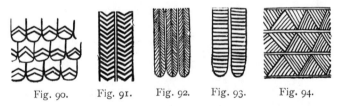

Fig. 90.   Fig. 91.   Fig. 92.   Fig. 93.   Fig. 94.

Now when we have thus been shown
the conventional types which were used to
represent feathers, we can identify these
again in many other places, where pro-

bably the original idea of feather work was entirely lost ; and we have a new light on some representations not yet understood.

On the kings of the XVIIIth–XXth dynasty we often see a wide belt covering the whole stomach, which is decorated with what is commonly called scale pattern. But this occurs in scenes which are not at all war-like, and where no defensive scale armour is likely to be shown—

95.— Amen- hotep I. R.S. xxix.

Amenhotep I. is seated as a god receiving adoration after his death; Amenhotep II. is represented adoring Ra. And in the second case the pattern is identical with the feathers on the Antef coffin. The only conclusion is that these

96.—Amenhotep II. R.S. xxxvii.

represent belts of feather work worn around the body to prevent chill, like the voluminous waist shawl of modern Orientals. Such a feather belt would be admirable for lightness and warmth, but that it is not scale armour is seen from the absence of it in fighting scenes. On the contrary, in the royal campaigning dress another form of feather work is seen in the large wings of feathers which encircle the shoulders (Ramessu II., R.S. lxxxi.).

This feather pattern is also very usual on the sides of thrones, from the XVIIIth dynasty down to the latest times. Here again it is evident that it cannot be scale armour; and a feather rug thrown across the seat, in place of the fur rug otherwise used, is a very likely thing to find in such a position.

We may, then, take this pattern, when

used on dress or on thrones, to represent feather work. But in later times it is also used on very incongruous objects. As early as the XVIIIth dynasty the feather pattern occurs around columns as an architectural ornament (Tell el Amarna), and with the characteristic mark-

97.—P. 79.

ing also about the XIXth dynasty (P. 79); also on metal work (vase, P. 97), where it must be purely an artificial marking.

98.—P.R. lix.

It became elaborated under Seti I., with markings upon it, both on a dress of a god and on a throne-cover. And it became degraded into an unintelligible pattern under Ramessu II., when it appears as the dress of the god Amen.

99.—R.S. lxxix.

In later times the same pattern was

used on columns at Philæ, in an
inverted and very corrupt form.

The other forms of feather
pattern shown on the Antef 100.—L.D. I.
108.
coffin were also found later. But they
merge so readily into mere line patterns
that it is not likely that they were re-
garded as feathers in their later use.
The V pattern is found on the columns
at Tell el Amarna, on belts of the kings
(L.D. III. I), on painted wooden columns
(P. 73), on the harps of Ramessu III.
(P. 114), and many other places.

The use of flowers for ornament is so
natural that their occurrence in the
earliest times is what might be expected.
Yet but few flowers were adopted for
decoration. The lotus is far the com-
monest, after that the papyrus, the daisy,

and the convolvulus, together with the vine and palm, almost complete the material of vegetable designs. There is also, however, what may be called a generic flower ornament — the rosette — which is treated so conventionally that it can hardly receive any precise name. Sometimes in the XVIIIth dynasty it is clearly a daisy, very seldom has it the pointed petals of the lotus; and it fluctuates between the geometrical and the natural so as to defy details. One cause of this is the evident effect of leather work. The coloured leather funereal tent of Isimkheb, found at Deir el Bahri, opens our eyes to a great deal. We there see an elaborate design, descending to long inscriptions of small hieroglyphs, all worked by cutting and stitching of leather. After this we can see in many of the Egyptian designs the influence of leather work; and nowhere is this plainer than in the rosettes. The earliest rosettes we know, those on the head-band of Nefert, at the very beginning of monumental history, are plain discs of colour divided into segments by white lines across them. These are discs of leather secured by radiating threads; and the same are seen in the XVIIIth dynasty, more varied by concentric circles of colours, probably succes-sive superposed discs stitched down one over the other.

101.—
P. 81.

Another stitch ornament is seen on the stuffs used for covering thrones in the XXth dynasty. There star and cross patterns are used which are evidently stitch work or embroi-dery; and in the spaces

102.—P. 116.

103.—P. 116.

are discs of colour with white spots around, probably pieces sewn on by stitches round the edge. On a dress of

Fig. 104.—R.S. lxxxiii. Ramessu II. also are little six-pointed stars, which were doubtless stitch work.

There can be no doubt of the effect that stitching has had on the use of rosettes, but other varieties are probably independent of that. The great series of rosettes is in the moulded glazed ware of Tell el Amarna ; there several dozen varieties are found, varying from four petals to thirty-two. The more elaborate

Fig. 105. of these have an unmistakable daisy centre of yellow in the midst of white petals, and this indicates what was probably the flower in mind for most of them.

The rosette is found in varied use. On metal vases it is very general, and

may either be a separate ornament of
beaten work riveted on, like the rosettes
on the silver ox head at Mykenae, or else
embossed *repoussé* in the metal. Carved
in wood or ivory, rosettes decorated the
furniture; and they are constantly found
as centre ornaments in square patterns,
and along borders with the lotus or other
subject.

In patterns a fre-
quent form is only
four petals, or a cruci-
form flower, as at
Benihasan in the
XIIth dynasty; and
this is varied by alter-

106.—L.D. 11. 130.

107.—P. 84.

nations of square and diagonal arrangement.

A graceful, simple
form, which again re-
calls leather *appliquée*, is
yellow on a blue ground.

108.—P. 84.

An allied pattern is the disc surrounded by spots. This is very usual on early Greek pottery, and is found on the Aegean pottery also. This is very rarely seen in pure Egyptian design, and only in the XVIIIth dynasty, when Mykenaean in-fluence was strongest. On Nefer-hotep's ceiling two forms are found,

Fig. 109.

put between the horns of the bulls' heads, like the rosette on the My-kenaean ox head. Elsewhere it is

Fig. 110.—
P. 81.

usually seen on the scarves of the negroes as a characteristic decora-

Fig. 111.

tion, and on the dress of the Amu (C.M. cclviii.). Hence it appears to be distinctly a foreign ornament, like the other spot pattern on a zigzag line. Only three examples are published from Egyptian decoration, and those may well be due to foreign influence.

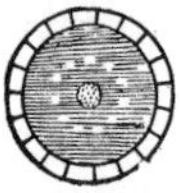

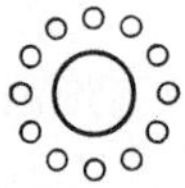

We now reach the largest and most
complex growth of Egyptian ornament in
the lotus, so widely spread that some
have seen in it the source of all ornament. Without going so far, we shall
find plenty in it to tax our reasoning and
imagination. If I prefer, in dealing with
this, to ignore the developments of it
seen outside of Egypt as aids to understanding it, this is only because those
foreign examples are so much later that
they are a reflex of various Egyptian
periods, and cannot show anything certainly as to the long anterior course of
development in Egypt itself.

The debated question of lotus and papyrus disappears at once when we look at
the feathery head of minute flowers which
the papyrus bears. That some flower,

such as a *nelumbium*, was confused with the lotus seems, however, very likely. There is no doubt that in ornament different flowers were sometimes confused, and their details mixed; hence it is of no use for us to be too particular in trying to separate them. We shall therefore use the name lotus in general without necessarily entering on botanical reasons for and against it on each occasion.

112.—L.D.
II. 33; I. 27.

The oldest use of the lotus was in groups of two flowers tied together by the stalks; such are found on the prehistoric pottery at Koptos, and on the earliest tombs. But in later times this became corrupted, and the origin apparently forgotten, by the XVIIIth dynasty.

113.—L.D.
III. 68.
XVIIIth dyn.

The plain flower was also used very early, as we see on the head-band of Nefert at the

Fig. 114.

begining of the IVth dynasty. And as architectural ornament it appears as a capital in wood of the Vth dynasty in the tomb of Imery. At Karnak there is a celebrated pair of granite pillars, one with the papyrus, the other with the

115.—L.D. II. 52. P. 74.

lotus; and this form, with the sepals turned over at the end, became the more usual in the Empire and later times.

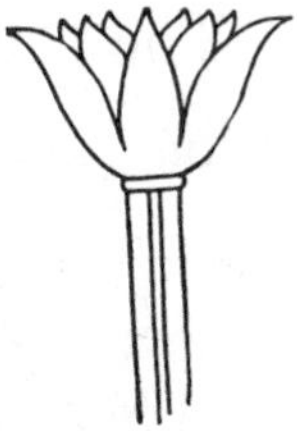

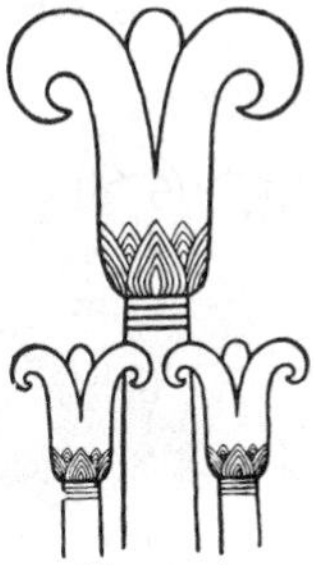

Fig. 116.

The variety of lotus capital is very great. The bud capital and the opened flower are

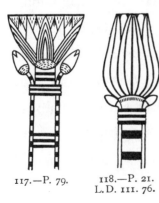

117.—P. 79.   118.—P. 21.
                  L.D. III. 76.

both shown in the XVIIIth dynasty (tomb
of Khaemhat); and many composite, complicated, and impossible combinations were
piled together in the decadent age of the
Ramessides.

The lotus was also much used in repetition as a border pattern, but not ap-

119.—P. Mon. L.

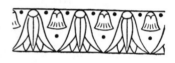

120.—R.C. lviii.

parently before the XVIIIth dynasty;
and usually it is in alternation with buds,

121.—P. 88.

which fit harmoniously
into the curves between
the flowers. This line
of flowers and buds
was varied as flowers
and grapes, and ap-
pears very often in

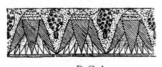

122.—R.C. lxx.

the XVIIIth dynasty.

The flower and bud was further developed in a mechani-
cal fashion, and we
can trace a continu-
ous series of forms
beginning in a flower

123.—P. 89. 8.

and bud pattern and modifying the inter-

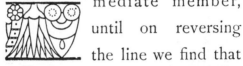

mediate member,
until on reversing
the line we find that

Fig. 124.   Fig. 125.
89. 9. 90. 4.   90. 5. 90. 6.

something has been
evolved which is in-
distinguishable from

126.—P. 90. 5.

the Greek palmetto alternating with the
lotus. The isolated anthemion, which is
so much like this, has probably a different
origin, as we shall soon see.

Beside using the separate flowers, the
whole plant was also a favourite subject
as a group. In the earliest days we find

it entwined around the hieroglyph of union, as we shall notice in considering

127.—R.C. xciii.

the hieroglyphs. In the XIIth dynasty the plant appears as a recurrent group in surface decoration; though from the varying form of the flower it might be intended for lotus or papyrus.

128.—L.D. III. 109.

In the XVIIIth dynasty it is more free, as might be expected in the time of Akhenaten.

It is also seen as a foreign ornament on the dress of a Syrian slain by Ramessu II. at Abu Simbel, but in this case perhaps the tufted papyrus is intended. And in

129.—R.S. lxxxiii.

place of the rounded group which is usual

in the XVIIIth–XIXth dynasties we find
a different treatment
on the throne of Ra-
messu III., in which
it is kept more as
a parallel pattern.
This parallelism be-
came general in later

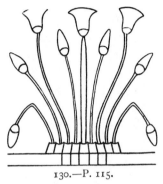

130.—P. 115.

times, and the Ptolemaic walls are ruled
over with stiff friezes of lotus and bud.

These wall basements are
preceded by groups of flower
and bud in scenes, which are

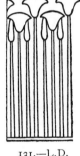

of the same style,
as early as the
IVth dynasty, on
the tomb of Debu-

131.—L.D.
II. 35.

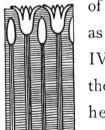

hen. Here it may be the
papyrus; but in the Vth

132.—L.D.
II. 64.

dynasty, on a basket-work
screen, the lotus and bud is clearly shown.

This pattern, however, is very seldom found as a general architectural ornament until we

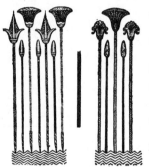

133.—P. 88. L.D. iv. 84.

come down to the dull sterility of the Ptolemaic and Roman age. Then the lower part of each wall is uniformly ruled with an endless series of flowers and buds on long stems in monotonous order.

We now come to the ornamental development of the flower into a monstrosity, which is only decorative and not natural, and which requires some thought and comparison to understand its origin.

134.—P. 79.

First there is the *fleur-de-lys* type, with curled-over sides and a middle projection. This has not been yet explained satisfactorily; but a principle which was first clearly formulated by Borchardt (A.Z. xxxi. 1) will show the origin of this as well as of the succeeding forms. The Egyptian, it seems, consistently drew the interior or top view of an object above the side view. In short, they suppose things to be seen in a bird's-eye view, and expressed that by drawing—for instance, a cup—in side view and partly in top view above that. A dish would be

drawn in side view, and a top view of its compartments and contents placed over it, and the bunch of flowers that lay on it is again placed over the top view. Now on this prin-

135.—
T.A. 1.

ciple we can see that the projection in the midst of the lotus flower is the third sepal at the back of the flower, the fourth, in front, being so foreshortened as to disappear altogether.

This view is further complicated by showing not only some of the four outer sepals, but also some of the petals, usually three. Here the near sepal is shown rising in front, and then above these everted sepals are three of the inner petals of the flower. These might be increased to five or seven, but were generally an odd number; and they were at last evolved to a fan of petals, in which the treatment of the dish of fruit just shown is exactly reproduced, a side view of the flower being crowned by a top view of it showing the radiating petals in the interior.

136.—
T.A. 368.

137.—
T.A.
381.

138.—
T.A.
388.

So far we are on clear ground. Now we come to a more complex form, which has also not yet been explained. In the XVIIIth dynasty (from which we must mainly draw, as we have the long series

of varieties in the glazed ornaments of
Tell el Amarna) a strange form
appears, with reversed curling arms
above the calyx. Now we have
seen that a third sepal is shown
139.—
T.A. 375.
from the back of the flower, and the
fourth is omitted which lay in front. But
this was an imperfect flower, and so a
diagonal point of view was taken, in which
two sepals lay nearest and were seen in
side view, and the two behind them were
seen over them. Sometimes they
are curled alike, but more generally
they are curled different ways, the
140.—
T.A.
374.
nearer ones downwards, the further
ones upwards. Hence we get this very
mechanical form, which was greatly developed in Assyrian and Greek types of
the pattern. If it can be proved that the
Assyrian tree pattern is earlier than this
development, we could then grant what

seems a likely influence on the development of this pattern. It was so
far removed from a natural view
that it soon became greatly varied
and amplified, as on a bracelet in
the Louvre.

141.—P. 113.

In Assyria this became a staple design,
in which the top was greatly
increased at the expense of the
lotus sepals below; but still the
four sepals, two front and two
back, are shown. In the Greek designs,
however barbarous they may seem in comparison, owing to their hopeless divergence
from any rational type, yet the
same elements remain, and the
four sepals can be traced below
the view of the petals in the
flower. Thus the anthemion
with its double curves is fully
accounted for, the lower and

142.—P. and C. Ass. 127.

143.—Tanis II. xxxi.

144.— Goodyear. 75.

upper sepals being still distinguishable in
the two spirals on each side at the base
of it.   The later changes of this necessarily belong to Greek art, and we cannot
here follow them out.

A late development of the lotus in
Ptolemaic Egypt was with a
central spike through the face of
petals. As this spike rises from
the base, it appears to be the
front sepal rising before the petals.

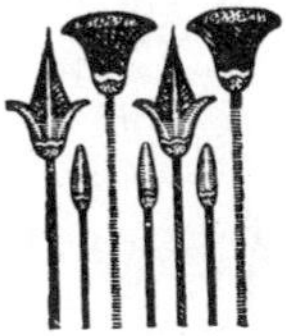

Fig. 145.

Another variety in this pattern remains
to be noticed.   On very many compound
lotus patterns there is a pendant from each end of the
side sepals. This does not
appear until the XVIIIth

146.—P. 111.

dynasty on the monuments : it is then
sometimes single and sometimes double.
But here, as in the spirals, the scarab
type is an earlier stage than the archi-

tectural. On the architecture it is quite unintelligible, and a mere conventional

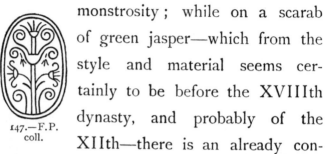

147.—F.P. coll.

monstrosity; while on a scarab of green jasper—which from the style and material seems certainly to be before the XVIIIth dynasty, and probably of the XIIth—there is an already conventionalised lotus group, with the four sepals and inner petals already developed into a sort of "tree pattern," and the lower two sepals have a pendant, partly worn away, but clearly showing a triply-branching line like a small lotus flower. This is the earlier stage of this conventional pendant; but even here, although the pendant itself is rational, the position of it is hard to explain. Probably we must wait for some early scarab to clear up the real origin of this curious and puzzling form.

We have now traced the evolution of the various forms of the lotus pattern in Egypt, and seen how the main Assyrian and Greek types of the palmetto and the anthemion arose, which were confounded together owing to their similarity.

Other plants were often confounded with the lotus in decoration, by the ancients as well as by moderns. We have noticed some examples of this; and it is well shown in the group of boat-builders, to whom, apparently, bundles of papyrus with lotus flowers are being brought, in the IVth dynasty tomb of Shepseskau (L.D. 11. 12).

Much use was made of papyrus in the floral work of Tell el Amarna. On the painted pavement groups of papyrus with large red fluffy heads of seed vessels are figured; and on the coloured tiles the landscape view of the papyrus plant in strictly natural treatment is a frequent subject. But these belong rather to artistic than to ornamental work.

In architecture the lotus and papyrus were largely used, in fact they form the basis of columnar decoration as distinct from that of pillars. The earliest figure of a column that is known is as far back as any dated monument we possess at the beginning of the IVth dynasty; and there it is fashioned as a stem and flower, pro-bably carved in wood. The contracting connection with the tenon above, in a bell form, on the top of the flower, is the same as columns of the VIth dynasty (L.D. ii. iii); and is the source of the much later columns of Tahutmes III. at Karnak,

Fig. 148.

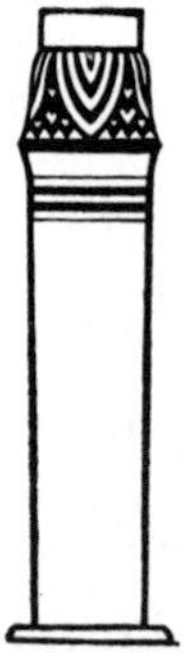

Fig. 149.

which otherwise seems to be an unaccountable "sport."

In the figures of
wooden columns in
the Vth and VIth
dynasties, the lotus
form prevails, as we

Fig. 150.　　　Fig. 151.

have already noticed, and here repeat.

In the Vth dynasty, in the
tomb of Ptahshepses at Abusir
the clustered papyrus stems are
a new feature; at Benihasan
they are well developed; and
they continued in use to the

Fig. 152.

XVIIIth dynasty. But a different type then arose into predominance
in the wide bell‑topped lotus capitals,
and with long sheath‑leaves around the
root; and this continued for several
dynasties. But this was displaced
by the elaborate composite capitals of

Ptolemaic and Roman age, which were made up of varied elements of incongruity.

The palm, though the most important tree of the country, has had but little effect on the architecture. There is not a single example of columns copied from a palm stem; and the only instances of the imitation of the stem are in two or three instances of copies of roofing beams.

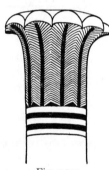

Fig. 153.

The branches are not copied on columns until other subjects were well used. In the XIIth dynasty the imitation of a bundle of palm branches was made in the capitals, and it became common in the XVIIIth. Perhaps, however, as we shall see in considering the hieroglyphs, the palm column originates with a bundle of palm sticks bound together. It is strange that the simple element of grouping branches round a post should not have been a very usual early motive. Was the palm really common in early Egypt? It does not enter into the hieroglyphs, and it is seldom shown on monuments till the XVIIIth dynasty; while grapes, figs, and pomegranates all seem to have been commoner than dates.

In late times not only the branches but the fruit was sculptured; and at Esneh and other Roman temples the bunches of dates are carefully rendered.

The vine is one of the oldest cultivated plants in Egypt, and all the designs copied from it are based on the idea of its climbing and trailing over the houses. It appears mainly in the florid work of the XVIIIth dynasty. The ceiling was often painted of a golden yellow, with

vine leaves and bunches of grapes hanging from a trellis pattern which covers
it.   At Tell el Amarna some fragments

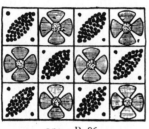

found were very free
and natural, but in
the XXth dynasty it
became a stiff and
formal affair. (Tomb of
Aimadua, Ramessu X.).

154.—P. 86.

Bunches of grapes also formed favourite

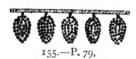

155.—P. 79,

pendants ; as such they
are painted in rows
hanging from architraves
of wooden buildings (tomb of Ra, Amenhotep II.); and frequently in blue glazed

ware bunches of grapes are
found of varying sizes, with
half of the upper part cut
away so as to affix them by

Fig. 156.

a peg-hole to a square wooden beam of
the ceiling.

In the Greco-Roman decoration of capitals the vine and grapes also appears, and is often very beautifully treated, as at Esneh, though essentially as a mere surface decoration, and not as an organic element.

The convolvulus has scarcely, if at all, been acknowledged as an Egyptian ornament. Yet it often occurs during the XVIIIth and XIXth dynasties. On a coffin in the Ghizeh Museum a long trail of convolvulus is beautifully modelled and painted; and during the tide of naturalism under Akhenaten the wild flowing stems were a favourite element of decoration.

Subsequently the convolvulus is often shown as a climber on the lotus or papyrus stems in bouquets; and though its leaves then have been miscalled lotus buds, or "tabs," yet they are clearly intended for a natural leaf of this climber, which

157.—P. 91.

is so common in the Egyptian fields.

Another field plant which played a great part in the glazed decorations was

158.—P. 91.

the thistle. This is naturally painted on the glazed tiles; and the glazed pendants of necklaces and wall decoration showed an abundance of thistles with green calices and purple petals. But this, like the convolvulus, was rarely used except during the beautiful period of naturalism which was most developed by Akhenaten.

Artificial combinations of flowers also became used decoratively. We have just instanced two examples from the great bouquets or staves of flowers which the Egyptians used in ceremonies.

The garlands of flower petals which are seen on the heads of women, or as collars, in the XVIIIth–XXth dynasties were also placed around the water-jars; and hence a painted pattern of garlands came to be used on those jars.

In architecture also the garland came into use, sometimes carved on the stone

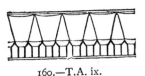

Fig. 159.

around the columns, sometimes made in coloured glaze and inlaid in the surface.

Wreaths of lotus flowers and buds were also represented around

160.—T.A. ix.

the columns at Tell el Amarna.

The great pectorals, or breast-plates, of successive strings of flowers and leaves were prominent in the personal and religious decoration. The sacred barks of the gods were adorned with large and complex breast-plates, probably made of bronze, gilded and inlaid (L.D. III. 235).

161.—P. Mon.
xlix. 2.

A small example of such we have in London, with the details all inlaid in gold. These pectorals were also represented on the later vases as a complete whole.

Turning now to the men and animals shown in decoration, in the period of the Empire we constantly see figures of captives introduced to emphasise the power of the king. These first appear in the great change which overcame Egyptian art consequent upon the Asiatic conquests. Before Tahutmes III. the character and style of work continually recalls that of the XIIth dynasty; but within one or two generations a profound difference changed for ever the nature of the art, and this is reflected in the national handwriting, which

shows a similar break. Amenhotep II. appears on his nurse's knee with an emblematic
group of foreigners under his feet, while he
grasps cords tied to their necks; and in
the same spirit he is shown, when grown
up, as smiting at one blow a whole bunch
of captives whom he holds in his left
hand (L.D. iii. 62; L.D. iii. 61).
Tahutmes IV. similarly is seen seated on
his tutor's knee, with his feet on a footstool ornamented with prostrate captives
(L.D. iii. 69). Amenhotep III. appears
with figures of a negro
and a Syrian bound to
the *sam* sign on the
sides of his throne, and
henceforward the
abasement of captives
was an essential idea

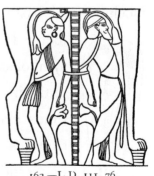

162.—L.D. iii. 76.

to Egyptians. But it should be remembered that common as the notion was in

late times, it is originally Asiatic and not Egyptian ; the king trampling on the nations and making foes a footstool are ideas not found in Egypt until the Semitic conquests of Tahutmes III., though the earliest figure of a sphinx trampling on a captive is under the XIIth dynasty.

Under Akhenaten six various races are represented on the sides of his great balcony (L.D. iii. 109), and the alternate negroes and Syrians are painted on the passage floors of his palace, or carved in blocks of alabaster to be trodden under foot.

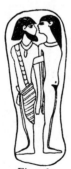

Down the various ages this symbolism recurs in decoration until in Ptolemaic and Roman times every decent Egyptian had captives painted on the soles of his sandals in which he was buried, so that for all eternity he might tread down the Gentiles.

Fig. 163.

Among animals a favourite in decoration
was the ibex, but it
was not introduced till
the XVIIIth dynasty.
It often appears on
the finger - rings of
Akhenaten's time, and
later upon the funeral

Fig. 164.

tent of Isiemkheb, ingeniously adapted to
fill a square space.

The bull or young calf was more frequently introduced ; on the wooden boxes
and trays it is shown as bounding in the
meadows, and it is continually used in the
groups of the painted pavement at Tell el
Amarna.

Birds are also a common subject for
decoration, though only dating from the
same period as the other animals. Besides
the symbolic or sacred use of the hawk
and vulture, the very secular duck was a

favourite bird. On the great pavements of Akhenaten it appears above every group of plants.

Fig. 165.

On rings it is often engraved fluttering above its nest; and in the decadence of Egyptian art in the XXth dynasty the incongruous idea was adopted of birds, eggs, and nests all upon a ceiling.

The natural ceiling pattern adopted from the early days of Egyptian art was of

Fig. 166.

golden stars on a deep blue ground; not a dark daylight blue, as in modern imitations, but a black night blue. These are always five-pointed stars, with a circular spot, usually of red, in the centre.

It is noticeable that the Egyptian views

a star as surrounded by long streamers of
light ; because to a long-sighted person, or
any one with proper spectacles, the stars
appear as points of light without radia-
tions.   Hence it seems as if the Egyptians were short-sighted people from the
early ages.

Lastly we may notice the base imitation
of nature in copying the grain of
wood, which we find done in the
earliest times of the IVth dynasty,
and continued down to the period
of the Empire.   Stones were also
imitated by painting, and red granite

Fig. 167.—
L.D. II. 19.
is frequently copied in the earlier days, on
the recessed doorways of tombs.   In later
times vases of valuable stone were
imitated by painting over a pottery
vase, and such cheap substitutes
were commonly placed in the tombs.

Fig. 168.

These base imitations are of æsthetic

interest as showing in what a different manner the Egyptian viewed his materials from that of our standpoint. He stuccoed and painted over his hard stone statues ; it was enough for him to know that the stone was hard and imperishable—he did not need to see it always exposed. The imitation of nature was the standpoint from which he started, and he had no objection to carry out that imitation with paint or otherwise ; our abstract standpoint of an artistic effect which must never involve falsity, but which may have little or nothing to do with nature, was altogether outside of his æsthetic.

CHAPTER IV

STRUCTURAL DECORATION

IN the persistence of certain forms which
were the direct result of the structure of
a building or object, we have a very con-
siderable source of decoration.   In Greek
architecture many of the details are entirely
the product of wooden construction translated into stone.   The triglyphs, the imitation of nail heads, of the ends of the poles
supporting the roofing, of the crossing of
beams at the coffers, are all details which
are retained as decoration long after they
ceased to have any structural meaning, owing
to an entire change of material.   Such is

structural decoration in its best known forms.
But the same principles equally apply to
Egyptian architecture; there the original
material was not sawn wood as in Greece,
but rather the papyrus and palm branch,
with the ever-present mud plastering and
mud bricks. The decorative details of the
stone architecture have come down from
this stage of building, translated point for
point into stone, just as the Greek translated his wooden architecture into marble.

But pottery preceded stone in Egypt,
and one of the simplest of ornaments
arose from structural necessity. To this
day may be seen in the Egyptian pottery
yards bowls and jars held together by a
twist of rough palm fibre cord, while they
dry in the sun before baking. This accidental marking by the rope in the wet
clay is seen on the pottery of all ages;
but it became developed as a pattern ap-

parently in the twist or guilloche, which

169.—H.S. 383.

170.—Kahun Pot.

may perhaps be rather derived from this than from the chain of coils or wave pattern.

Basket-work was elaborately developed in the Old Kingdom. There were beautiful screens represented behind the figures of the owners of the early tombs; they might in some cases be matting instead of basket-work, but others of the patterns appear certainly to be of a rigid material. In no case are they likely to be " mats on which the kings stand," as styled by Owen Jones. Among the various patterns of platting which are readily developed, squares, waves, zig - zags, chequers, &c., there are some

171.—L.D. ii. 63.

made by binding the fibres into bundles,

and so making a kind of open work, which may well have led to the pattern of connected rhombs which is so usual on

172.—L.D.
II. 63.

Oriental pottery.

One of the most familiar early motives is wooden framing. This is continually imitated in the stone figures of doorways in the tombs. The details of it show that a frame or grate of joinery must

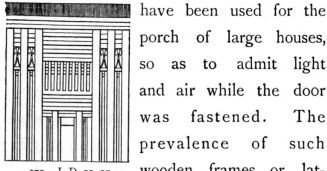

have been used for the porch of large houses, so as to admit light and air while the door was fastened. The prevalence of such

173.—L.D. II. 17.

wooden frames or lat-

tices in modern times in Egypt — known as mushrabiyeh work—shows how suited such a system is to the climate. Long

after the use of stone was general the
frames were imitated, and the pattern survived as a decoration. The same style
of framing was used in the upper part of
a house, with decora-
tive uprights of the
hieroglyph *tat*, and
was copied as a
fancy decoration in

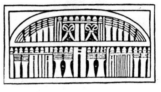

174.—Ghizeh.

furniture, as seen in a beautiful ivory carv-
ing in the Louvre. This style survived
until the XVIIIth dynasty, when it is
seen in a tomb at Thebes (Amenhetop
II., Prisse Art) and at the temple of
Sedeinga under
Amenhotep III.

Fig. 175.

Much akin to this
wood framing is the panelling of the brickwork which is seen in the earliest examples

in Egypt, and is identical with the panelling of walls in early Babylonia, one of the indications of a common civilisation of the two great valleys. This panelling  does not seem to have lasted beyond the Old Kingdom ; there was

176.—P.M. vii. (plan).

no trace of it found at Kahun or Gurob, in the buildings of the XIIth and XVIIIth dynasties, nor does it appear in any drawings or imitations of buildings.

One of the best known characteristics of Egyptian architecture is the sloping face of the walls and pylons. This is directly copied from brickwork. In order to give more cohesion to a wall it was the custom  to build it on a curved bed, so that the courses all sloped up outwards at the

Fig. 177.

outer corners. Thus the outer faces sloped

inwards, and the wall had more stability. So wedded were the builders to this method, that where a long wall of a fort or city was to be built they preferred to begin with a row of towers of brickwork thus arranged, and then to fill in the spaces between them with more plain walling. This slope of the walls was copied in stone at the earliest time. The temple of Sneferu at Medum has a slope on the face of about 1 in 16, and it was continued down to the very latest age of Roman building.

Another familiar feature is the roll or torus down the corners of the buildings. It is usually ornamented by a pattern of binding. This— as was well pointed out by Professor Conway—is evidently a bundle of reeds bound together, and put down the angle of the

178.—Perring.
L.D. 11. 44.

plastering in order to preserve it from breaking away. Such a construction was an ugly necessity at first, but when stone-working arose it had become so familiar that it was faithfully copied in stone as a decoration, and continued to be so copied for more than four thousand years, as long as Egyptian architecture lasted.

The well-known Egyptian cornice has been so long taken for granted that it might seem never to have required an origin. Yet in 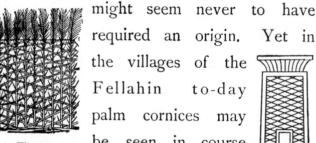 the villages of the Fellahin to-day palm cornices may be seen in course

Fig. 179.

Fig. 180.

of development. A fence is formed of palm-sticks, placed upright, and stripped of leaves for some way up. The tops are left bushy, and serve to prevent men or animals climbing over the court-yard wall. The upright sticks are tied together by a rope near the top, or lashed on to a cross line of sticks. The fence is stiffened below by interweaving other palm-sticks in both directions ; and then the whole is plastered with mud up to the tie level. Here we have the cavetto cornice being formed by the nodding tops of the branches ; and to clinch the matter, the earliest representations of that cornice are on figures of buildings which show the crossed sticks of the fence below the cornice. The ribbing of the cornice is seen on the earliest examples, on Men-kaura's sarcophagus in the IVth dynasty (Per-ring), in the Vth dynasty (L.D. II. 44) and the VIth (L.D. II. 112), and

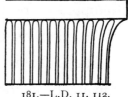

181.—L.D. II. 112.

such was copied until late times. But in
the more decorative cornices of the
XVIIIth dynasty the ribbing was broken

up by cross lines,
sometimes curved
upward, sometimes
downward. These

182.—L.D.   Fig. 183.
III. 115.

cross lines must be a degradation of the
leaves of the palm branch. In later times
they are omitted, and the pattern becomes
simply striped.

This cornice was copied in Syrian architecture, in the plain form without ribbing,
as in the tomb at Siloam and the slabs
of Lachish ; but it does not appear to
have ever taken root in Assyria, though
attempted there, nor is it known in Europe.

The other main type of Egyptian cornice
is what is known as the *Khaker*, from the
equivalent of the sign as a hieroglyph in
inscriptions. This only means " to cover "

or "to ornament," and therefore refers to the position of the decoration and not to its origin. The clue to the real nature of this decoration is given in a tomb of the IVth dynasty (Ptah-hotep, L.D. 11. 101. b.), where we see the *khaker* ornament not as a mere painting, but represented as standing up solid around the tops of the cabins of boats. It cannot therefore be anything very heavy or solid, such as spear-heads, as has been proposed. It probably results in some way from the

construction of the cabins. They must have had roofs of very light material. Papyrus was generally used for building boats, and therefore for cabins also, most likely. This gives us

Fig. 184.

the clue to interpret it. Suppose a screen of papyrus stems; the roofing stems tied on to the uprights; and the loose wiry leaves at the head tied together, to keep them from straggling over and looking untidy. Here we have all the details of the *khaker* ornament simply resulting from structural necessity. The leaves are gathered together at the lower tying; there the end view of the concentric coats of the papyrus stems of the roof are seen as concentric circles; above which the leaves bulge out and are tied together near the top. Though this structural decoration is seen on the top of boat cabins as early as the IVth dynasty, yet we have not found it as decoration on a flat surface until the XIIth. Then it is very common; but its meaning became confused in the XVIIIth dynasty, and in Ptolemaic times it is seen in absurd positions, as on a base, and on architraves above an

185.—
Prisse 88.

empty space, where no stems below it were possible.

We have just mentioned one use of reeds or papyrus in the torus roll on the edge of buildings; but on interior decoration we meet again with the same motive. The borders of Egyptian scenes from the earliest times are framed with a variety of bindings; and so suitable did such bordering seem that it was continued with but little variation throughout all the history. The oldest forms are—

plain binding

186.—L.D. II. 43.

a diagonal binding,

187.—L.D. II. 44.

or

188.—L.D. II. 44.

and crossed binding.

189.—L.D. II. 54.

The latter became modified into—

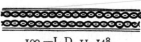

190.—L.D. ii. 148.

by the XIth dynasty, showing that its meaning was already becoming forgotten.

191.—
L.D.
ii.
132.

But a modification of the tower ends of this pattern in the XIIth dynasty is difficult to understand; unless we can look on it as an irregular winding of the ends of the cord around the reed bundle in place of the regular crossing which is shown above it.

The modification of colours and arrangement in the plain binding is interminable. In the XVIIIth dynasty we find

192.—L.D. iii. 115.

in the XIXth

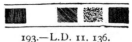

193.—L.D. ii. 136.

in late times

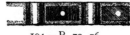

194.—P. 72. 76.

and in all ages a binding with a number
of lines between coloured spaces was
common

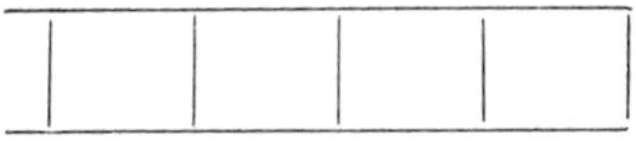

Fig. 195.

and on borders of architecture and statuary
thrones

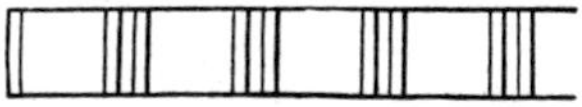

Fig. 196.

CHAPTER V

SYMBOLIC DECORATION

THE Egyptian who expressed all his thoughts by a symbolical writing, full of determinatives, was naturally much given to symbolism in his decoration. Not, however, that all his decoration was symbolic in a recondite sense; the ever-present lotus ornament was merely a thing of beauty; the lotus was not a sacred plant, it is not associated with any divinity in particular, and only in one unusual instance does it ever occur in the hieroglyphs. The fanciful habit of Europe, in seeing a hidden sense in every flower, was not akin to the simple and elementary mind of the Egyptian. But certain striking emblems he used continually; and one of the earliest of these is the uraeus snake, or cobra in his wrath, reared up with expanded body ready to strike. The dignity and power of the animal made it to be an emblem of the king, or rather perhaps of the royal power of death. That capital punishment was used in Egypt is seen in the Westcar Tales, which probably date from the Old Kingdom, where a condemned malefactor is ordered to be brought forth for a magician to try his power in bringing him to life when slain. The king, as having the power of death, bore the uraeus always on his head-dress; and from the earliest days (at Medum) the royal court of justice was adorned with a cornice of uraei, implying that there resided the royal right of judgment and of condemnation. This cornice seems, however, to

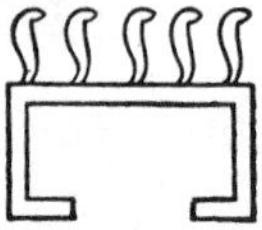

Fig. 197.

have been regarded as merely royal in later times, and was freely used to adorn any royal structure, even a wooden summer-house (Amenhotep II.); or the uraei formed a band around columns (Akhenaten), or appear as supporters of the royal cartouche

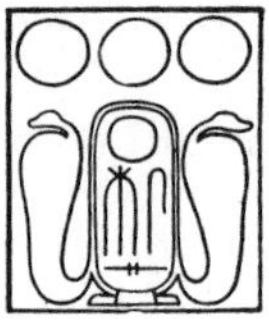

198.—P. 72.

(P. 72), either plain (Ramessu II.) or winged

Fig. 199.

(Horem-heb) L.D. III. 122).

A symbolism closely connected with this is that of the globe and wings. This certainly dates to the beginning of the monu-

200.—Khufu.

mental age, as it is seen above the figure of Khufu seated before a table of offerings

201.—Unas.

on an amulet. In that instance it is on too small a scale to show the details; but in the next dynasty it appears above Unas at Elephantine, with the globe flanked by two uraei and two wings. What the symbolism of it was we have no direct information. But when we consider that the wings are those of the vulture spread out, as it appears on the roofs of the passages as a protecting and preserving maternal emblem, and the uraeus is associated with it, we can hardly view it as other than the same idea of the power of life and death, of preservation and destruction. But in this emblem it is not the king who wields these powers, but Ra the Sun, whose disc appears in the midst. That the wings have thus the meaning of protection is shown by the globe with drooping

202.—L.D. III. 122a.

wings embracing the royal name, expressing the protection given by Ra to the king, without associating the deadly or punitive power of the uraeus. A curious

203.—L.D. III. 8

form of this emblem which was common in the early part of the XVIIIth dynasty is with only one wing.

One of the most perfect and beautiful examples of the winged disc is on

204.—P. 72.

the temple of Tahutmes III., but it continued to be used down to the latest times of Egyptian architecture as a lintel decoration.

In the XIXth dynasty an addition to the symbolism appears; the horns of a ram are added to the wings; sometimes without the uraei (Ramessu I., L.D. III. 131), sometimes with the uraei (Ramessu II., L.D. III. 204). These rams' horns can hardly be other than those of the ram-headed god Khnum, "the maker" or "modeller" of men. The idea then of

the wings and horns is that Ra makes as
well as protects; and where the uraeus is
added it implies that Ra is creator, pre-
server, and destroyer.

The vulture alone as the emblem of protection is frequently figured with out-
stretched wings across the ceilings of the
passages, particularly those of the royal
tombs of the XIXth dynasty.   There is
perhaps no sight in the animal world more
imposing than one of these birds, stretched
out with a span of some nine or ten feet,
hanging in the air close overhead; it is
natural that it should have excited the
admiration of man, and not being hurtful
it readily came to be honoured as a type
of maternal care.

The scarab was another such typical
animal, rolling the pellet containing an egg

to a safe place where it buries it. Though very common as an amulet for the living and the dead, yet it is not often seen in symbolical or decorative use otherwise. With what idea the amulet was used we do not know for certain. The scarab itself is often figured as holding the disc of the sun between its claws: and it is at least possible that the symbolic idea of the scarab as the maker or creator arose from the burial of its ball being an emblem of the setting of the sun, from which new life will arise in due course. It occurs with the wings extended and the disc

between the claws as a centre figure

205.—P. 81.

206.—L.D.
III. 235.

in the space of a ceiling pattern (Neferhotep, XVIIIth dynasty), and on the border of the covering of a shrine under Ramessu X., and is occasionally met with later in decoration.

The lion as a noble and royal animal
frequently figures in
the XVIIIth dynasty.
The Egyptians, with
their marvellous in-
stinct for taming every

207.—R.C. cxxx.

animal they could find, actually trained
lions or leopards to live as domesticated

208.—P. 78.

animals, with the same sort
of allowed wildness as modern
hunting dogs. The lion accompanied the king in battle;
but in camp it lay down as peaceably as

an ox. It was fre-
quently carved on
the sides of the
thrones of the
XVIIIth – XXth
dynasties, and also

209.—L.D. III. 100.

seated in pairs, facing or backing, on the

temple walls, a usage reminding us of the lion gate of Mykenae of the same age.

Some of the Egyptian divinities also ap-

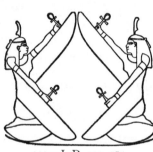

210.—L.D. III. 114.

pear as symbolic orna-
ments. The figures
of the goddess Maat
with spread wings
adorned the ark of
Amen-ra under Ta-
hutimes II. ; and in

earlier times similar cheru-
bic figures stand guarding
the name of Antef V. on
a scarab.

Fig. 211.

Hathor also appears on various objects.
A mirror handle carved in wood during
the XIIth dynasty has the head of Hathor (P. I. xiii.) ; columns with heads of
Hathor, crowned with a shrine occupied

by a uraeus, are found introduced by
Amenhotep III. in his temples at El
Kab and Sedeinga, and were copied by
Ramessu II. at Abu Simbel.
The similar head of Hathor
was frequently made in glazed
pottery as a pendant in the
time of Akhenaten. And in
later times these Hathor
headed capitals became usual   212.—L.D. I. 100.
under the Ptolemies, as in the well-known
case of the portico of the great temple at
Dendera.

Bes was one of the favourite popular
deities of the Egyptians ; restricted to no
place in particular, every votary of music
and the dance patronised Bes.   The little
statuette of a dancing girl with a Bes
mask on, besides an actual mask in cer-
tonnage, found at Kahun, show the popu-
larity of the god in the XIIth dynasty.

In later times his figure is frequently seen. At Tell el Amarna ornaments for necklaces made in glazed pottery followed two types of Bes, the god dancing with the tambourine seen in side view, and the earlier grotesque front view, with arms akimbo. These familiar little figures continued to be made till late times; and in the Roman age Bes was elevated to architectural dignity on the dies above the columns at Dendereh in the small temple of the Mammeisi.

Another and more artificial mode of symbolical decoration was by means of the hieroglyphic signs. Having a mode of writing in which a single mark could express an abstract idea, it was possible to adapt writing to a purely decorative

design. Even with alphabetic characters
this has been done, as in the elaborate
crossing patterns of the earlier Arab
period in Egypt, in which no untrained
eye would see anything but a complex
ornament.

Four of the hieroglyphs most usually
worked into ornamental designs are
the *ankh*, a girdle, or symbol of life;
the *thet*, another form of girdle, with
longer bow-tie in front, which, as
always identified with Isis, may have
been a primitive feminine girdle,
the ankh being masculine; the

213.—
Ankh.

214.—
Thet.

215.—
Uas.

216.—
Dad.

uas, a stick of authority, or
symbol of power; and the
dad, a row of columns, or
symbol of stability.

As early as the Old Kingdom
we find wooden framings, or lattices,
ornamented with *dad* signs; and

this continued at least as late as Amen-

217.—L.D.
III. 131.

hotep II. The *dad* also appears in what is probably copied from pierced woodwork, in a relief at Qurneh of Ramessu I.

The combination of *thet dad uas*, and of *ankh dad uas*, is found in the XIIth dynasty at Benihasan, appa-

Fig. 218.

rently carved in relief, on the wooden panels of a litter (R.C. xciii.). The same occur similarly carved on the ebony doors of Hatshepsut at Deir el Bahri. The group begins to appear as an architectural design early in the XVIIIth dynasty, and continues down to Roman times, especially on bases of scenes and groups, thus forming a continuous border of good wishes. The hieroglyphs, *ankh*, *dad*, and *uas*, are all found on pendants for necklaces, in the blue glazed pottery of

the XVIIIth dynasty, and also combined
in one as a ring bezil. And the *thet*
girdle tie of Isis appears repeated as a
pattern, probably of pierced woodwork,
along the sides of a shrine of Tahutimes
III. at Semneh, and on the base of a
couch in the birth scene of Amenhotep
III. (R.S. xxxviii.). As funeral amulets
the *thet*, *dad*, and *ankh* occur commonly,
but that branch is outside of the subject
of decoration.

Another hieroglyph often appearing as an
ornament is the *sam*, or symbol of union.
The origin of it is yet unexplained.   It
certainly is a column of some kind;
it has a well-marked capital and an
abacus. The capital is formed much
like the palm-leaf capital; and the
stem is clearly bound round, and
must therefore be composite. This
suggests that it might be a column of

219.—
Khafra.

palm sticks bound together, with some tops left projecting for ornament. Such might well be more conventionalised at the beginning of Egyptian sculpture in the IVth dynasty than the other kinds of capitals; and the immigrant race came from the region of the palm, while the lotus and papyrus only were reached by them in Egypt itself. The base is a main difficulty to explain. It might be conventionalised clods of earth, with two curled-over side branches of the palm; but it has been so modified that we must await more evidence. In any case the stem is formed of several parts bound to-

220.—Khafra.

gether, and hence it was very naturally adopted as a symbol of union. It was further grouped with two plants, the stalks of which were linked around it. It is always supposed that these symbolise northern and southern Egypt, and that the group means the union of all the land. Still it is yet uncertain what plants are intended to be represented, though on the throne of Tahutimes IV. they are clearly lotus and papyrus : but the evidence is too late to be of much value. This group was a favourite decoration from beginning to end of Egyptian history. At the beginning of the XIIth dynasty an addition was made by placing a figure of Hapi or the Nile on each side of the group (Tanis i. i.), each figure holding one of the two plants. As these figures were crowned, one with the sign of south the other of north, they point to the plants being emblems of the south and north also. This group with the figures is found as late as the XXth dynasty (L.D. iii. 237). Another design came into fashion during the great foreign wars of the XVIIIth dynasty, representing two captives, one negro, one Syrian, bound back to back against the *sam ;* thus it symbolised not only the union of upper and lower Egypt, but also of the northern and southern races outside of Egypt. Later on, four or even six such racial types are figured as bound together.

INDEX.

A CATALOG OF SELECTED
DOVER BOOKS
IN ALL FIELDS OF INTEREST

A CATALOG OF SELECTED DOVER
BOOKS IN ALL FIELDS OF INTEREST

CONCERNING THE SPIRITUAL IN ART, Wassily Kandinsky. Pioneering work by father of abstract art. Thoughts on color theory, nature of art. Analysis of earlier masters. 12 illustrations. 80pp. of text. 5⅜ x 8½. 23411-8 Pa. $4.95

ANIMALS: 1,419 Copyright-Free Illustrations of Mammals, Birds, Fish, Insects, etc., Jim Harter (ed.). Clear wood engravings present, in extremely lifelike poses, over 1,000 species of animals. One of the most extensive pictorial sourcebooks of its kind. Captions. Index. 284pp. 9 x 12. 23766-4 Pa. $14.95

CELTIC ART: The Methods of Construction, George Bain. Simple geometric techniques for making Celtic interlacements, spirals, Kells-type initials, animals, humans, etc. Over 500 illustrations. 160pp. 9 x 12. (USO) 22923-8 Pa. $9.95

AN ATLAS OF ANATOMY FOR ARTISTS, Fritz Schider. Most thorough reference work on art anatomy in the world. Hundreds of illustrations, including selections from works by Vesalius, Leonardo, Goya, Ingres, Michelangelo, others. 593 illustrations. 192pp. 7⅛ x 10¼. 20241-0 Pa. $9.95

CELTIC HAND STROKE-BY-STROKE (Irish Half-Uncial from "The Book of Kells"): An Arthur Baker Calligraphy Manual, Arthur Baker. Complete guide to creating each letter of the alphabet in distinctive Celtic manner. Covers hand position, strokes, pens, inks, paper, more. Illustrated. 48pp. 8¼ x 11. 24336-2 Pa. $3.95

EASY ORIGAMI, John Montroll. Charming collection of 32 projects (hat, cup, pelican, piano, swan, many more) specially designed for the novice origami hobbyist. Clearly illustrated easy-to-follow instructions insure that even beginning papercrafters will achieve successful results. 48pp. 8¼ x 11. 27298-2 Pa. $3.50

THE COMPLETE BOOK OF BIRDHOUSE CONSTRUCTION FOR WOOD-WORKERS, Scott D. Campbell. Detailed instructions, illustrations, tables. Also data on bird habitat and instinct patterns. Bibliography. 3 tables. 63 illustrations in 15 figures. 48pp. 5¼ x 8½. 24407-5 Pa. $2.50

BLOOMINGDALE'S ILLUSTRATED 1886 CATALOG: Fashions, Dry Goods and Housewares, Bloomingdale Brothers. Famed merchants' extremely rare catalog depicting about 1,700 products: clothing, housewares, firearms, dry goods, jewelry, more. Invaluable for dating, identifying vintage items. Also, copyright-free graphics for artists, designers. Co-published with Henry Ford Museum & Greenfield Village. 160pp. 8¼ x 11. 25780-0 Pa. $10.95

HISTORIC COSTUME IN PICTURES, Braun & Schneider. Over 1,450 costumed figures in clearly detailed engravings—from dawn of civilization to end of 19th century. Captions. Many folk costumes. 256pp. 8⅜ x 11¾. 23150-X Pa. $12.95

BRASS INSTRUMENTS: Their History and Development, Anthony Baines. Authoritative, updated survey of the evolution of trumpets, trombones, bugles, cornets, French horns, tubas and other brass wind instruments. Over 140 illustrations and 48 music examples. Corrected and updated by author. New preface. Bibliography. 320pp. 5⅜ x 8½. 27574-4 Pa. $9.95

HOLLYWOOD GLAMOR PORTRAITS, John Kobal (ed.). 145 photos from 1926-49. Harlow, Gable, Bogart, Bacall; 94 stars in all. Full background on photographers, technical aspects. 160pp. 8⅜ x 11¼. 23352-9 Pa. $12.95

MAX AND MORITZ, Wilhelm Busch. Great humor classic in both German and English. Also 10 other works: "Cat and Mouse," "Plisch and Plumm," etc. 216pp. 5⅜ x 8½. 20181-3 Pa. $6.95

THE RAVEN AND OTHER FAVORITE POEMS, Edgar Allan Poe. Over 40 of the author's most memorable poems: "The Bells," "Ulalume," "Israfel," "To Helen," "The Conqueror Worm," "Eldorado," "Annabel Lee," many more. Alphabetic lists of titles and first lines. 64pp. 5³⁄₁₆ x 8¼. 26685-0 Pa. $1.00

PERSONAL MEMOIRS OF U. S. GRANT, Ulysses Simpson Grant. Intelligent, deeply moving firsthand account of Civil War campaigns, considered by many the finest military memoirs ever written. Includes letters, historic photographs, maps and more. 528pp. 6⅛ x 9¼. 28587-1 Pa. $12.95

AMULETS AND SUPERSTITIONS, E. A. Wallis Budge. Comprehensive discourse on origin, powers of amulets in many ancient cultures: Arab, Persian Babylonian, Assyrian, Egyptian, Gnostic, Hebrew, Phoenician, Syriac, etc. Covers cross, swastika, crucifix, seals, rings, stones, etc. 584pp. 5⅜ x 8½. 23573-4 Pa. $15.95

RUSSIAN STORIES/PYCCKNE PACCKA3bl: A Dual-Language Book, edited by Gleb Struve. Twelve tales by such masters as Chekhov, Tolstoy, Dostoevsky, Pushkin, others. Excellent word-for-word English translations on facing pages, plus teaching and study aids, Russian/English vocabulary, biographical/critical introductions, more. 416pp. 5⅜ x 8½. 26244-8 Pa. $9.95

PHILADELPHIA THEN AND NOW: 60 Sites Photographed in the Past and Present, Kenneth Finkel and Susan Oyama. Rare photographs of City Hall, Logan Square, Independence Hall, Betsy Ross House, other landmarks juxtaposed with contemporary views. Captures changing face of historic city. Introduction. Captions. 128pp. 8¼ x 11. 25790-8 Pa. $9.95

AIA ARCHITECTURAL GUIDE TO NASSAU AND SUFFOLK COUNTIES, LONG ISLAND, The American Institute of Architects, Long Island Chapter, and the Society for the Preservation of Long Island Antiquities. Comprehensive, well-researched and generously illustrated volume brings to life over three centuries of Long Island's great architectural heritage. More than 240 photographs with authoritative, extensively detailed captions. 176pp. 8¼ x 11. 26946-9 Pa. $14.95

NORTH AMERICAN INDIAN LIFE: Customs and Traditions of 23 Tribes, Elsie Clews Parsons (ed.). 27 fictionalized essays by noted anthropologists examine religion, customs, government, additional facets of life among the Winnebago, Crow, Zuni, Eskimo, other tribes. 480pp. 6⅛ x 9¼. 27377-6 Pa. $10.95

AUTOBIOGRAPHY: The Story of My Experiments with Truth, Mohandas K. Gandhi. Boyhood, legal studies, purification, the growth of the Satyagraha (nonviolent protest) movement. Critical, inspiring work of the man responsible for the freedom of India. 480pp. 5⅜ x 8½. (USO)   24593-4 Pa. $8.95

CELTIC MYTHS AND LEGENDS, T. W. Rolleston. Masterful retelling of Irish and Welsh stories and tales. Cuchulain, King Arthur, Deirdre, the Grail, many more. First paperback edition. 58 full-page illustrations. 512pp. 5⅜ x 8½.   26507-2 Pa. $9.95

THE PRINCIPLES OF PSYCHOLOGY, William James. Famous long course complete, unabridged. Stream of thought, time perception, memory, experimental methods; great work decades ahead of its time. 94 figures. 1,391pp. 5⅜ x 8½. 2-vol. set.
Vol. I: 20381-6 Pa. $13.95
Vol. II: 20382-4 Pa. $14.95

THE WORLD AS WILL AND REPRESENTATION, Arthur Schopenhauer. Definitive English translation of Schopenhauer's life work, correcting more than 1,000 errors, omissions in earlier translations. Translated by E. F. J. Payne. Total of 1,269pp. 5⅜ x 8½. 2-vol. set.
Vol. 1: 21761-2 Pa. $12.95
Vol. 2: 21762-0 Pa. $12.95

MAGIC AND MYSTERY IN TIBET, Madame Alexandra David-Neel. Experiences among lamas, magicians, sages, sorcerers, Bonpa wizards. A true psychic discovery. 32 illustrations. 321pp. 5⅜ x 8½. (USO)   22682-4 Pa. $9.95

THE EGYPTIAN BOOK OF THE DEAD, E. A. Wallis Budge. Complete reproduction of Ani's papyrus, finest ever found. Full hieroglyphic text, interlinear transliteration, word-for-word translation, smooth translation. 533pp. 6½ x 9¼.
21866-X Pa. $11.95

MATHEMATICS FOR THE NONMATHEMATICIAN, Morris Kline. Detailed, college-level treatment of mathematics in cultural and historical context, with numerous exercises. Recommended Reading Lists. Tables. Numerous figures. 641pp. 5⅜ x 8½.
24823-2 Pa. $11.95

THEORY OF WING SECTIONS: Including a Summary of Airfoil Data, Ira H. Abbott and A. E. von Doenhoff. Concise compilation of subsonic aerodynamic characteristics of NACA wing sections, plus description of theory. 350pp. of tables. 693pp. 5⅜ x 8½.   60586-8 Pa. $14.95

THE RIME OF THE ANCIENT MARINER, Gustave Doré, S. T. Coleridge. Doré's finest work; 34 plates capture moods, subtleties of poem. Flawless full-size reproductions printed on facing pages with authoritative text of poem. "Beautiful. Simply beautiful."—*Publisher's Weekly.* 77pp. 9¼ x 12.   22305-1 Pa. $7.95

NORTH AMERICAN INDIAN DESIGNS FOR ARTISTS AND CRAFTSPEOPLE, Eva Wilson. Over 360 authentic copyright-free designs adapted from Navajo blankets, Hopi pottery, Sioux buffalo hides, more. Geometrics, symbolic figures, plant and animal motifs, etc. 128pp. 8⅜ x 11. (EUK)   25341-4 Pa. $8.95

SCULPTURE: Principles and Practice, Louis Slobodkin. Step-by-step approach to clay, plaster, metals, stone; classical and modern. 253 drawings, photos. 255pp. 8⅛ x 11.
22960-2 Pa. $11.95

PHOTOGRAPHIC SKETCHBOOK OF THE CIVIL WAR, Alexander Gardner. 100 photos taken on field during the Civil War. Famous shots of Manassas Harper's Ferry, Lincoln, Richmond, slave pens, etc. 244pp. 10⅝ x 8¼. 22731-6 Pa. $10.95

FIVE ACRES AND INDEPENDENCE, Maurice G. Kains. Great back-to-the-land classic explains basics of self-sufficient farming. The one book to get. 95 illustrations. 397pp. 5⅜ x 8½. 20974-1 Pa. $7.95

SONGS OF EASTERN BIRDS, Dr. Donald J. Borror. Songs and calls of 60 species most common to eastern U.S.: warblers, woodpeckers, flycatchers, thrushes, larks, many more in high-quality recording. Cassette and manual 99912-2 $9.95

A MODERN HERBAL, Margaret Grieve. Much the fullest, most exact, most useful compilation of herbal material. Gigantic alphabetical encyclopedia, from aconite to zedoary, gives botanical information, medical properties, folklore, economic uses, much else. Indispensable to serious reader. 161 illustrations. 888pp. 6½ x 9¼. 2-vol. set. (USO) Vol. I: 22798-7 Pa. $9.95
Vol. II: 22799-5 Pa. $9.95

HIDDEN TREASURE MAZE BOOK, Dave Phillips. Solve 34 challenging mazes accompanied by heroic tales of adventure. Evil dragons, people-eating plants, blood-thirsty giants, many more dangerous adversaries lurk at every twist and turn. 34 mazes, stories, solutions. 48pp. 8¼ x 11. 24566-7 Pa. $2.95

LETTERS OF W. A. MOZART, Wolfgang A. Mozart. Remarkable letters show bawdy wit, humor, imagination, musical insights, contemporary musical world; includes some letters from Leopold Mozart. 276pp. 5⅜ x 8½. 22859-2 Pa. $7.95

BASIC PRINCIPLES OF CLASSICAL BALLET, Agrippina Vaganova. Great Russian theoretician, teacher explains methods for teaching classical ballet. 118 illustrations. 175pp. 5⅜ x 8½. 22036-2 Pa. $5.95

THE JUMPING FROG, Mark Twain. Revenge edition. The original story of The Celebrated Jumping Frog of Calaveras County, a hapless French translation, and Twain's hilarious "retranslation" from the French. 12 illustrations. 66pp. 5⅜ x 8½. 22686-7 Pa. $3.95

BEST REMEMBERED POEMS, Martin Gardner (ed.). The 126 poems in this superb collection of 19th- and 20th-century British and American verse range from Shelley's "To a Skylark" to the impassioned "Renascence" of Edna St. Vincent Millay and to Edward Lear's whimsical "The Owl and the Pussycat." 224pp. 5⅜ x 8½. 27165-X Pa. $5.95

COMPLETE SONNETS, William Shakespeare. Over 150 exquisite poems deal with love, friendship, the tyranny of time, beauty's evanescence, death and other themes in language of remarkable power, precision and beauty. Glossary of archaic terms. 80pp. 5³⁄₁₆ x 8¼. 26686-9 Pa. $1.00

BODIES IN A BOOKSHOP, R. T. Campbell. Challenging mystery of blackmail and murder with ingenious plot and superbly drawn characters. In the best tradition of British suspense fiction. 192pp. 5⅜ x 8½. 24720-1 Pa. $6.95

PLANS OF CARE FOR
SPECIALTY PRACTICE

Surgical Nursing

BONNIE ALLBAUGH, RN, MS, CDE
Clinical Nurse Manager
University of Wisconsin Hospitals and Clinics
Madison, Wisconsin

KATHY V. GETTRUST, RN, BSN ~ *Series Editor*
Case Manager
Midwest Medical Home Care
Milwaukee, Wisconsin

Delmar Publishers Inc.™

I(T)P™

NOTICE TO THE READER

Publisher does not warrant or guarantee any of the products described herein or perform any independent analysis in connection with any of the product information contained herein. Publisher does not assume, and expressly disclaims, any obligation to obtain and include information other than that provided to it by the manufacturer.

The reader is expressly warned to consider and adopt all safety precautions that might be indicated by the activities described herein and to avoid all potential hazards. By following the instructions contained herein, the reader willingly assumes all risks in connection with such instructions.

The publisher makes no representations or warranties of any kind, including but not limited to, the warranties of fitness for particular purpose or merchantability, nor are any such representations implied with respect to the material set forth herein, and the publisher takes no responsibility with respect to such material. The publisher shall not be liable for any special, consequential or exemplary damages resulting, in whole or in part, from the readers' use of, or reliance upon, this material.

Delmar publishing team:
Publisher: David C. Gordon
Administrative Editor: Patricia Casey
Associate Editor: Elisabeth F. Williams
Project Editor: Danya M. Plotsky
Production Coordinator: Mary Ellen Black
Art and Design Coordinator: Megan K. DeSantis
                              Timothy J. Conners

For information, address

Delmar Publishers Inc.
3 Columbia Circle, Box 15015
Albany, NY 12212-5015

Printed in the United States of America
Published simultaneously in Canada
by Nelson Canada,
a division of The Thomson Corporation

1 2 3 4 5 6 7 8 9 10 XXX 00 99 98 97 96 95 94

Library of Congress Cataloging-in-Publication Data

Surgical nursing / (edited by) Bonnie Allbaugh.
      p.   cm.—(Plans of care for specialty practice)
   Includes index.
   ISBN 0-8273-6297-8
   1. Surgical nursing.   2. Nursing care plans.   I. Allbaugh, Bonnie.   II. Series.
   [DNLM: 1. Surgical Nursing—methods.   2. Patient Care Planning.
WY 161 S9611   1994]
RD99.S94   1994
610.73′677—dc20
DNLM/DLC
for Library of Congress   93-26626
                                                                              CIP

TABLE OF CONTENTS

PLANS OF CARE FOR
SPECIALTY PRACTICE

Surgical Nursing

CONTRIBUTORS

Bonnie Allbaugh, RN, MS, CDE
Clinical Nurse Manager, Diabetes,
  Renal and Geriatric Clinics
University of Wisconsin Hospitals
  and Clinics
Madison, WI
• Diabetes Mellitus: Effects of
  Hospitalization and Surgery
• Diabetes Mellitus: Initiating
  Insulin

Penny M. Bernards, RN, MS, GNP
Clinical Nurse Specialist, Peripheral
  Vascular Nursing
University of Wisconsin Hospitals
  and Clinics
Madison, WI
• Arteriography (Angiogram)
• Carotid Endarterectomy
• Thrombophlebitis/Deep-Vein
  Thrombosis

Linda A. Briggs, RN, MS, CCRN
Clinical Nurse Specialist,
  Cardiovascular Nursing
Rural Wisconsin Hospital
  Cooperative
Sauk City, WI
• Digitalis Toxicity

Rochelle M. Carlson, RN, MS,
  CRRN
Clinical Nurse Specialist—Geriatrics
  and Rehabilitation
William S. Middleton Memorial
  Veterans Hospital
Madison, WI
• Lumbar Puncture

Mercy Galicia, RN, BSN
Nurse Manager—Orthopedic,
  Gynecology, Urology, Plastic, and
  Oral Surgery
St. Vincent Hospital and Medical
  Center
Portland, OR
• Breast Reconstruction
• Hysterectomy
• Mastectomy
• Nephrectomy
• Nephrostomy
• Prostatectomy

Gail Gaustad, RN, MS
Director, Project Access
Sauk Prairie Memorial Hospital
Prairie du Sac, WI
(previously, Manager, General
  Surgery Unit, Meriter Hospital,
  Madison, WI)
• Breast Reconstruction
• Hysterectomy
• Mastectomy
• Nephrectomy
• Nephrostomy
• Prostatectomy

LuAnn Greiner, RN, BSN
Assistant Clinical Nurse Manager—
  General Medicine Unit
University of Wisconsin Hospitals
  and Clinics
Madison, WI
• Acquired Immunodeficiency
  Syndrome: Opportunistic
  Infections, Secondary Cancers and
  Neurological Disease

Deborah R. Johnson, RN, MS, CNSN
Clinical Nurse Specialist—Medical/ Surgical Nursing
Meriter Hospital
Madison, WI
- Basic Standards for Preoperative and Postoperative Care
- Pain Management: Patient- Controlled Analgesia
- Cholecystectomy
- Nutrition Support: Enteral Nutrition
- Nutrition Support: Total Parenteral Nutrition

Ellen M. Jovle, RN, MS
Clinical Nurse Specialist—Chronic Illness
Meriter Hospital
Madison, WI
- Corticosteroid Therapy
- Pleural Effusion

Barbara King, RN, MS, CCRN, ANP
Geriatric Nurse Practitioner
University of Wisconsin Hospitals and Clinics Regional Services
Madison, WI
- Prevention and Care of Pressure Ulcers

Susan Murray, RN, MS
Clinical Nurse Manager—General Surgery/Enterostomal Therapy
University of Wisconsin Hospitals and Clinics
Madison, WI
- Appendectomy
- Basic Standards for Preoperative and Postoperative Care
- Bowel Resection With or Without Ostomy
- Gastrectomy: Bilroth I, Bilroth II, Antrectomy, Vagotomy
- Hiatal Hernia Repair: Nissen Fundoplication
- Hernia Repair: Ventral Herniorraphy
- Pancreatic Surgery: Wipple Procedure
- Prevention and Care of Pressure Ulcers

Lynn Schoengrund, RN, MS
Director of Nursing
Meriter Hospital
Madison, WI
- Hemodialysis
- Peritoneal Dialysis

Andrea Strayer, RN, MS, CNRN
Clinical Nurse Specialist— Neuroscience and Epilepsy
William S. Middleton Memorial Veterans Hospital
Madison, WI
- Altered Consciousness
- Brain Tumors
- Craniotomy
- Ventricular Shunts

Mary A. Vassalotti, RN, MS
Clinical Nurse Specialist—Oncology
Meriter Hospital
Madison, WI
- Long-Term Venous Access Devices

Linda Wonoski, RN, MSN
Manager—Intermediate Care Unit
Meriter Hospital
Madison, WI
- Cardiac Catheterization
- Chest Tubes
- Femoral-Popliteal Bypass
- Laryngectomy
- Pneumonectomy
- Thoracotomy
- Tracheostomy

PREFACE

Medical-surgical nursing is one of the largest specialties within the nursing profession. Medical or surgical nursing is most often selected by nurses as they begin their nursing career. The body of knowledge required to practice surgical nursing is growing constantly. The skilled nurse faces a multiplicity of surgical diagnoses and problems requiring familiarity with extensive pathophysiology, human psychosocial needs, and current nursing diagnoses and treatments. While the roles and responsibilities of the nurse are expanding, the time to carry these out is decreasing. Care must be planned and coordinated to be accomplished efficiently. The plans of care in this book are designed to assist the experienced nurse with prioritizing care, to give direction, and to provide continuity of care during hospitalization and after discharge.

In surgical nursing, the professions of nursing and medicine are closely interrelated. Recognizing this fact, this book is organized by surgical procedure and/or medical diagnosis. The most common surgical procedures and diagnoses requiring hospital admission have been included. The plans are comprised of background information on the surgical procedure or diagnosis: etiologies or indications, clinical manifestations, and clinical diagnostic findings; nursing diagnoses, expected patient outcomes, and nursing interventions and rationales; and discharge planning/continuity of care strategies.

Practicing nurse experts from all areas of medical-surgical nursing have contributed to this project. Their knowledge, practical experience and high standards of care are reflected in the content of each plan of care.

ACKNOWLEDGMENTS

This book could not have been written without the willingness and interest of the contributors to share their expertise and time in writing the plans of care. Much can be learned from each. I would like to thank Trish Casey, Administrative Editor, Health Sciences, Beth Williams, Health Sciences Editor, and Elena Mauceri, Project Editor, for their support and assistance and Delmar Publishers for this opportunity. For assistance with typing and manuscript development, I want to thank Trisha Borgrud, who cheerfully gave up many evenings and weekends. I especially want to thank my husband, Stu, for his encouragement, patience, and willingness to take over house and dog responsibilities during the long hours of preparing this book, and my daughter, Gaylin, for her moral support from afar.

SERIES INTRODUCTION

Scientific and technological developments over the past several decades have revolutionized health care and care of the sick. These rapid and extensive advancements of knowledge have occurred in all fields, necessitating an ever-increasing specialization of practice. For nurses to be effective and meet the challenge in today's specialty settings, the body of clinical knowledge and skill needs to continually expand. *Plans of Care for Specialty Practice* has been written to aid the practicing nurse in meeting this challenge. The purpose of this series is to provide comprehensive, state-of-the-art plans of care and associated resource information for patient situations most commonly seen within a specialty that will serve as a standard from which care can be individualized. These plans of care are based on the profession's scientific approach to problem solving—the nursing process. Though the books are written primarily as a guide for frontline staff nurses and clinical nurse specialists practicing in specialty settings, they have application for student nurses as well.

DOCUMENTATION OF CARE

The Joint Commission on Accreditation of Healthcare Organizations (JCAHO) assumes authority for evaluating the quality and effectiveness of the practice of nursing. In 1991, the JCAHO developed its first new nursing care standards in more than a decade. One of the changes brought about by these new standards was the elimination of need for every patient to have a handwritten or computer-generated care plan in his or her chart detailing all or most of the care to be provided. The Joint Commission's standard that describes the documentation requirements stipulates that nursing assessments, identification of nursing diagnoses and/or patient care needs, interventions, outcomes of care, and discharge planning be permanently integrated into the clinical record. In other words, the nursing process needs to be documented. A separate care plan is no longer needed; however, planning and implementing care must continue as always, but using whatever form of documentation that has been approved by an institution. *Plans of Care for Specialty Practice* can be easily used with a wide variety of approaches to documentation of care.

ELEMENTS OF THE PLANS OF CARE

The chapter title is the presenting situation, which represents the most commonly seen conditions/disorders treated within the specialty setting. It may be a medical diagnosis (e.g., diabetes mellitus), a syndrome (e.g., acquired immunodeficiency syndrome), a surgical procedure (e.g., mastectomy), or a diagnostic/therapeutic procedure (e.g., thrombolytic therapy).

An opening paragraph provides a definition or concise overview of the presenting situation. It describes the condition and may contain pertinent physiological/psychological bases for the disorder. It is brief and not intended to replace further investigation for comprehensive understanding of the condition.

Etiologies

A listing of causative factors responsible for or contributing to the presenting situation is provided. This may include predisposing diseases, injuries or trauma, surgeries, microorganisms, genetic factors, environmental hazards, drugs, or psychosocial disorders. In presenting situations where no clear causal relationship can be established, current theories regarding the etiology may be included.

Clinical Manifestations

Objective and subjective signs and symptoms which describe the particular presenting situation are included. This information is revealed as a result of a health history and physical assessment and becomes part of the data base.

Clinical/Diagnostic Findings

This component contains possible diagnostic tests and procedures which might be done to determine abnormalities associated with a particular presenting situation. The name of the diagnostic procedure and the usual abnormal findings are listed.

Nursing Diagnosis

The nursing management of the health problem commences with the planning care phase of the nursing process. This includes obtaining a comprehensive history and physical assessment, identification of the nursing diagnoses, expected outcomes, interventions, and discharge planning needs.

Diagnostic labels identified by NANDA through the Tenth National Conference in April 1992 are being used throughout this series. (Based on North American Nursing Diagnosis Association, 1992. *NANDA Nursing Diagnoses: Definitions and Classification 1992*.) We have also identified new diagnoses not yet on the official NANDA list. We endorse NANDA's recommendation for nurses to develop new nursing diagnoses as the need arises and we encourage nurses using this series to do the same.

"Related to" Statements

Related to statements suggest a link or connection to the nursing diagnosis and provide direction for identifying appropriate nursing interventions. They are termed contributing factors, causes, or etiologies. There is frequently more than one related to statement for a given diagnosis. For example, change in job, marital difficulties, and impending surgery may all be "related to" the patient's nursing diagnosis of anxiety.

There is disagreement at present regarding inclusion of pathophysiological/medical diagnoses in the list of related to statements. Frequently, a medical diagnosis does not provide adequate direction for nursing care. For example, the nursing diagnosis of chronic pain related to rheumatoid arthritis does not readily suggest specific nursing interventions. It is more useful for the nurse to identify specific causes of the chronic pain such as inflammation, swelling, and fatigue; these in turn suggest more specific interventions. In cases where the medical diagnosis provides

the best available information, as occurs with the more medically oriented diagnoses such as decreased cardiac output or impaired gas exchange, the medical terminology is included.

Defining Characteristics

Data collection is frequently the source for identifying defining characteristics, sometimes called signs and symptoms or patient behaviors. These data, both subjective and objective, are organized into meaningful patterns and used to verify the nursing diagnosis. The most commonly seen defining characteristics for a given diagnosis are included and should not be viewed as an all-inclusive listing.

Risk Factors

Nursing diagnoses designated as high risk are supported by risk factors that direct nursing actions to reduce or prevent the problem from developing. Since these nursing diagnoses have not yet occurred, risk factors replace the listing of actual defining characteristics and related to statements.

Patient Outcomes

Patient outcomes, sometimes termed patient goals, are observable behaviors or data which measure changes in the condition of the patient after nursing treatment. They are objective indicators of progress toward prevention of the development of high-risk nursing diagnoses or resolution/modification of actual diagnoses. Like other elements of the plan of care, patient outcome statements are dynamic and must be reviewed and modified periodically as the patient progresses. Assigning realistic "target or evaluation dates" for evaluation of progress toward outcome achievement is crucial. Since there are so many considerations involved in when the outcome could be achieved (e.g., varying lengths of stay, individual patient condition), these plans of care do not include evaluation dates; the date needs to be individualized and assigned using the professional judgment and discretion of the nurse caring for the patient.

Nursing Interventions

Nursing interventions are the treatment options/actions the nurse employs to prevent, modify, or resolve the nursing diagnosis. They are driven by the related to statements and risk factors and are selected based on the outcomes to be achieved. Treatment options should be chosen only if they apply realistically to a specific patient condition. The nurse also needs to determine frequencies for each intervention based on professional judgment and individual patient need.

We have included independent, interdependent, and dependent nursing interventions as they reflect current practice. We have not made a distinction between these kinds of interventions because of institutional differences and increasing independence in nursing practice. The interventions that are interdependent or dependent will require collaboration with other professionals. The nurse will need to determine when this is necessary and take appropriate action. The interventions include assessment, therapeutic, and teaching actions.

Rationales

The rationales provide scientific explanation or theoretical bases for the interventions; interventions can then be selected more intelligently and actions can be tailored to each individual's needs.

The rationales provided may be used as a quick reference for the nurse unfamiliar with the reason for a given intervention and as a tool for patient education. These rationales may include principles, theory, and/or research findings from current literature. The rationales are intended as reference information and, as such, should not be transcribed into the permanent patient record. A rationale is not provided when the intervention is self-explanatory.

Discharge Planning/Continuity of Care

Because stays in acute care hospitals are becoming shorter due to cost containment efforts, patients are frequently discharged still needing care; discharge planning is the process of anticipating and planning for needs after discharge. Effective discharge planning begins with admission and continues with ongoing assessment of the patient and family needs. Included in the discharge planning/continuity of care section are suggestions for follow-up measures, such as skilled nursing care; physical, occupational, speech, or psychiatric therapy; spiritual counseling, social service assistance; follow-up appointments, and equipment/supplies.

References

A listing of references appears at the conclusion of each plan of care or related group of plans. The purpose of the references is to cite specific work used and to specify background information or suggestions for further reading. Citings provided represent the most current nursing theory and/or research bases for inclusion in the plans of care.

A Word About Family

The authors and editors of this series recognize the vital role that family and/or other significant people play in the recovery of a patient. Isolation from the family unit during hospitalization may disrupt self-concept and feelings of security. Family members, or persons involved in the patient's care, must be included in the teaching to ensure that it is appropriate and will be followed. In an effort to constrain the books' size, the patient outcome, nursing intervention, and discharge planning sections usually do not include reference to the family or other significant people; however, the reader can assume that they are to be included along with the patient whenever appropriate.

Any undertaking of the magnitude of this series becomes the concern of many people. I specifically thank all of the very capable nursing specialists who authored or edited the individual books. Their attention to providing state-of-the-art information in a quick, usable form will provide the reader with current reference information for providing excellent patient care.

The editorial staff, particularly Patricia E. Casey and Elisabeth F. Williams, and production people at Delmar Publishers have been outstanding. Their frank criticism, comments, and encouragement have improved the quality of the series.

Finally, but most importantly, I thank my husband, John, and children, Katrina and Allison, for their sacrifices and patience during yet another publishing project.

Kathy V. Gettrust
Series Editor

LIST OF TABLES

Special Needs and Procedures

▼

BASIC STANDARDS FOR PREOPERATIVE AND POSTOPERATIVE CARE

Deborah R. Johnson, RN, MS, CNSN
Susan Murray, RN, MS

The preoperative period is the time between when the surgery is planned and the time surgery actually takes place. Inpatient preoperative time may be very short or nonexistent, making outpatient interventions necessary. These interventions are done to assure physical and emotional safety before and after the surgery.

ETIOLOGIES

See individual plans of care.

CLINICAL MANIFESTATIONS

See individual plans of care.

CLINICAL/DIAGNOSTIC FINDINGS

See individual plans of care.

NURSING DIAGNOSIS: KNOWLEDGE DEFICIT REGARDING PREOPERATIVE PROCEDURES, POSTOPERATIVE PROCEDURES, AND SELF-CARE

Related To
- New experiences
- No previous information

Defining Characteristics

Verbalization of unfamiliarity with routines and expectations
Requests information
Inaccurate follow-through of instructions
Inappropriate or exaggerated behaviors

Patient Outcomes

The patient will
- state the routine preoperative and postoperative care.
- demonstrate the ability to perform techniques designed to prevent postoperative complications.
- define a plan for ongoing care needs posthospitalization.

Nursing Interventions	Rationales
Provide information about the usual preoperative surgical routine, for example, blood work, electrocardiogram (ECG), chest x-ray, bowel and/or skin preps, insertion of tubes/lines, food/fluid restrictions, preoperative medications, and documentation of allergies.	
Inform about the anticipated postoperative care: 1. postanesthesia care unit routines 2. equipment [dressings, intravenous (IV) lines, tubes] 3. activity limitations and expectations 4. dietary modifications 5. assessments [intake and output (I&O), vital signs (VSs), bowel and breath sounds, neurological checks] 6. treatments (respiratory care, wound care, circulatory care) 7. pain control 8. medications	

Nursing Interventions	Rationales
Demonstrate techniques the patient will be expected to perform post-operatively: 1. cough and deep breathing 2. incentive spirometry 3. leg exercises 4. correct method for ambulation	
Provide with educational materials specific to the surgical intervention.	Written materials are helpful for later reference.
Assess patient's capability to perform anticipated self-care posthospitalization.	Discharge planning must begin as soon as the patient enters the hospital.

NURSING DIAGNOSIS: ANXIETY/FEAR

Related To
- Surgical experience
- Hospitalization

Defining Characteristics
Inability to relax
Apprehensive, uncertain
Fearful, overexcited
Distressed, worried
Anxious, withdrawn

Patient Outcomes
The patient will
- verbalize fears.
- identify coping mechanisms.
- describe hospital routines, diagnostic tests, preoperative procedures, the surgery, and its anticipated results.
- state feeling less anxious, less fearful.

Nursing Interventions	Rationales
Assess for signs and symptoms of anxiety and fear and effectiveness of current coping skills.	
Include significant others in orientation and instructional sessions.	

Nursing Interventions	**Rationales**
Implement measures to reduce anxiety or fear: 1. Orient to hospital environment and preoperative and postoperative routines. 2. Introduce staff who will be participating in patient's care. 3. Respond to call signal as soon as possible. 4. Encourage to verbalize fears and anxiety. 5. Clarify any misconceptions the patient may have about the surgery. 6. Provide a calm, restful environment. 7. Reassure patient that pain will be controlled postoperatively. 8. Inform patient that a visit from clergy can be arranged if desired.	

Post-Operative Care

The postoperative period begins after surgery and includes interventions to assist the patient in returning to his or her normal level of functioning.

ETIOLOGIES

See individual plans of care.

CLINICAL MANIFESTATIONS

See individual plans of care.

CLINICAL/DIAGNOSTIC FINDINGS

See individual plans of care.

NURSING DIAGNOSIS: INEFFECTIVE AIRWAY CLEARANCE

Related To
- Pain
- Anesthesia
- Anxiety

Defining Characteristics

Abnormal breath sounds (crackles, wheezes)
Changes in rate or depth of respirations
Ineffective cough with or without sputum production

Patient Outcomes

The patient will maintain clear open airways, as evidenced by normal breath sounds and effective cough.

Nursing Interventions	Rationales
Assess for signs and symptoms of ineffective breathing pattern (shallow or slow respirations, hyperventilation, dyspnea, use of accessory muscles).	
Auscultate lung fields and assess sputum production at least every 4 hr.	
Implement measures to promote effective airway clearance: 1. Ensure adequate pain control: positioning, splinting, premedication prior to activity or procedure. 2. Increase activity as prescribed and tolerated. 3. Ensure adequate and balanced fluid intake. 4. Provide humidified air or oxygen as prescribed. 5. Assist patient with coughing, deep breathing, and incentive spirometry every 2 hr.	Adequate fluids help liquefy tenacious secretions.

NURSING DIAGNOSIS: PAIN

Related To
- Surgical incision
- Surgical manipulation
- Reflex muscle spasm

Defining Characteristics
Muscle tension, guarded body posture
Inability to participate in activities to facilitate recovery
Facial grimacing, moaning, diaphoresis, restlessness, irritability
Blood pressure and pulse changes
Verbally expresses complaints of pain

Patient Outcomes
Patient will
- express satisfaction with pain relief.
- participate in postoperative activities that facilitate recovery.

Nursing Interventions	Rationales
Assess the nature of the patient's pain, including location, quality, and intensity, utilizing a pain-rating scale of 1–10 (1 being minimal pain and 10 being the worst pain imaginable).	
Assess factors that seem to alleviate and/or aggravate the patient's pain.	

Nursing Interventions	Rationales
Implement measures to reduce pain: 1. Perform measures to decrease the patient's fear and anxiety about the pain experience. 2. Assure the patient of efforts to reduce the pain. 3. Provide for, or assist with, non-pharmacological comfort measures: splint and support the surgical area during activity; position the patient in a manner that minimizes tension at the surgical site; provide a quiet, restful environment for the patient; administer back rubs or massage muscles to ease tension; and apply heat or cold remedies to affected area(s) if not contraindicated, as prescribed. 4. Administer analgesics as prescribed: medicate patient on a schedule; medicate the patient in anticipation of painful activities such as dressing changes, coughing, turning, deep breathing, or ambulation.	
Implement a combination of pharmacological and nonpharmacological therapeutic interventions to facilitate the patient's comfort.	
Evaluate the therapeutic effectiveness of each nursing intervention used to reduce patient's pain and modify plan accordingly.	

NURSING DIAGNOSIS: ACTIVITY INTOLERANCE

Related To
- Generalized postoperative weakness
- Bedrest
- Immobility
- An imbalance between oxygen supply and demand

Defining Characteristics
Verbally reports fatigue or weakness
Abnormal heart rate or blood pressure response to activity
Exertional discomfort or dyspnea

Patient Outcomes
The patient will
- demonstrate increased activity tolerance.
- verbalize feeling less fatigued or weak.
- demonstrate the ability to perform the activities of daily living without exertional chest pain, dyspnea, dizziness, diaphoresis, or a significant change in VSs.

Nursing Interventions	Rationales
Assess for patient's verbalization of fatigue and weakness.	
Assess for presence or absence of exertional chest pain, dyspnea, dizziness, or diaphoresis.	
Assess for presence of pulse rate not returning to preactivity level within a few minutes after stopping activity.	
Assess for presence of blood pressure changes with activity (hypotension or increased diastolic blood pressure).	
Implement measures to balance rest with activity: 1. Schedule nursing care activities to allow for periods of uninterrupted rest. 2. Limit the number of visitors and their length of stay. 3. Maintain activity restrictions as prescribed. 4. Instruct in energy-saving techniques; assure all supplies and personal articles are within reach. 5. Assist with self-care activities as needed.	
Increase patient's activity as prescribed and as tolerated.	

Nursing Interventions	Rationales
Instruct to stop and report any activity that causes shortness of breath, chest pain, dizziness, diaphoresis, extreme fatigue, or weakness.	

NURSING DIAGNOSIS: IMPAIRED PHYSICAL MOBILITY

Related To
- Postoperative pain
- Anxiety
- Activity intolerance
- Decreased strength and endurance

Defining Characteristics
Inability to move in bed, transfer, or ambulate
Reluctant to attempt movement
Limited range of motion
Decreased muscle strength

Patient Outcomes
Patient will demonstrate maximum physical mobility within the limitations imposed by the surgical intervention and postoperative care management.

Nursing Interventions	Rationales
Position the nurse call light within reach of patient at all times when patient is unattended.	
Assess for factors that may impair physical mobility; pain, fear of falling, surgical dressings or drains, and nausea.	
Implement measures to reduce pain.	
Implement measures to reduce nausea.	
Schedule interventions to increase activity when antiemetics and analgesics are at their peak therapeutic blood levels.	

Nursing Interventions	Rationales
Schedule activities after patient's rest periods, and not immediately after treatment or meals.	
Secure all dressings, drains, and tubes to decrease the chance of inadvertent removal during the patient's activities.	
Provide encouragement and praise for all efforts to increase physical mobility.	
Reinforce that the level of prescribed activity progression will enhance, not compromise, postoperative recovery and the healing process.	
Allow patient realistic, adequate time frames to complete expected activities.	
Increase activity and participation in self-care activities as prescribed and tolerated.	
Allow significant others to assist the patient with increased activity.	
Assess for and collaborate with the physician for a physical therapy consultation to maximize activity/ mobility progression.	
Collaborate with the physical therapist to coordinate care activities; set realistic mutual goals and outcomes for success.	

NURSING DIAGNOSIS: HIGH RISK FOR ALTERED PERIPHERAL AND/OR PULMONARY TISSUE PERFUSION

Risk Factors
- Venous stasis, intraoperative positioning, postoperative immobility, dehydration

- History of venous trauma/venous insufficiency
- Malignancy
- Concurrent hypercoagulability states
- Obesity

Patient Outcomes
Patient will
- not develop a venous thrombus.
- not experience a pulmonary embolism.

Nursing Interventions	Rationales
Instruct and assist with dorsiflexion, plantar flexion, and ankle-rolling exercises while in bed or in chair. Perform passive range of motion for patients unable to do active exercises.	Helps to reduce venous stasis and prevent peripheral pooling of blood.
Elevate foot of bed, if tolerated, and avoid positions that compromise lower extremity blood flow, for example, pillows under knees, crossing legs, use of knee gatch, or sitting for long periods of time.	An elevation of 10° can increase venous blood flow by 30%.
Encourage and assist with ambulation as prescribed. Ensure patient picks up feet and does not shuffle feet.	Maximizes muscular contraction to prevent peripheral pooling of blood.
Monitor intake and output to maintain proper fluid balance; avoid dehydration.	Prevents fluid volume deficit and increased blood viscosity, which lead to hypercoagulability.
Apply and remove antiembolic hose, elastic wraps, or intermittent venous compression devices as prescribed.	
Assess for and report signs and symptoms of venous thrombosis; for example, calf tenderness, warmth, redness, swelling, and pain with dorsiflexion.	
Do not massage or exercise any extremity suspected of thrombosis.	Prevent a pulmonary embolism.
Avoid activities that create a Valsalva response.	Prevent dislodgement of existing thrombi.

Nursing Interventions

Report signs and symptoms of pulmonary embolism immediately to physician, for example, dyspnea, cyanosis, restlessness, sudden shortness of breath, and chest pain.

Rationales

This is a medical emergency.

NURSING DIAGNOSIS: HIGH RISK FOR INFECTION—WOUND, URINARY TRACT, PNEUMONIA

Risk Factors
- Inadequate primary defenses: broken skin, traumatized tissue, decrease in ciliary action, stasis of body fluids
- Inadequate secondary defenses: decreased hemoglobin, leukopenia
- Suppressed inflammatory response; immunosuppression
- Tissue destruction, surgical incision, increased environmental exposure to pathogens
- Chronic disease, invasive procedures
- Malnutrition, trauma
- Immobility

Patient Outcomes
- Patient will remain free of wound infection, as evidenced by
  - absence of redness, warmth, and swelling around incision(s) or open wound(s)
  - absence of fever and chills
  - white blood cell count normal or returning toward normal
  - no unusual drainage from wound
  - negative wound drainage cultures
  - intact well-approximated wound edges when healing is done by primary intention
  - presence of granulation tissue when healing is done by secondary or tertiary intention
- Patient will remain free of urinary tract infection, as evidenced by
  - clear yellow urine
  - no unusual urine odor
  - absence of urgency, frequency, or dysuria
  - absence of fever and chills
  - absence of white blood cells or bacteria in urine
  - negative urine culture
- Patient will not develop pneumonia, as evidenced by
  - absence of fever and chills
  - normal breath sounds
  - normal breathing pattern, rate, and depth

– nonproductive cough
– absence of pleuritic pain
– white blood cell count normal or returning to normal
– clear chest x-ray
– negative sputum culture
– arterial blood gases within normal range for specific patient

Nursing Interventions	Rationales
Assess temperature at least every shift and monitor for presence of fever and chills. Report elevated temperatures and chilling episodes to physician.	
Monitor white blood cell count and report increased values or persistent elevations.	
Implement measures to prevent wound infection. 1. Assess wound for signs and symptoms of infection: redness, warmth, unusual tenderness, swelling, odor from wound site, and unusual wound drainage. 2. Use good hand-washing technique before caring for patient's wounds, drains, incisions, or tubes. 3. Maintain meticulous sterile or aseptic technique during all dressing changes or wound care interventions. 4. Reinforce the importance of good hand-washing technique and instruct patient not to touch incisions, drainage tubes, open wounds, or dressings unless patient is competent with wound care. 5. Obtain wound drainage cultures as prescribed, monitor results, and report accordingly. 6. Protect patient from others with documented infections or open contaminated wounds.	

Nursing Interventions

Implement measures to prevent urinary tract infection:

1. Assess for signs and symptoms of urinary tract infection: cloudy, foul smelling urine; dysuria; and frequency, urgency, and/or burning upon urination.
2. Monitor urinalysis and report presence of bacteria, white blood cells, or nitrites.
3. Obtain a urine specimen for culture and sensitivity as prescribed; report any abnormal results.
4. Implement measures to minimize occurrence of urinary tract infection:
   - Instruct patient to void when urge is felt.
   - Offer bedpan, urinal, or help to bathroom or commode at least twice a shift.
   - Perform actions to facilitate voiding (e.g., run water, pour warm water over perineum, provide privacy).
   - Instruct female patients to clean perineum front to back after urinating or defecating.
   - Instruct/assist patient with perineal care every day and after each bowel movement.
   - Monitor intake and output to assure adequacy and balance of fluid status.
   - Provide a minimum of 2,000–2,500 mL/day if not contraindicated.
   - Maintain sterile technique during urinary irrigations and/or catheterizations.

Rationales

Nursing Interventions	**Rationales**

5. If indwelling urinary catheter is needed or present:
  • Keep urine-collecting device below the level of the bladder at all times to prevent stasis or reflex of urine.
  • Maintain patency of catheter by keeping the tube free of kinks and irrigate catheter as prescribed.
  • Secure catheter to minimize risk of trauma to urethra or bladder.
  • Perform catheter care as needed to prevent mucous accumulation around the meatus.
  • Remove indwelling urinary catheter as soon as it is no longer needed.	

Nursing Interventions	Rationales

Implement measures to prevent pneumonia:

1. Assess for signs and symptoms of pneumonia: abnormal breath sounds (crackles, rubs); absent or diminished breath sounds; pleuritic chest pain; productive cough with purulent, green, or rust-colored sputum; presence of fever.
2. Monitor chest x-ray results.
3. Monitor white blood cell counts and arterial blood gas results.
4. Monitor intake and output to assure an adequate and balanced fuid status; provide a minimum of 2,000–2,500 mL/day if not contraindicated.
5. Obtain a sputum culture as prescribed; report any abnormal results.
6. Implement measures to improve breathing patterns:
   • Decrease fear and anxiety
   • Decrease pain.
   • Assist patient with coughing, turning, deep breathing, and use of incentive spirometer at least every 2 hr, while awake.
7. Reinforce the need for frequent oral hygiene and assist patient, as needed, with these practices.
8. Protect patient from others with documented respiratory tract infections.

NURSING DIAGNOSIS: HIGH RISK FOR INJURY—FALLS AND ASPIRATION

Risk Factors
• Reduced coordination
• Altered mentation
• Weakness and fatigue

- Orthostatic hypotension
- Central nervous system (CNS) depressant effects of medications
- Decreased level of consciousness
- Diminished gag reflex
- Flat positioning in prolonged supine position

Patient Outcomes
The patient will
- not experience falls.
- not aspirate secretions, foods, or fluids, as evidenced by normal breath sounds, afebriel state, and clear chest x-ray.

Nursing Interventions	**Rationales**
Assess for prior history of falls and/or aspiration.	
Identify predisposing factors that could increase the incidence of falls and/or aspiration.	
Implement measures to prevent falls: 1. Keep bed in low position with siderails up and needed items within reach. 2. Instruct to wear nonskid slippers or shoes when ambulating. 3. Position tubes and equipment so they do not interfere with ambulation. 4. Instruct to change position slowly (i.e., dangle patient at bedside for a few minutes before standing); slower movements will help decrease an orthostatic drop in blood pressure. 5. Assist with ambulation the first two times and as needed thereafter.	

Nursing Interventions	Rationales
Implement measures to reduce the risk of aspiration: 1. Position patient on side until awake, unless contraindicated. 2. Maintain NPO until alert and gag reflex present. 3. Have suction equipment nearby. 4. Place in semi-Fowler's position during eating and drinking and for 30 min after. 5. Suction patient and provide oral care as needed to remove secretions.	

NURSING DIAGNOSIS: HIGH RISK FOR FLUID VOLUME DEFICIT

Risk Factors
- Intraoperative blood loss
- Excessive vomiting
- Prolonged and/or excessive nasogastric tube drainage
- Profuse wound drainage
- Insensible fluid loss

Patient Outcomes
The patient will maintain an adequate fluid balance, as evidenced by
- normal skin turgor
- moist mucous membranes
- normal VSs
- normal urine specific gravity
- no evidence of confusion

Nursing Interventions	Rationales
Assess for signs and symptoms of fluid volume deficit at least every 8 hr, for example, decreased urine output, increased urine concentration, hypotension, thirst, increased pulse rate, decreased skin turgor, dry mucous membranes, weakness, and change in mental state.	

Nursing Interventions	Rationales
Maintain an accurate intake and output record.	
Monitor urine specific gravity every 8 hr.	A result greater than 1.030 may indicate a fluid volume deficit.
Weigh daily.	A weight loss greater than 0.5 kg/day may indicate a fluid volume deficit.
Administer prescribed IV fluids and encourage oral intake, maintain an intake of 2,500 mL/day unless contraindicated.	

NURSING DIAGNOSIS: HIGH RISK FOR URINARY RETENTION

Risk Factors
- Depressant effect of medications
- Altered mobility

Patient Outcomes
The patient will demonstrate normal adequate urine output and elimination pattern.

Nursing Interventions	Rationales
Assess every 4 to 8 hours for signs and symptoms of urinary retention, for example, small frequent voidings, dribbling, presence of residual urine, and decrease or absence of urine output.	
Monitor for an output of at least 30 mL of urine per hour.	
Instruct to urinate whenever the urge is felt.	
Offer bedpan or urinal every 2–3 hr.	
Encourage to use nonnarcotic analgesics once severe pain has subsided.	Narcotics can have a depressant effect on bladder muscle tone.

Nursing Interventions	Rationales
If urinary retention occurs, contact physician regarding intermittent catheterization or insertion of an indwelling catheter.	

DISCHARGE PLANNING/CONTINUITY OF CARE

- Assure understanding of the self-care management plan, for example, wound care, assessments and dressing changes, any dietary restrictions, activity level progression, medication administration, and when to notify the physician.
- Refer to a home care agency if continued nursing care, teaching, or assistance with self-care management is needed.
- Assist with obtaining prescriptions and supplies. Establish a plan for replenishing necessary materials and refilling prescriptions as needed.
- Arrange for the initial postoperative physician office visit.

REFERENCES

Lawler, M. (1991). Managing other complications. *Nursing, 21*(11), 40–46.

Lewis, S. M. & Collier, I. C. (1992). *Medical surgical nursing: Assessment and management of clinical problems* (3rd ed). St. Louis, MO: Mosby.

McConnell, E. A. (1991). Minimizing respiratory problems. *Nursing, 21*(11), 34–39.

Thompson, J. M., McFarland, G. K., Hirsch, J. E., Tucker, S. M., & Bowers, A. C. (1993). *Mosby's manual of clinical nursing* (3rd ed.). St. Louis, MO: Mosby.

LONG-TERM VENOUS ACCESS DEVICES

Mary A. Vassalotti, RN, MS

Long-term venous access devices are used to administer intravenous (IV) antibiotics, chemotherapy, hydration fluids, and total parenteral nutrition in either the home or the hospital setting. They may be inserted peripherally, centrally through the chest or implanted in a pocket on the chest. These devices are either external catheters or implanted ports accessed through the skin with a noncoring needle. There are two types of catheters: closed end (Groshong) and open end (Hickman). Placement of either an external catheter or implanted port can be performed as an outpatient procedure under local anesthetic. This plan encompasses centrally placed access devices.

ETIOLOGIES

None.

CLINICAL MANIFESTATIONS

- Poor peripheral access for short-term IV catheters
- Receiving vesicant/irritating medication
- Potential for prolonged therapy (months)
- Fear of repetitive needle sticks
- Need for frequent blood draws/blood products

CLINICAL/DIAGNOSTIC FINDINGS

None.

NURSING DIAGNOSIS: KNOWLEDGE DEFICIT—PROCEDURE AND POSTOPERATIVE CARE

Related To
- New experience
- No previous exposure to information.

Patient Outcomes

The patient will

- state reasons for and process of placement of device.
- state immediate postoperative complications: bleeding, pneumothorax.
- demonstrate site care, dressing change, inspection of the site, cap changes, and flushing technique appropriate for the type of catheter.
- state who and when to call for assistance.
- define comfort measures to relieve pain and discomfort after placement of the line.

Nursing Interventions	Rationales
Discuss reason(s) for device being placed (see Clinical Manifestations and Table 2.1).	
Explain process for placement: 1. sterile procedure 2. IV placed prior to procedure 3. potential IV sedation with placement 4. use of local anesthetic 5. actual procedure time as little as 30 min 6. chest x-ray taken to confirm placement	Implanted ports are placed in the right infraclavicular fossa (see Figure 2.1). The catheter is threaded through the subclavian vein and terminates at the junction of the superior vena cava and the right atrium. Incision will be approximately 3 in. long with internal stitches. External catheters are threaded through the subclavian vein and terminate at the junction of the superior vena cava just above the right atrium (see Figure 2.2). The proximal end is tunnelled from the entrance site in the subclavian vein through the subcutaneous fascia of the chest wall and brought out through an exit site on the chest. The catheter will have a Dacron polyester fiber cuff placed about 2 mm from the exit site. This cuff promotes fibrin growth, which helps anchor the catheter in place. The cuff will also prevent bacteria from migrating up the catheter.

Nursing Interventions	Rationales
Instruct patient to expect shoulder stiffness and soreness for 24–72 hr after placement of the line. Comfort measures could include 1. nonsteroidal analgesics (NSAIDs) Tylenol, or mild narcotics 2. heat to shoulder area 3. ice to exit site if bleeding occurs	
Discuss the potential for pneumothorax induced with placement of the line, signs and symptoms, and how treated.	
Teach site care, dressing change. See steps under High Risk for Infection and Table 2.2.	
Review care of healed site. When site is healed, exit site may be cleansed in the shower.	
Teach patient cap changes. See steps under High Risk for Infection.	
Teach patient flushing solution/ technique appropriate for type of catheter.	
Instruct to observe for signs of complications daily while device is present and appropriate resource persons to call if problems occur. The following problems and/or their symptoms should be reported immediately: 1. infection: locally at site—redness, drainage, erythema, tenderness; systemically—fever and chills 2. catheter malfunction: leakage, breakage of line 3. catheter thrombosis: swelling of arm, discomfort in chest and arm catheter displacement: cuff becomes visible, catheter falls out, unable to draw or infuse	These complications need immediate attention to prevent increasing problems. None are life threatening, but they could lead to major problems.

Table 2.1 • General Comparison of Venous Access Devices

External Silastic Catheter	Implantable Ports
May remain in place as long as trouble free.	Silicone septum good for 1000–2000 punctures (varies per manufacturer).
Open-system catheter capped with injection cap.	Completely closed system.
Barrier against infection: tunnelled Dacron cuff.	Barrier against infection: skin.
Surgically inserted, may be removed in office setting.	Surgically inserted and removed.
Features: single, double, and triple lumens available.	Features: single and double lumens/septums available.
Maintenance: requires daily to weekly flush with normal saline or heparin, 10 U/mL). Regular dressing change and injection cap change. Care is done by patient, family, or home health agency. Maintenance costs include heparin or saline, syringes, needles, alcohol wipes, dressing supplies, injection caps, etc.	Maintenance: requires heparin or normal saline flush every 4 weeks. Usually done by nurse or trained phlebotomist. Maintenance cost minimal.
Appearance: tube outside of body and limits to physical freedom. Four to 5 inches of external catheter present.	Appearance: minimal alteration in body image because port is totally under the skin. Minimal limits on physical freedom.
Access: catheter accessed directly into catheter or through needle into injection cap.	Access: special needle (Huber non-coring) required to puncture skin and septum of catheter.
Placement: exit site of catheter will vary depending on surgical technique.	Placement: placed over bony prominence to allow stability during accessing. Potential areas of placement are limited, especially in overweight patients.
Complications:	*Complications*:
1. Catheter-related infections.	1. Port-related infections.
2. Occluding thrombosis.	2. Occluding thrombosis.
3. Infuses, but cannot draw.	3. Infuses but cannot draw.
4. Catheter damage, leakage, or dislodgment.	4. Catheter, migration, damage, or leakage.
5. Spontaneous blood backflow (open-ended catheters).	5. Catheter-needle dislodgment.

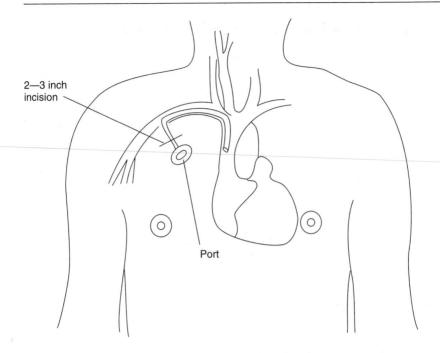

Figure 2-1. Implanted Port

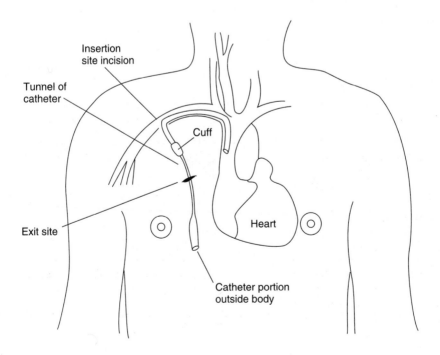

Figure 2-2. Central Catheter Placement:
Insertion and Exit Site

Table 2.2 • Postoperative Care of Long-Term Venous Access Devices

	External	Implanted Port
Dressing change exit site	Change initial dressing after 24–48 hr. Dressing may need reinforcement if bleeding present after placement.	Anticipate 3-inch incision with absorbable sutures. Dressing removed after 24–48 hr. Usually requires no further dressing.
Dressing change entrance site	Remove initial dressing after 24–48 hr. Observe for redness or drainage. Cover with Band-Aid, clear dressing, or no dressing.	No entrance site.

NURSING DIAGNOSIS: HIGH RISK FOR IMPAIRED GAS EXCHANGE

Risk Factors
- Potential for pneumothorax with surgical procedure
- Difficulty placing line

Patient Outcomes
The patient will not exhibit symptoms of pneumothorax, as evidenced by an absence of pain with inspiration, shortness of breath, and anxiety.

Nursing Interventions	Rationales
Assess patient for signs and symptoms of pneumothorax; assess for pain with inspiration, shortness of breath, or anxiety frequently after catheter placement.	
If patient is discharged on the same day as placement, instruct on the symptoms to assess at home.	If symptoms occur, patient should call physician immediately.

NURSING DIAGNOSIS: HIGH RISK FOR INFECTION

Risk Factors
- Traumatized tissue with placement
- Altered immune system/chronic disease
- Poor personal hygiene

Patient Outcomes
The patient and/or caregiver will
- demonstrate site care, dressing change, inspection of the site, cap changes, and flushing technique appropriate for the type of catheter.
- identify resources to call with questions/problems.

Nursing Interventions

Protect insertion and exit site (see Figure 2.2).
1. Remove initial dressing on *insertion site* after 24 hr. Keep site clean and observe for signs of infection.Remove sutures (if present) once healing occurs (2–3 weeks).

2. Leave the initial, occlusive, pressure dressing on the *exit site* intact for 2–3 days after surgery. Then change the dressing every 2–3 days until the exit site is healed (2–3 weeks). At this time, the sutures anchoring the catheter in place should be removed. Once healed, the site may be washed daily in the shower and a Band-Aid placed. Some patients may want to continue to use a transparent dressing. Depending on the patient situation and institution policy, the healed site may require no dressing.

3. Change dressing immediately when soiled, wet, or no longer intact.

Rationales

The initial dressing is left in place to permit surgical healing and lessen the risk of bacteria being introduced.

Nursing Interventions

Aseptically change dressing wearing nonsterile gloves (universal precautions).

1. Remove old dressing and discard. Never use scissors to remove dressing as the catheter could be inadvertently severed or damaged.
2. Remove gloves and wash hands.
3. Inspect catheter *exit site* for leaking fluid, bloody or purulent drainage, redness, swelling, or induration.
4. Palpate along tunnel route for swelling or tenderness. Notify appropriate personnel if these problems occur.
5. Organize supplies on work area. Put on sterile examination gloves and maintain aseptic technique.
6. Cleanse *exit site* if bloody or crusty drainage is present with hydrogen peroxide. Then cleanse with povidone-iodine swabs as for the exit site.
7. Clean exit site with 2 povidone-iodine swabsticks. Cleansing must begin at the *exit site* and move away from the catheter. Clean in a circular motion covering an area of 3 in. in every direction. Never return to the *exit site* with the same swabstick. Let dry for at least 60 s.
8. With the swabstick, clean the catheter from the *exit site* distally. Allow the povidone-iodine to dry.
9. Antimicrobial ointment may be applied to the *exit site* with sterile cotton tip applicators.

Rationales

The antimicrobial activity of povidone-iodine occurs as the solution dries on the skin.

The efficacy of using antimicrobial ointment to decrease exit site colonization remains controversial.

Nursing Interventions	Rationales
10. A skin protective preparation (i.e., Skin Prep) may be applied to the area around the catheter and allowed to dry.	Use of Skin Prep may decrease skin irritation and create better adhesion of dressing.
11. Apply dressing of choice (see Table 2.3).Ensure dressing is occlusive.	Randomized studies have found no statistical difference between use of transparent gauze or no dressing.
12. Secure the catheter and its tubing to the dressing or skin with tape.	If catheter is inadvertently pulled on, the tape will help prevent the initial tug from the catheter from being pulled out.
13. Label dressing with date and initials.	
Change the cap of external catheters weekly and as needed. Each manufacturer has recommendations for frequency of cap changes.	
1. Use only short luer-lock injection caps.	Short luer-lock injection caps will not require injection of flushing solution into cap before flushing entire line.
2. Clamp catheter (Hickman).	
3. Clean the junction between the catheter or extension tubing and old injection cap with disinfectant. Allow to dry.	
4. Put on nonsterile gloves (universal precautions).	
5. Remove old injection cap and attach the new injection cap.	
6. Secure external catheter to chest with tape.	
Flush catheter using aseptic technique (see Table 2.4).	
If unable to flush catheter, consider using antithrombolytic agent such as urokinase 5000 IU (1 mL) per physician and manufacturer's recommendation.	

Nursing Interventions

For implanted ports, aseptically a insert noncoring needle (straight or 90° bent) into implanted port to flush or use the port.

1. Locate the portal septum by palpating it under the skin.
2. Cleanse the injection site with povidone-iodine (or alcohol). Allow to dry.

3. While the port is held firmly between two fingers of the non-dominant hand, grasp the wings of the noncoring needle with the dominant hand and insert needle, perpendicular to the septum, through the skin and septum until it reaches the bottom of the portal system.

4. If the needle is to be left in, place a 2 x 2 gauze under the wings of the extension tubing; use a 3 x 5 clear dressing over the entire site to anchor.

Rationales

Noncoring needles are available in straight or right-angle configurations in various lengths and gauges. The noncoring needle has a deflected point that helps avoid damage to the septum.

Care should be taken when inserting a noncoring needle into an implanted port. Excessive insertion pressure or "grinding" of the needle against the portal base may damage the needle point. A "barbed" needle point may damage the resealing septum.

NURSING DIAGNOSIS: HIGH RISK FOR BODY IMAGE DISTURBANCE

Risk Factors
- Tube hanging outside the body (Groshong, Hickman)
- Bulge present in the body (port)
- Required physical restrictions

Patient Outcomes
The patient will
- be involved in choice (if treatment plan allows) of type of line to be used preoperatively.
- express feelings/concern over having the catheter present in the body.
- identify coping mechanisms that will be of assistance.

Table 2.3 • Catheter Exit Site Dressings

Type	Advantages	Disadvantages
Transparent	Permeable membrane allows oxygen, moisture out; impermeable to bacteria. Allows visualization of site. Can remain in place 3–7 days. Greater patient comfort. Provides barrier for catheter dislodgment.	Expense. Allows cleansing of site with dressing change only. May increase colonization of bacteria. Poor adhesion with diaphoresis or bleeding at site.
Gauze	Absorbs moisture or drainage. Less expensive. Provides barrier for catheter dislodgment.	No visualization of site. Risk of irritation from tape. Increased frequency of dressing change: daily to every 3 days.
No dressing	Daily cleansing of site. Allows visualization of site. No irritation related to adhesive. No expense.	Greater risk of catheter dislodgment. No barrier to contamination.

Table 2.4 • Flushing Solutions

Catheter Type	Frequency	Solution/Amount
Groshong (closed end) with two-way valve	Brisk flush after each use, or every 7 days	5 mL normal saline (*do not flush with heparin*) 20 mL normal saline following viscous solutions such as lipids.
Hickman (open end)	Before and after each use Above followed by heparin (10 U/mL) after each use or every 12–24 hr	3–5 mL normal saline 3–5 mL 10 U/mL heparin solution

▼

Nursing Interventions	**Rationales**
Assure patient understanding of care and maintenance and the effect the required restrictions will have on his or her lifestyle.	Patient may not be clear about the care and maintenance of a particular line.
Allow patient to express any concerns over the existence of a line. Provide strategies on how to incorporate the addition of the line into patient's lifestyle, i.e., types of clothing to wear, dealing with small children.	

DISCHARGE PLANNING/CONTINUITY OF CARE

- Assure understanding of and ability to perform care and maintenance of line.
- Provide patient with needed supplies (usually 1 month's supply) and establish a plan for obtaining refills as needed.
- Assure follow-up with physician/nurse for questions and continued management.
- Refer to a home care agency if further assistance is needed for teaching or ongoing follow-up.

REFERENCES

Access Device Guidelines Module I—Recommendations for Nursing Education and Practice. Module I—Catheters. (1989). Pittsburgh, PA: Oncology Nursing Society.

Burke, M., Berg, W., Ingwersen, B. et al. (1991). *Cancer chemotherapy: A nursing process approach*. Boston: Jones and Bartlett.

Lucas, A.(1992). A critical review of venous access devices: The nursing perspective. *Current Issues in Cancer Nursing Practice, 1*(7), 1–10.

Tillman, K. R. (1991). Venous access devices: Guidelines for home healthcare nurses. *Home Healthcare Nurse, 9*(5), 13–17.

NUTRITION SUPPORT: ENTERAL NUTRITION

Deborah R. Johnson, RN, MS, CNSN

Enteral nutrition is the delivery of nutrients directly into a functioning gastrointestinal (GI) tract. Total enteral nutrition is delivered by a tube when normal GI motility and absorption are present but caloric needs are unmet by usual oral intake because of some underlying illness or deficit. Malnourished patients requiring tube feeding may or may not outwardly appear clinically starved. Patients may present in a simple starvation state and appear cachetic; the body's adaptive mechanism (decreased metabolic rate and gradual wasting of body fat and skeletal muscle) operates to preserve protein stores. The patient with sepsis or trauma or one requiring an extensive surgical procedure may not appear malnourished or starved on physical exam but is significantly metabolically stressed. The metabolically stressed patient also requires enteral nutritional support to meet his or her needs because of limited body adaptive mechanisms, accelerated protein catabolism, and increased energy expenditure. See Decision Tree for Enteral vs. Parenteral Nutrition Support Delivery System.

ETIOLOGIES

- Neuromuscular impairments (usually permanent enteral access is needed with feeding into stomach or past the pylorus):
  - impaired gag or swallow reflexes
  - head trauma, cerebral vascular accidents, multiple sclerosis, or comatose state
- The lack of desire or incapability to ingest adequate oral intake to meet metabolic needs
  - chemo- or radiation therapy with mucositis, stomatitis
  - obstructive lesions of the esophagus, pharynx
  - the transition time during weaning from total parenteral nutrition and introducing oral feedings
- Inability to eat as a result of underlying illness (access temporary or permanent with feeding tube placed past the pylorus)
  - trauma

– burns
– sepsis

CLINICAL MANIFESTATIONS

- Muscle weakness, fatigue
- Anorexia, poor oral intake
- Aversion to food
- Weight loss, lack of interest in food
- Aspiration of food/fluids

Signs of severe malnutrition
- Subcutaneous fat loss, generalized muscle wasting
- Scaly dermatitis
- Dilated veins
- Petechia
- Poor skin turgor
- Dry mucous membranes
- Extremity edema
- Brittle thin nails
- Lack of hair luster, thinning hair
- Blepharitis
- Bitot's spots (grey triangular spots related to vitamin A deficiency)
- Lethargy, irritability, confusion
- Glossitis, cheilosis, angular stomatitis
- Parotid or thyroid enlargement

CLINICAL/DIAGNOSTIC FINDINGS

- Inadequate calorie counts or a dietary history assessment that indicates food intolerances, aversions, poor oral intake, or underlying clinical conditions causing decreased nutrient intake
- Somatic protein compartment assessment
  – weight less than normal for height
  – abnormal skin fold anthropometric measurements
- Visceral protein compartment assessment
  – decreased serum albumin
  – decreased serum transferrin
  – decreased hemoglobin and hematocrit levels.
- Immunocompetence assessment
  – delayed cutaneous hypersensitivity (anergic response)
  – decreased total lymphocytic count
- Abnormal swallow study
  NOTE: The above diagnostic findings may not be absolute indicators to diagnose the need for enteral nutrition. Certain diagnostic findings can be influenced by nonnutritional factors such as general anesthesia, steroid use, and fluid resuscitation. The decision to tube feed a patient with

a functioning GI tract should be made only after examining the patient holistically.

NURSING DIAGNOSIS: ALTERED NUTRITION—LESS THAN BODY REQUIREMENTS

Related To
- Inability to ingest nutrients orally
- Inability to ingest adequate nutrient amounts
- Increased metabolic demand for nutrients

Defining Characteristics

Demonstrated protein/calorie malnutrition for more than 5–7 days
Inability to take over 50% of necessary calories by mouth
Greater than 10% unintentional weight loss despite oral intake
Altered level of consciousness
Impaired swallowing
Muscle weakness, anorexia, depression
Inability to meet increased nutritional needs by oral intake due to accelerated metabolic demands caused by sepsis, major trauma, or illness

Patient Outcomes

Patient will progress toward an improved nutritional state, as evidenced by
- weight increases towards normal range for age, sex, height, and activity level
- serum albumin, transferrin, hemoglobin, hematocrit, lymphocyte count, blood sugar, and electrolytes within normal range or improved
- urine area nitrogen balanced or positive
- improved strength, energy, and activity tolerance
- healing wounds or improved tissue integrity/skin turgor
- predictable bowel elimination patterns
- anthropometric measurements progressing toward normal

Nursing Interventions

Consult dietitian or nutrition support team, if available, for recommended calorie, protein, carbohydrate, fat requirements, assistance with enteral formula selection and enteral access route (nasogastric, nasoduodenal, percutaneous endoscopic gastrostomy (PEG), or jejunostomy tube. See Decision Tree for Enteral vs. Parenteral Nutrition Support Delivery System, p. 39.

Rationales

Nursing Interventions

Weigh patient every other day at same time with the same amount of clothing and equipment using the same scale.

Maintain accurate intake and output measurement. Intake includes colloid, crystalloid, and enteral feeding formula. Output includes all urine, loose stool, gastric losses, wound drainage, and presence of febrile episodes.

Implement techniques to maintain feeding tube patency:

1. Flush feeding tube with at least 20–30 mL of water every 4 hr during continuous feeding, before and after giving medications, and after each intermittent gravity feeding or gastric residual check.

2. Insert a feeding tube made of a polyurethane material if available.

3. Administer medications in elixir form if available. Consult with the pharmacist.

4. Use an infusion pump when viscous enteral formulas are being used or if feedings are given at a slow rate.

5. If feeding tube becomes obstructed, attempt to irrigate it with water or cola. Avoid using meat tenderizer or pancreatic enzyme mixtures.

Rationales

Accurate serial measurements are important to establish patient response to therapy.

Attention to insensible losses is important to assure additional free water requirements are being met to prevent dehydration.

Tubes that are routinely and prophylactically irrigated with water have a lower incidence of obstruction. Tubes irrigated with cranberry juice have a higher rate of tube obstruction and shorter duration of use than tubes irrigated with water.

Formula flows more quickly through tubes made of polyurethane than silicone.

Pill fragments from inadequately crushed medications are a frequent cause of tube obstruction.

A slow, low-pressure formula flow can promote feeding formula to adhere to the feeding tube lumen and cause obstruction.

Although meat tenderizer solutions can dissolve protein coagulated materials and pancreatic enzyme materials are often superior to meat tenderizer solutions, in dissolving some obstructions, use of these materials is discouraged because they can cause severe lung damage if given through a feeding tube that is accidently malpositioned in the respiratory tract.

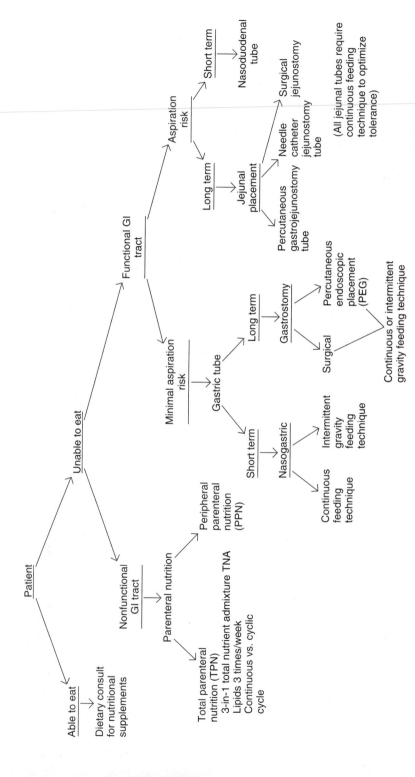

Figure 3–1. Decision Tree for Enteral vs. Parenteral Nutrition Support Delivery System

NURSING DIAGNOSIS: HIGH RISK FOR ASPIRATION

Risk Factors
- Malpositioned feeding tube
- Inability to maintain airway
- Impaired cough and gag reflexes
- Altered level of consciousness
- Incompetent esophageal sphincter (history of reflux or hiatal hernia)
- Delayed gastric emptying (gastroparesis associated with diabetes)
- Demonstrated GI intolerance to feeding with nausea, vomiting, abdominal fullness, and gastric residuals > 100–150 mL
- Inability to elevate head of bed 30°–45° at all times during continuous feeding or 1 hr before, during, and after intermittent gravity feeding

Patient Outcomes
Patient will demonstrate no aspiration, as evidenced by
- unlabored respirations
- normal complete blood cell count and differential
- adequate aeration in all lung fields via auscultation
- warm, dry, pink skin
- clear chest x-ray
- no unexplained fever

Nursing Interventions	Rationales
Insert a small-bore (7–8 French size) nasal enteral feeding tube to deliver formula.	Small-bore tubes are less likely to disrupt the esophageal sphincter and cause reflux compared to larger bore (14–16 French size) nasal tubes.
Assure proper enteral tube placement:	Pulmonary complications are generally caused by improper tube placement during insertion or from formula aspiration.
1. Measure tube for insertion landmarks and place tube as instructed on manufacturer's recommendation.	

Nursing Interventions	Rationales
2. After tube is placed, attempt to aspirate gastric contents to confirm gastric placement.	It may be impossible to aspirate gastric contents from a small-bore feeding tube because the tube may collapse during attempts to aspirate. Be aware that fluid can be aspirated from pleural space and mistaken for gastric contents.
3. Auscultate air insufflation over abdomen to confirm gastric placement.	This may also be misleading. The tube could be in the pleural space and sounds transmitted below the diaphragm can be mistaken for proper gastric placement.
4. Verify placement with x-ray.	This is the most accurate and reliable way to verify proper placement of a small-bore enteral feeding tube.
Tape nasal tube securely, after x-ray verification, and measure tube from nose to a predetermined point. Check this measurement at least once a shift.	Prevents migration of the tube and provides clues if the tube is migrating out of position.
If patient is at very high risk for aspiration, anticipate the need to place a weighted transpyloric feeding tube (jejunal or duodenal).	Placing a transpyloric tube minimizes incidence of gastric reflux and subsequent aspiration.
Elevate head of bed to 30°–45° while on continuous tube feeding or 1 hr before, during, and after each intermittent gravity feeding, if possible.	Optimizes stomach emptying and prevents reflux.
Encourage ambulation if not clinically contraindicated.	Optimizes stomach emptying and prevents reflux.
Add a small amount of vegetable-based food coloring to tube feeding in all patients at risk for aspiration.	Color will indicate presence or absence of tube feeding in sputum when coughing or suctioning.
Assure presence of bowel sounds by auscultating abdomen at least once a shift.	

Nursing Interventions	Rationales
Check gastric residuals every 4 hr and as needed when patient is on a continuous tube feeding or before each intermittent gravity feeding. Stop tube feeding or hold scheduled intermittent gravity feeding if residuals are above 100–150 mL. Slowly refeed the residual. Recheck residuals after 1 hr and resume feeding if residuals are below 100–150 mL.	Stomach may not be emptying well and distention and vomiting could occur. It may be difficult to check residuals with a small-bore (7–8 French size) nasal tube, hence assess patient for feeling of fullness, nausea, or increased abdominal girth. NOTE: There will be no residuals when a jejunostomy tube is placed because unlike the stomach, the jejunum is not a reservoir for food. The enteral formula should be delivered continuously via an enteral pump to maximize GI tolerance when a jejunostomy tube is used.

NURSING DIAGNOSIS: HIGH RISK FOR IMPAIRED SKIN INTEGRITY

Risk Factors
- Enteral tube pressure on skin
- Enteral tube shearing motion on skin
- Drainage from enteral tube site
- Existing alteration in nutritional state

Patient Outcomes
Area at enteral tube site is clean and dry without redness, swelling, pain or drainage.

Nursing Interventions	Rationales
Assess skin around enteral tube for redness, swelling, tenderness, and drainage daily, and more frequently as needed.	
If nasal feeding is indicated, attempt to place a small (7–8 French size) soft polyurethane nasal enteral tube.	It is less irritating to nares and throat than the larger (14–18 French size) polyvinyl nasal gastric tubes.

Nursing Interventions	Rationales
If a nasal enteral tube is in use:	
1. Assess security of tape at nose regularly. Secure and position feeding tube to patient's gown/clothing to prevent shearing, friction, and unnecessary motion.	A secured tube without shearing motion minimizes tissue breakdown or areas of pressure necrosis.
2. Lubricate nares regularly; cleanse nose if crusting; provide mouth care every 2–4 hr.	
If a surgically and percutaneously placed gastric or jejunal tube is used:	
1. Cleanse tube site regularly with soap and water; apply split gauze or a sterile transparent dressing.	
2. Apply half-strength hydrogen peroxide to tube site if area is crusted and make sure to rinse peroxide from the skin.	
3. Tape the tube securely to minimize any shear, drag, and/or tension on tube.	
4. Apply abdominal binder over the tube if the patient is confused or agitated and pulling at tube.	
5. Avoid application of any topical ointments to the tube site unless specifically preserved.	Betadine ointment applied to a tube site for any length of time can destroy healthy granulation tissue. Chronic use of antibiotic ointment can foster a yeast infection.

NURSING DIAGNOSIS: HIGH RISK FOR DIARRHEA

Risk Factors
- Non-tube-feeding related

- low serum albumin levels
- antibiotic administration
- antacid administration
- medications in elixir form (sorbital based)
- Tube-feeding related
  - bacterial contamination
  - improper feeding formula composition, hyperosmolar solution, absence/presence of fiber, solution high in fat
  - Formula infusion rate is too fast.

Patient Outcomes

Patient tolerates tube feeding volume, concentration, rate, and formula type, as evidenced by
- soft, formed, stools evacuated on a regular predictable schedule
- no more than 3 stools a day
- improved serum albumin

Nursing Interventions	Rationales
Assess for all non-tube-feeding related causes of diarrhea, including	
1. low serum albumin	Hypoalbuminemia disrupts intestinal cell osmotic pressure, hence compromising tube-feeding formula absorption.
2. drug therapy that may cause diarrhea, such as antibiotics, histamine 2 (H_2) blockers, oral medications in elixir form, and magnesium antacid	Antibiotics alter normal intestinal flora and bacterial overgrowth occurs; may need to administer a lactobacillus acidophilus preparation to restore GI flora. Histamine 2 blockers alter gastric pH, which causes bacterial overgrowth and diarrhea. Elixirs can contain sorbitol or another hypertonic base, which if given undiluted, may increase diarrhea. Alternating magnesium antacids with calcium- or aluminum-containing antacids may decrease diarrhea.

Nursing Interventions	Rationales
3. bacterial contamination	Prevent bacterial contamination by: using good hand washing technique when handling tubes, formula, or other equipment; avoid touching the inside of the tube-feeding delivery set during refilling and decanting; use only enough formula for 4–6 hr of tube feeding at one time; rinse tube-feeding delivery set with water before adding new formula; change tube-feeding delivery sets every 24 hr; when possible use full-strength, commercially prepared, ready-to-use formula.
4. presence of fecal impaction if not clinically contraindicated.	May be stooling around fecal impaction.
Assess for causes of diarrhea related to the tube-feeding formula.	
1. Consult dietitian for assistance.	
2. Examine enteral formula composition, including • fat content • fiber content • osmolality • lactose content	A fat content greater than 20 g fat/L can induce diarrhea. Dietary fiber and bulking agents may prevent or help control diarrhea in tube-fed patients. Hyperosmolar solutions greater than 280 mOsm/L may be poorly tolerated by the GI tract of a severely malnourished patient. The patient with a malabsorption problem may produce a "dumping syndrome" characterized by cold sweats, dizziness, distention, weakness, tachycardia, nausea, and diarrhea; the nurse may need to dilute this hyperosmolar formula to a more isotonic formula. Lactose intolerance is rarely a problem, as most commercially prepared enteral formulas do not contain lactose.

▼

DISCHARGE PLANNING/CONTINUITY OF CARE

- Assure patient/family understands self-care management plan:
    - feeding tube site care, assessments, and dressing changes
    - medication administration
    - tube-feeding formula storage
    - proper administration of formula by intermittent gravity feeding or continuous feeding technique
    - troubleshooting equipment
    - troubleshooting signs/symptoms of GI distress or feeding intolerance
    - when to call the physician
- Refer patient to a home health care agency if continued nursing care, teaching, or assistance with a self-care management plan is needed.
- Arrange follow-up with nurse and/or physician for continued management after discharge.
- Assist patient with obtaining prescriptions and establish a plan of refilling prescriptions.
- Assure that the financial arrangements (cost and reimbursement) for the enteral nutrition supplies be reviewed, discussed, and accepted by the patient prior to discharge.
- Establish a workable plan with the patient to deliver additional enteral supplies when materials need replenishing.

REFERENCES

Eisenberg, P. (1989). Enteral nutrition—indications, formulas and delivery techniques. *Nursing Clinics of North America, 24,* 315–338.

Keithley, J. K. & Kohn, C. L. (1992). Advances in nutritional care of medical-surgical patient. *Medical Surgical Nursing, 1,* 13–21, 67.

Kennedy-Caldwell, C. & Guenter, P. A. (1988). *Nutrition support nursing core curriculum* (2nd Ed.). Silver Spring, MD: American Society for Parenteral and Enteral Nutrition.

Kohn, C. L. & Keithley, J. K. (1989). Enteral nutrition: Potential complications and patient monitoring. *Nursing Clinics Of North America, 24,* 339–353.

Rombeau, J. L. & Caldwell, M. D. (1990). *Clinical nutrition enteral and tube feeding* (2nd Ed.). Philadelphia, PA: Saunders.

NUTRITION SUPPORT: TOTAL PARENTERAL NUTRITION

Deborah R. Johnson, RN, MS, CNSN

Patients who cannot meet their caloric needs by the usual oral route or through a tube feeding because of abnormal gastrointestinal (GI) absorption or motility may be candidates for total parenteral nutrition (TPN). Total parenteral nutrition, also called hyperalimentation, is the administration of intravenous (IV) nutrients directly into the peripheral or central venous circulation. Peripheral parenteral nutrition (PPN) is administered through a large peripheral vein when nutrition support may only be needed for a short time, protein and calorie requirements are not high, or the placement of a central venous catheter (CVC) would be dangerous or technically difficult. Parenteral solutions that contain glucose as the primary energy source have a high osmolality, which can be *very irritating* to peripheral veins; hence PPN solutions rely on isotonic lipid emulsions for the main source of nonprotein calories. Phlebitis is frequently reported with PPN, and there are often times it is not possible to meet an adult's total nutritional needs with PPN. Central parenteral nutrition is most often given through a catheter inserted into the subclavian vein and threaded into the superior vena cava; the jugular or femoral vein may be used if the subclavian is inaccessible. A CVC enables the administration of hypertonic dextrose solutions to meet the nutritional needs of severely stressed or hypermetabolic patients. Central parenteral solutions may be compounded as a dual mixture of carbohydrates and amino acids (protein) or with a lipid (fat) source which is infused, *separately*, two to three times a week, or the lipids may be combined *with* the carbohydrate and amino acids in one large bag. This latter option is referred to as a "3-in-1" solution or a total nutrient admixture (TNA). All 3-in-1 solutions, including bags and tubing, must be changed every 24 hr.

ETIOLOGIES

- Conditions requiring complete bowel rest:
  - pancreatitis, enteric fistulas
  - inflammatory bowel disease
- Conditions that interfere with GI nutrient absorption
  - Short bowel syndrome
  - radiation enteritis
  - bowel obstruction/ileus
  - Congenital malformations
- Persistent uncontrollable vomiting or diarrhea related to
  - chemotherapy/radiation therapy
  - hyperemesis gravidarum
  - pseudomembranous colitis

CLINICAL MANIFESTATIONS

- Weight loss
- Persistent vomiting/diarrhea
- Documented intolerance to oral intake
- Documented intolerance to tube feeding

CLINICAL/DIAGNOSTIC FINDINGS

- Fluid and electrolyte imbalances
- Abnormal abdominal x-ray: obstruction or motility disturbance
- Elevated serum amylase/lipase
- Decreased serum albumin
- Decreased serum transferrin
- Weight outside of referenced normal for recorded height

OTHER PLANS OF CARE TO REFERENCE

- Nutrition Support: Enteral Nutrition
- Long-Term Venous Access Devices

NURSING DIAGNOSIS: ALTERED NUTRITION—LESS THAN BODY REQUIREMENTS

Related To
- Inability to ingest foods orally
- Inability to absorb nutrients in adequate amounts
- Increased metabolic demand for nutrients

Defining Characteristics
Weight loss
Reported inadequate food intake less than recommended daily allowance
Aversion to eating
Abdominal pain with associated pathology
Satiety immediately after ingesting food
Abdominal cramping
Diarrhea
Vomiting
Weakness, fatigue
Poor muscle tone

Patient Outcomes
Patient will progress toward an improved nutritional state, as evidenced by
- weight increases toward normal range for age, sex, height, and activity level
- serum albumin, transferrin, hemoglobin, hematocrit, electrolytes, blood sugar, and chemistries within normal range or improved
- urine urea nitrogen balanced or positive
- improved strength, energy, and activity tolerance
- healing wounds or improved tissue integrity/skin turgor
- predictable bowel elimination patterns
- anthropometric measurements progressing toward a normal range

Nursing Interventions	Rationales
Consult dietitian, pharmacist, or nutrition support team, if available.	These resource people can provide recommendations for caloric needs, fat, carbohydrate, and protein requirements. They can also assist with monitoring blood chemistries and fluid and electrolyte balance as well as compounding the TPN solution.
Administer TPN at a constant rate using an infusion pump: 1. Do not interrupt the flow of TPN. 2. Do not increase or decrease the TPN rate to accommodate total IV fluids that could have fallen behind or infused too quickly. 3. If TPN catheter clots and TPN cannot be infused, notify physician, start a peripheral IV with at least a 5% dextrose solution at same rate as TPN.	An infusion pump regulates the flow rate more accurately than gravity and decreases the likelihood of fluid, metabolic, and electrolyte imbalances. Hyperglycemia or hypoglycemic reactions can occur if TPN solutions are not given at a steady rate or if the TPN is suddenly discontinued.

Nursing Interventions	Rationales
Monitor serum or capillary glucose levels as needed (e.g., every 6–8 hr when TPN is at a final rate and more frequently when TPN is initiated) to establish patient's baseline serum glucose levels and their tolerance to the infused glucose load. Serum glucose levels should stay between 100–200 mg/dL.	Blood glucose levels above 200 mg/dL may indicate the following: the need for supplemental insulin to increase tolerance to the infused glucose load; an expected short-term postoperative surgical stress response; and impending infection or sepsis. Blood glucose monitoring is more sensitive and allows tighter control/titration than urine glucose testing because urine is only positive for glucose when levels exceed renal threshold at approximately 240 mg/dL.
Infuse IV fat (lipid) emulsions as prescribed:	Lipids prevent essential fatty acid deficiency and provide caloric source:

1. If lipids are given separately, infuse through an additional peripheral IV line or through a Y connector attached to the TPN catheter:
  • Infuse each fat emulsion over 4–8 hr two to three times per week.
  • Administer separate fat emulsion slowly over the first 15–30 min (60 mL/hr 10% lipid emulsion, and 30 mL/hr, 20% lipid emulsion); if tolerated increase to maximum of 125 mL/hr (10% lipid emulsion) or 160 mL/hr (20% lipid emulsion).
  • Observe for dyspnea, chest or back pain, and pain at IV site during infusions.
	Infusion of fats separately prevents breakdown of fat emulsions and decreases risk of fat emboli. Slower rates allow body to assimilate the fat and prevent hyperlipidemia. Allergic reactions to fat emulsions may be local or systemic.

Nursing Interventions	**Rationales**
2. Infuse lipids in the specially pre-pared TPN, 3–in-1/TNA solution.	There is better normalization of blood glucoses when all nutrients are combined. Fat sources may be better tolerated when combined together with carbohydrates and amino acids and not given sepa-rately. There may be reduced in-fection rates because no addi-tional breaks in IV tubing are done to hang fat emulsions sepa-rately. The TNA solutions may be more cost effective and time saving for Pharmacy and Nursing when compared to hanging sepa-rate bags of solution throughout the patient's course of TPN therapy.
3. Do not hang the TNA solution if there is any fat separation ob-served, as evidenced by a yel-low-colored ring around the edges of the bag. Notify the pharmacy.	These solutions can separate if not correctly mixed by pharma-cist. This may cause fat emboli.
4. Do not use IV filters with any fat emulsion infusions.	Fat particle size exceeds filter pore size and solution will not infuse.
Weigh patient daily or every other day at the same time with the same amount of clothing and equipment utilizing the same scale.	Accurate serial measurements are important to establish patient re-sponse to therapy.
Monitor and record accurate in-take and output. Assess for signs and symptoms of fluid imbalances.	Overhydration or underhydration may occur with TPN and TPN solutions need to be reformulated accordingly.
Monitor serum electrolytes and blood chemistries.	Chemical and metabolic imbal-ances may occur in patients re-ceiving TPN.
Assess for continued improvement in GI function, e.g., improved tol-erance to oral intake, decreased nausea, vomiting, and diarrhea. Collaborate with physician and/or dietitian to follow progress.	Patients receiving TPN should be transitioned to enteral feeding when appropriate as the enteral route is the preferred method to provide nutrition support to pa-tients with a functioning GI tract.

Nursing Interventions

Collaborate with nutrition support team, physician, pharmacist, and/or dietitian when TPN is to be discontinued for assistance with weaning or tapering parameters. Total parenteral nutrition can usually be discontinued within 4–6 hr.

Rationales

Proper tapering rates/weaning parameters prevent hypoglycemia. Hypoglycemia is less common with the TNA 3-in-1 solutions.

NURSING DIAGNOSIS: HIGH RISK FOR INJURY

Risk Factors
- Central venous catheter insertion and removal
- Bleeding
- Pneumothorax, hemopneumothorax
- Air emboli, thromboemboli

Patient Outcomes
Patient is not harmed during catheter insertion, catheter usage, or removal, as evidenced by
- unlabored symmetrical respirations
- bilateral breath sounds
- normal chest x-ray
- chest x-ray confirmation of proper catheter placement
- patent catheter
- no evidence of catheter emboli

Nursing Interventions

Maintain patient in Trendelenburg position with rolled towel between the scapulae while physician, using a sterile technique, inserts the CVC.

Rationales

The Trendelenburg position increases venous pressure in the subclavian vein, thus distending it for easier cannulation. This helps to prevent air from entering the venous system during catheter insertion. A sterile technique minimizes the potential for infectious complications.

Nursing Interventions	**Rationales**
Observe for signs/symptoms of shock and respiratory distress during CVC insertion, including tachycardia, hypotension, tachypnea, dyspnea, use of accessory muscles, and absent or decreased breath sounds on affected side.	Shock and/or respiratory distress can occur with complications. The lung may be punctured during insertion and a pneumothorax may occur. An artery may be cannulated, in error, during line insertion. Bleeding may compress the trachea.
After the CVC is inserted, arrange for an immediate chest x-ray. Auscultate lungs in all fields postinsertion and at least once a shift.	The x-ray confirms catheter tip placement in the superior vena cava and rules out pneumo-, hemo-, or chylothorax. Comprehensive auscultation of lung fields assures full-lung aeration. A pneumothorax may not manifest itself immediately on the initial postinsertion x-ray.
Begin TPN only after CVC tip placement is confirmed by x-ray in the superior vena cava.	The hyperosmolar TPN solution can be irritating to smaller vessels (subclavian, innominate, jugular) and can cause thrombophlebitis.
Securely tape all TPN tubing connections and/or use a standardized male-female leur-lock connector system.	Prevents accidental disconnections. Disconnections could result in air emboli, bleeding, clot formation, loss of catheter patency, contamination, and sepsis.
Assess for signs/symptoms of air emboli: sharp chest pain, sudden in nature, extreme anxiety, cyanosis, and churning precordial murmur.	Large amounts of air in the venous circulation may cause an air lock in the heart with subsequent cardiac arrest related to blocked blood flow and ischemia.
If air emboli are suspected, immediately place patient in Trendelenburg with left side down. Administer oxygen and notify physician immediately.	This position allows air to collect at the apex of the right ventricle. Small amounts of air may pass into the pulmonary circulation and be reabsorbed. Air may need to be aspirated by the physician from the right atrium with a needle to relieve the air lock. This is a *medical emergency*.

Nursing Interventions	Rationales
If the CVC intravenous system must be opened to air (e.g., cap changes, catheter repair), instruct the patient to perform a Valsalva maneuver by taking a deep breath, holding it, and bearing down as if having a bowel movement, before opening the CVC intravenous system. Use any CVC clamps provided by the manufacturer to prevent air from entering the system.	The Valsalva maneuver increases intrathoracic pressure and prevents air from entering the IV system and the bloodstream.
Assess chest wall for presence of visible collateral circulation.	This is a sign of venous thrombosis.
Observe for the presence of a suture at the insertion site of a temporary CVC, or if a more permanent, long-term CVC was placed (Broviac, Hickman, Groshong), the suture will be at the exit site. Observe the catheter for any notable increase in external catheter length.	Sutures stabilize the catheter, and an increased external length indicates catheter movement with potential displacement.
Assess for swelling around the CVC insertion site, shoulder, clavicle, and upper extremity. Note any complaints of chest pain, burning, or fluid leaking at the insertion site. Any inability to withdraw blood from a previously patent CVC warrants further investigation.	May indicate vein thrombosis and/or catheter displacement.
When catheter removal is indicated: 1. Assist patient to supine position.	Allows optimal visualization for suture removal and application of occlusive dressing.
2. Instruct patient to perform the Valsalva maneuver prior to CVC removal.	
3. Immediately after catheter removal, apply ointment (betadine or antibiotic) to exit hole and a sealed, airtight, occlusive dressing.	If ointment and an airtight sealed dressing is not applied, the CVC sinus tract allows air to enter the venous system during inspiration, potentially causing air emboli.
4. Measure catheter length and observe integrity of catheter.	Ensure entire catheter was completely removed.

NURSING DIAGNOSIS: HIGH RISK FOR INFECTION

Risk Factors
- Indwelling (CVC)
- Administration of contaminated TPN solution

Patient Outcomes
Patient is without infection as evidenced by
- normal white blood cell (WBC) count
- afebrile response
- normal serum blood glucose
- negative blood cultures
- negative catheter tip culture
- CVC site without redness, swelling, drainage, warmth, or tenderness

Nursing Interventions	Rationales
Monitor WBC, blood glucose levels, temperature, and pulse rate. Notify physician of any increases (subtle or more dramatic) that may be above the patient's established baseline.	Increases may indicate impending line infection/sepsis.
Monitor results of blood cultures if obtained.	
Assess CVC site daily and as needed. Observe for redness, swelling, drainage, or tenderness.	
Change CVC dressing following institution protocol or any time dressing is damp or nonocclusive using sterile technique.	
Adhere to institution protocol for TPN tubing changes and antibacterial preparation of all IV tubing connector sites.	
Refrigerate TPN until ready to use. Each TPN solution should not hang longer than 24 hr.	
Never add any additional substances to the TPN solutions specially prepared in the pharmacy.	

Nursing Interventions	Rationales
Do not infuse any cloudy or pre-cipitated TPN solutions. Notify the pharmacy if cloudy or precipitated TPN solutions are found.	
Infuse only TPN solutions through the dedicated TPN line. Do not use a dedicated TPN CVC for drawing blood samples or administering medications.	Minimizes chance of infection.

NURSING DIAGNOSIS: KNOWLEDGE DEFICIT

Related To
- New information
- No previous experience

Defining Characteristics
Verbalizes a lack of knowledge about use of TPN at home
Willing to learn procedure

Patient Outcomes
The patient/family will
- infuse TPN solution aseptically using an infusion pump.
- test blood glucose accurately.
- perform CVC care, dressing change, and cap change and flush correctly.
- state signs, symptoms, and problems to report.

Nursing Interventions	Rationales
Collaborate with physician, dietitian, pharmacist, certified nutrition support nurse, nutrition support team, and/or discharge planning nurse to establish a discharge plan that is reasonable with clear expectations: 1. Assure insurance coverage is verified and/or authorization of benefits is obtained prior to discharge. 2. Determine how home care supplies can be ordered and delivered on a regular basis.	

Nursing Interventions	Rationales
Provide educational materials about: 1. TPN–storage; setup and administration; proper technique for adding additional medications to premade TPN solution as prescribed, if needed, at home (e.g., vitamins). 2. CVC care—dressing change, cap change; site assessment; signs and symptoms of infection; flushing technique to maintain catheter patency, if/when catheter not in use (e.g., heparinized saline or normal saline). 3. infusion pump—operation and programming; trouble shooting alarms. 4. blood glucose monitoring—signs and symptoms of hypo-/hyperglycemia; technique for self-testing of blood sugars; administration of insulin, as needed, if prescribed.	
Incorporate teaching into patient's daily routine by having patient/family member perform infusion skills, gradually adding new pieces of information, but taking care not to overwhelm patient/family with too much information.	
Increase patient/family independence with infusions, testing, and catheter care on a daily basis and document progress.	
Investigate potential for establishing a cyclic TPN schedule with physician, dietitian, pharmacist, or nutrition support team.	Allows patient some time off of TPN. Many patients prefer a nighttime cycle.

Nursing Interventions	**Rationales**
Investigate potential for placing an external long-term CVC (Hickman, Groshong) when home TPN is necessary and patient has a short-term CVC in place.	Long-term external CVCs are uniquely designed for safer extended usage. Infection rates and thromboembolitic events are reduced.

DISCHARGE PLANNING/CONTINUITY OF CARE

- Assure patient/family understands self-care management plan and demonstrates competency with TPN self-care skills, e.g., CVC dressing changes, equipment setup, and when to call the physician.
- Refer to a home care agency if continued nursing care, teaching, or assistance with self-care management is needed.
- Arrange for follow-up with physician or nurse for continued management postdischarge.
- Assist patient with obtaining TPN supplies, equipment, and prescriptions; establish a plan for replacing, restocking, and refilling.
- Assure patient/family understands the financial arrangements (cost and reimbursement) of home TPN equipment, supplies, and nursing care as outlined by the patient's payment source.

REFERENCES

American Society For Parenteral And Enteral Nutrition. (1988). Standards for home nutrition support. *Nutrition In Clinical Practice, 3,* 202–205.

Keithley, J. K. & Kohn, C. L. (1992). Advances in nutritional care of medical-surgical patients. *Medical Surgical Nursing, 1,* 13–21, 67.

Lewis, S. M. & Collier, I. C. (1992). *Medical surgical nursing: Assessment and management of clinical problems* (3rd ed). St. Louis, MO: Mosby.

Shekleton, M. E. & Litwack, K. (1991). *Critical care nursing of the surgical patient.* Philadelphia, PA: Saunders.

Worthington, P. H. & Wagner, B. A. (1989). Total parenteral nutrition. *Nursing Clinics of North America, 24,* 355–370.

PAIN MANAGEMENT: PATIENT-CONTROLLED ANALGESIA

Deborah R. Johnson, RN, MS, CNSN

Patient-controlled analgesia (PCA), or "demand analgesia," is a useful clinical tool that represents a major advancement in the treatment of acute, chronic, or postoperative pain. Patient-controlled analgesia is designed so that patients self-administer a predetermined therapeutic amount of narcotic (referred to as the incremental dose) through a patent venous access system within preset time intervals (referred to as the delay) at times of discomfort. The most common medications used are morphine sulfate, hydromorphone, and meperidine. Intravenous narcotics administered in smaller dosages and at a greater frequency create a more optimal serum analgesic level when compared to the conventional intermittent intramuscular (IM) injection dosing regimes.

ETIOLOGIES

See individual plans of care.

CLINICAL MANIFESTATIONS

See individual plans of care.

CLINICAL/DIAGNOSTIC FINDINGS

See individual plans of care.

OTHER PLANS OF CARE TO REFERENCE

- Basic standards for preoperative and postoperative care.

NURSING DIAGNOSIS: KNOWLEDGE DEFICIT—USE OF PCA

Related To
- New experience
- No previous information

Defining Characteristics
Verbalizes a lack of knowledge
Demonstrates inaccurate follow-through of instructions

Patient Outcomes
The patient will
- demonstrate an understanding of PCA principles.
- demonstrate accurate follow-through with plan of care while hospitalized.

Nursing Interventions	Rationales
Distribute PCA teaching materials.	
Explain principles of PCA to patient/family. Also include the following:	
1. No IM narcotics or "hypos" given while on PCA.	Titration of comfort and sedation is more difficult when IM and intravenous (IV) administration routes are combined.
2. May receive antiemetics or smooth-muscle relaxants to treat any nausea or vomiting that occassionally occurs postoperatively.	
3. No pain management modality can relieve all discomfort. An optimal comfort level is that which permits participation in activities to promote recovery.	
4. May notice an increased level of alertness.	

Nursing Interventions	Rationales
Dispel fears of overdosage: 1. Modality is controlled by the patient (and not other family members) in response to an individualized discomfort level. 2. Dose is titrated and monitored by the nurse and physician. 3. Computerlike system with programmed safety delays is used.	
Reinforce that there is no addiction potential with short-term usage.	
Teach patient to use PCA button in anticipation of activity (cough, turn, ambulation), special treatments (dressing changes), and procedures.	
Reassess patient understanding of PCA principles and reinforce concepts as necessary.	
Respect and support patient's decision to discontinue PCA if requested.	

NURSING DIAGNOSIS: PAIN

Related To
- Inflammation
- Surgical incision
- Surgical manipulation
- Reflex muscle spasm

Defining Characteristics
Muscle tension, guarded body posture
Inability to participate in activities to facilitate recovery
Facial grimacing, moaning, irritability, restlessness
Diaphoresis, blood pressure and pulse changes
Verbal complaints of pain

Patient Outcomes
- Patient expresses satisfaction with pain relief.
- Patient participates in activities that facilitate recovery.

Nursing Interventions	Rationales
Assess comfort level using verbal and nonverbal cues.	
Assess patency of IV and assure correct setup of PCA equipment.	An infiltrated IV will not allow infusion of medication into the bloodstream.
If patient experiences little or no pain relief:	
1. Assess/monitor the number of attempts and injections.	Attempts should about equal injections for optimal comfort.
• If attempts are much more frequent than injections, consider increasing incremental dose or giving a bolus dose.	This may be necessary to increase analgesic therapeutic blood levels for optimal comfort.
• If attempts and injections are infrequent, encourage patient to press PCA button more often.	Smaller dosages at a greater frequency may create a more optimal serum analgesic level.

Nursing Interventions	Rationales
Plan or contract with patient for nighttime usage to maintain an optimal analgesic blood level throughout the night and in anticipation of next day's activities. Options include: 1. Nurse pushes PCA button for patient on hourly rounds. 2. Patient continues self-administration throughout the night and nurse encourages increased usage in the early morning hours (5:00–6:30 a.m.) 3. The PCA/basal mode may be prescribed by the physician for nighttime use. This is a continuous analgesic infusion with the patient having the capability to use additional incremental doses for "breakthrough" pain when the button is pushed. If the PCA/basal mode is prescribed, assess the total amount of narcotic administered via basal rate and incremental dose with delay for appropriateness/safety.	
Position patient for optimal comfort.	
Encourage/teach/reinforce relaxation techniques.	
Maintain optimal room temperature according to patient preferences.	
Minimize environmental stimuli, for example, a quiet room, dim lights, TV off, monitor visitors, and close the door.	
Investigate other sources of potential discomfort, for example, a distended bladder, antiembolic stockings, nasogastric tubes, Foley catheter, tape, drains, and dressings.	

Nursing Interventions	Rationales
Assess/reassess efficacy of pharmacological and nonpharmacological interventions.	
Advise patient that PCA can/will be discontinued at any time if the patient is not satisfied with comfort level; more traditional narcotic dosing can be resumed.	
Notify physician if unrelieved pain persists.	

NURSING DIAGNOSIS: HIGH RISK FOR INEFFECTIVE BREATHING PATTERN

Risk Factors
- Excessive narcotic self-administration
- Obesity
- Anesthesia
- Other medications

Patient Outcomes
- Patient is alert or easily aroused.
- Patient will maintain clear open airways as evidenced by easy, spontaneous respirations with an acceptable rate, depth, and pattern.
- Patient maintains an effective cough.
- Patient skin and nailbeds are pink, warm, and dry.

Nursing Interventions	Rationales
Assess level of consciousness, respiratory rate, pattern, pupil size, muscle tone, and skin color with vital signs and as needed.	
Do not give IM narcotics while on PCA.	
Examine total medication regime for substances that may foster relaxation or potentiate PCA narcotics, for example, droperidol, Fentanyl, hydroxyzine, Versed, and diphenhydramine HCl.	

Nursing Interventions	Rationales
Decrease the incremental dose as prescribed if assessment suggests early signs of oversedation.	
If signs of overdosage occur, stop the PCA, administer 0.4 mg naloxone IV in 0.1-mg increments as prescribed. Stay with patient and notify physician.	Naloxone is short acting; reevaluate for reoccurrence of signs/symptoms of overdosage 30–45 min after naloxone is given.

NURSING DIAGNOSIS: HIGH RISK FOR PAIN (ITCHING)

Risk Factors
Systemic histamine release more commonly associated with morphine sulfate administration

Patient Outcomes
Skin redness, swelling, and/or itching is minimal, tolerable, or nonexistent.

Nursing Interventions	Rationales
Administer diphenhydramine HCl as prescribed.	Antihistamine will minimize itching.
Suggest changing PCA narcotic from morphine sulfate to hydromorphone.	Hydromorphone produces a lesser systemic histamine release compared to morphine sulfate.
If symptoms persist may need to discontinue PCA and resume more traditional IM narcotic regime.	

NURSING DIAGNOSIS: KNOWLEDGE DEFICIT—WEANING FROM PCA AND ADVANCING TO ORAL ANALGESICS

Related To
- New experiences
- No previous information

Defining Characteristics
Verbalizes a lack of knowledge
Demonstrates inaccurate follow-through of instructions

Patient Outcomes

The patient will

- state the reasons for advancement to oral medication.
- participate in the process of discontinuing PCA.
- describe the differences in onset/length of action between oral and IV narcotics (PCA) for pain control.

Nursing Interventions	Rationales
Attempt to wean from PCA when the patient has bowel sounds, a soft belly, and no nausea or vomiting, the patient is tolerating clear liquids, and the nasogastric (NG) tube is removed.	These are the same assessments used to transition from IM analgesics to oral (PO) analgesics.
Explain that the above assessments are normal, expected, positive progressions in the clinical course of recovery.	
Explain the differences in onset/length of action between IV (PCA) pain medication and the oral pain medication.	

Nursing Interventions	**Rationales**
The weaning process is: 1. Direct patient to self-administer a PCA incremental dose; then give the oral analgesic as prescribed. 2. Take the PCA button from the patient, but do not remove the PCA machine from the room. 3. Monitor frequently to assess comfort level. 4. Reinforce the differences in oral vs. IV analgesic action. 5. If patient is uncomfortable after oral medication is given (rare), it is acceptable for patient to administer another PCA incremental dose. Take PCA button away from patient after this PCA dose is given and monitor comfort level. 6. Administer second dose of oral analgesic at earliest prescribed frequency to maximize analgesic blood level. 7. Discontinue PCA if patient is comfortable after second dose of oral analgesic is given.	A successful weaning process is built on a trusting relationship between the patient and the nurse.

DISCHARGE PLANNING/CONTINUITY OF CARE

- Refer to individual plans of care.
- Assure that oral analgesics control discomfort so that patient can participate in activities that facilitate recovery.
- Reinforce that patient should not drive or operate machinery when taking prescribed oral analgesics.
- Assist patient with obtaining prescription and establish a plan for refilling prescriptions.

REFERENCES

Jacox, A., Ferrel, B., Heidrich, G., Hester, N., & Miaskowski, C. (1992). A guideline for the nation: Managing acute pain. *American Journal of Nursing, 92*(5), 49–55.

Kaiser, K. (1992). Assessment and management of pain in the critically ill trauma patient. *Critical Care Nursing Quarterly, 15*(2), 14–34.

McCaffery, M. & Beebe, A. (1989). *Pain: Clinical manual for nursing practice.* St. Louis, MO: Mosby.

Sheidler, V. (1987). Patient controlled analgesia. *Current Concepts In Nursing, 1* (1), 13–16.

U.S. Department of Health and Human Services (DHHS), Public Health Service, Agency for Health Care Policy and Research (AHCPR). (1992). *Acute pain management: Operative or medical procedures and trauma, clinical practice guideline,* publication No. 92–0032. Washington, DC: DHHS.

▼

Common Cardiovascular Conditions and Procedures

▼

ARTERIOGRAPHY (ANGIOGRAM)

Penny M. Bernards, RN, MS, GNP

An arteriogram is an invasive procedure involving insertion of a catheter into an artery and injecting contrast dye. The contrast dye allows x-ray pictures to be taken of the arterial blood flow to demonstrate the passage as well as any occlusions or abnormalities. A digital subtraction angiogram (DSA) is used more often than conventional arteriograms to evaluate the arterial system, since a better image is obtained with subtraction of over-lying bone and less contrast dye is used, which results in less trauma to the kidneys. Possible entry sites include the femoral artery at the groin, the axillary artery, the brachial artery, and the abdominal aorta via the trans-lumbar approach. An arteriogram usually takes between 1 and 2 hr.

ETIOLOGIES (INDICATIONS)

- Symptomatic peripheral arterial occlusive disease
- Extracranial vascular disease
- Preoperative assessment of arterial aneurysm disease
- Screening of hypertensive patients for renal artery disease
- Screening of potential donors for renal transplant
- Evaluation for pulmonary emboli
- Access for interventional radiology such as angioplasty and embolization

CLINICAL MANIFESTATIONS

- Intermittent claudication
- Rest pain
- Nonhealing ulcers
- Uncontrolled hypertension
- Acute shortness of breath
- Transient ischemic attacks

CLINICAL/DIAGNOSTIC FINDINGS

- Absent or diminished Doppler pulse signal
- Ankle-brachial index < 0.4 or higher if patient has functional deficits
- Dampening of pulse waveforms
- Increased velocities in an artery or bypass graft per ultrasound
- Presence of a large arterial aneurysm on ultrasound or computerized tomography (CT) scan

NURSING DIAGNOSIS: FEAR

Related To
- Unknown procedure
- Diagnosis
- Anticipated pain

Defining Characteristics
Apprehension
Verbalization of fear
Diaphoresis
Tachycardia
Avoidance behavior
Tenseness

Patient Outcomes
The patient will
- express fears related to the procedure and diagnosis.
- describe some of the sensations experienced during the procedure.
- utilize methods of coping to reduce anxiety.

Nursing Interventions	Rationales
Assess level of anxiety.	
Evaluate understanding of the procedure to clear up any misconceptions.	

Nursing Interventions	Rationales
Describe the sensations often felt during an angiogram such as the hardness of the examining table, coolness of the radiology room and the cleansing soap, burning of the local anesthetic, pressure of the catheter and warmth of the dye. Occasionally straps are used to hold an extremity in place while films are obtained or the head during carotid arteriograms.	Preparing patients for procedures using sensory events that they can expect decreases stress.
Encourage verbalization of feelings to help identify source of anxiety.	
Assess understanding and level of anxiety in family members and significant others and include them in patient teaching.	Patients can have increased anxiety when people around them are anxious or are providing conflicting information.
Explore successful coping strategies in previous experiences and relevance to current situation.	Drawing on past experiences with coping with stresses may help determine which intervention will be most beneficial.
Alert the radiology and medical staff if patient appears excessively anxious.	The physician may choose to use an antianxiety medication prior to the procedure.

NURSING DIAGNOSIS: KNOWLEDGE DEFICIT—PREPARATION AND POSTPROCEDURE CARE
- Lack of exposure to information

Defining Characteristics
Verbalization of inadequate understanding or misconception
Anger
Anxiety

Patient Outcomes
The patient will
- describe the procedure.
- identify the purpose of the procedure.
- verbalize understanding of preprocedure routines.
- verbalize understanding of postprocedure routines.

Nursing Interventions	Rationales
Evaluate understanding of the procedure.	Some patients confuse the procedure arteriogram with the surgery.
Explain that the purpose of the arteriogram is to provide a definitive diagnosis necessary to assess treatment options.	
Describe the different steps of the arteriogram procedure, including positioning on the examining table, preparation of the injection site, (most commonly femoral artery), placement of the catheter, injection of the dye, obtaining pictures, repositioning of the catheter and more pictures, removal of the catheter, and holding pressure at the site.	
Instruct patients on what will be expected of them during the arteriogram, such as holding their breath, deep breathing, and holding still.	
Instruct the patients that they will be on complete bedrest for 4–8 hr postprocedure with punctured extremity straight.	Care is provided to prevent dislodgement of a clot at the arterial injection site which may result in formation of a hematoma or hemorrhage.
Explain that vital signs will be monitored frequently for changes in blood pressure, pulse, and respiration, presence of discomfort, swelling or bleeding at the injection site, and circulation, movement, and sensation of involved extremity.	Frequent assessments are done to evaluate for bleeding or hemorrhage from the injection site that may not be apparent through visualization of the insertion site.

Nursing Interventions	Rationales
Instruct patient that intravenous fluids will be used before and after the arteriogram and that it is important to push oral fluids. A regular meal can be ordered postprocedure if there is no problem with nausea.	Hydration is used to flush dye out of kidneys.
Inform patient that ambulation can be resumed after 4–8 hr although prolonged sitting should be avoided.	
Instruct patient regarding care of the arterial puncture site after discharge. Wash area with soap and water, place a Band-Aid if desired, and monitor for signs of infection, swelling, or bleeding at the site.	
Inform patient of any follow-up care with the physician.	

NURSING DIAGNOSIS: HIGH RISK FOR INJURY

Risk Factors
- Chronic renal failure
- Allergy to contrast dye, iodine, or seafood
- Osmolarity of contrast dye
- Poor hydration
- Cardiovascular disease
- Diabetes

Patient Outcomes
The patient will have
- no allergic reaction to the contrast dye
- creatinine level within 0.2 of preprocedure
- a balanced intake and output
- blood glucose levels ranging from 80 to 200 if diabetic

Nursing Interventions	Rationales
Obtain list of all allergies and sensitivities and report them to the physician.	Patients with an allergy to iodine or seafood may be sensitive to the contrast dye.

Nursing Interventions	Rationales
Administer antihistamines and/or corticosteroids as prescribed prior to an arteriogram for patients with suspected allergy to contrast dye.	
Obtain renal history and baseline blood urea nitrogen (BUN) and creatinine. Repeat BUN and creatinine the following day or at clinic visit.	Patients with chronic renal disease or renal transplants may require alternative interventions such as decreased hydration, corticosteroids, or a dopamine drip. Laboratory values are used to evaluate damage to kidneys from the contrast dye.
Maintain intravenous (IV) hydration as prescribed pre- and post-procedure. Encourage oral fluids postprocedure if patient is not nauseated.	Hydration is used to flush dye from kidneys.
Monitor urine output.	Low urine output may be an indicator of acute renal failure.
Assess cardiopulmonary status ongoing.	Patients with cardiovascular or renal disease are at risk for fluid overload due to IV hydration during and after procedure.

NURSING DIAGNOSIS: HIGH RISK FOR ALTERED PERIPHERAL OR CEREBRAL TISSUE PERFUSION

Risk Factors
- Atherosclerosis
- Embolus
- Hypotension
- Bleeding from injection site

Patient Outcomes
The patient will have
- stable vital signs
- a flat, dry puncture site
- baseline peripheral pulses distal to insertion site
- absence of petechia distal to insertion site
- no neurological deficits
- no changes in functional status

Nursing Interventions	Rationales
If patients are on anticoagulation therapy, consult with physician on when to discontinue medication and when to resume postprocedure. Warfarin should be discontinued for 48–72 hr prior to the angiogram.	Anticoagulation therapy increases risk of hemorrhage postprocedure.
Monitor vital signs frequently postprocedure.	Elevated pulse and respirations with drop in blood pressure may indicate acute blood loss.
Assess insertion site for bleeding or swelling with vital signs. Apply continuous pressure for 10 min if bleeding is noted and contact physician immediately.	
Check pulses distal to insertion site with vital signs.	Diminished pulses may indicate bleeding at the site or acute occlusion.
Maintain proper positioning with extremity straight to prevent dislodgement of newly formed clot.	
Monitor for changes in sensation and movement of extremity with vital signs.	Embolus to extremity or thrombosis at insertion site may alter sensation and movement.
Obtain a hematocrit prior to the arteriogram	A baseline hematocrit is used to help estimate blood loss in suspected hemorrhage or hematoma.
Obtain serial hematocrit levels when translumbar approach is used or when bleeding is suspected.	A large hematoma can be concealed retroperitoneal in the abdomen. The use of sandbags at the puncture site is not always recommended due to risk of internal bleeding.
Administer IV fluids at prescribed rate and encourage oral fluids to replace fluid loss by diuresis.	The osmolarity of the dye may cause diuresis and a fluid deficit.
Check for color or temperature changes in extremities.	An embolus to the extremity may cause acute occlusion or petechia on skin.

Nursing Interventions	Rationales
Perform neurological exam, including extremity strength and function, speech, swallowing, visual acuity, facial symmetry, peripheral sensation, pupil reactivity, and mentation with vital signs after carotid arteriogram.	One risk of the carotid arteriogram is dislodgement of plaque during the procedure.

DISCHARGE PLANNING/CONTINUITY OF CARE

- Assure understanding of puncture site care.
- Instruct patient to call physician if bleeding, swelling, or signs and symptoms of infection are noted at the puncture site
- Review signs and symptoms of transient ischemic attacks for patients with carotid artery disease and impress importance of reporting these symptoms.
- Instruct patient to call physician if there are sudden changes in sensation and movement in extremity.
- Coordinate follow-up care, which may include surgical intervention, other procedures, consultations, or clinic visits.

REFERENCES

Rice, V. H., Sieggreen, M., Mullin, M., & Williams, J. (1988). Development and testing of an arteriography information intervention for stress reduction. *Heart & Lung, 17,* 23–28.

Vogelzang, R. L. (1988). Vascular imaging techniques and percutaneous vascular intervention. In V. A. Fahey (Ed.), *Vascular nursing.* Philadelphia, PA: Saunders.

Waugh, J. R. & Sacharias, N. (1992). Arteriographic complications in the DSA era. *Radiology, 182,* 243–246.

CARDIAC CATHETERIZATION

Linda Wonoski, RN, MSN

Cardiac catheterization is a diagnostic procedure used to obtain information about the structure and function of the cardiac chambers, valves, and vessels. Almost every type of cardiac anatomic or pathological condition or defect can be detected, quantified, and documented by the procedure. The technique involves inserting a radiopaque catheter into a vein or artery (femoral or brachial) and passing it through the various chambers and vessels. Pressure readings and oxygen concentrations are measured in the chambers and vessels of the heart.

ETIOLOGIES (INDICATIONS)

- Confirm the presence of valvular heart disease, myocardial disease, and/or coronary artery disease.
- Determine location and severity of disease process.
- Preoperative assessment for cardiac surgery.
- Evaluate ventricular function.
- Evaluate effect of medical treatment on cardiovascular function.
- Access for coronary angioplasty.

CLINICAL MANIFESTATIONS

- Angina, chest pain
- Myocardial infarction (MI)
- Hypertension
- Fatigue, weakness
- Dyspnea

CLINICAL/DIAGNOSTIC FINDINGS

- Presence of occlusions or partial occlusion in coronary arteries
- Presence of insufficient and/or stenotic heart valves

- Decreased cardiac output
- Areas of decreased contractility of myocardium
- Ventricular aneurysm
- Cardiac anomalies

NURSING DIAGNOSIS: KNOWLEDGE DEFICIT—PROCEDURE

Related To lack of previous exposure to information

Defining Characteristics
Expression of anxiety about the procedure
Statement of lack of knowledge and need for information
Asking many questions
Procedure new for the patient

Patient Outcomes
Patient will
- state reason for procedure
- describe pre- and postprocedure routine
- describe what to expect during the procedure
- state ways to cope with anxiety during the procedure

Nursing Interventions	Rationales
Assess patient/family understanding of the procedure and willingness to learn.	
Provide available teaching materials (pamphlets, videos) to supplement teaching.	
Explain preprocedure routine, including 1. consent for procedure	
2. identification of allergies or sensitivities, especially to contrast media, iodine, or seafood, to identify risk for allergic reaction	Contrast material used contains a hypertonic solution with iodine. Patients may be at risk for an allergic reaction. Physician may premedicate with prednisone or diphenhydramine.
3. chest x-ray, blood work, and electrocardiogram (ECG)	

Nursing Interventions	Rationales
4. nothing by mouth, or clear liquids only, prior to procedure to reduce risk of vomiting or aspiration	
5. intravenous (IV) fluids to be started before the procedure to decrease dehydration caused by contrast medium	
6. pedal pulses marked if femoral site used	
7. vital signs obtained	
8. voiding prior to procedure	
9. mild sedative given prior to procedure	
Explain routine and sensations experienced during catheterization:	
1. Patient will be awake and may be able to see x-ray monitor.	Understanding that certain sensations are expected during the procedure and are not complications will help to alleviate anxiety.
2. A local anesthetic will be administered at catheter puncture site. Pressure but no sharp or severe pain may be felt when the catheter is inserted.	
3. Notify physician or nurse of any sharp or severe pain experienced during the procedure. Nitroglycerin may be administered.	Contrast medium displaces coronary blood flow and may create transient ischemia.
4. Palpitations may be felt as the catheter is advanced because catheter manipulation can irritate the endocardium and produce ectopic beats.	
5. Contrast medium injection may create a warm, flushing sensation for a few seconds. Nausea and lightheadedness may also be experienced briefly at this time.	

Nursing Interventions	**Rationales**
6. May be asked to make a deep, abdominal cough.	Coughing clears contrast material from the coronary arteries and acts as a mechanical stimulus to the heart if ectopic beats occur.
7. Blood samples and pressure readings will be obtained to assess the condition of the cardiac chambers and valves and to determine oxygen saturation values.	

Explain postprocedure routine:
1. Catheters are removed at end of procedure. Manual pressure is applied for 20–30 min; then a pressure dressing is applied. A sandbag may be used on the puncture site.
2. Vital signs will be checked frequently to prevent bleeding and hematoma formation.
3. Bedrest will be maintained for 6–8 hr, with affected extremity held straight to prevent postprocedure bleeding. If femoral site is used, the head of the bed will be kept elevated to at most 30°.
4. Patient may eat and drink soon after procedure; fluids are encouraged.
5. Patient is instructed to notify the nurse if warmth or wetness is felt in the groin area because it may indicate bleeding.
6. Mild discomfort/pain may be experienced at puncture site. Patient is told to inform nurse; pain medication may be given.
7. Patient is told when results of procedure will be discussed.

NURSING DIAGNOSIS: HIGH RISK FOR DECREASED CARDIAC OUTPUT

Risk Factors
- Hypotension
- Tachypnea
- Dyspnea
- Angina
- Dysrhythmia
- Oliguria
- Hematoma at puncture site

Patient Outcomes
Cardiac output is adequate, as evidenced by
- vital signs within normal limits for patient
- absence of angina
- absence of dysrhythmias
- urine output > 30 mL/hr
- skin warm and dry
- no bleeding or hematoma at puncture site

Nursing Interventions	Rationales
Assess vital signs prior to procedure for baseline.	
Assess postprocedure vital signs and puncture site dressing every 15 min for first hour; every 30 min for 2 hr; hourly for 4 hr; and then every shift.	
Record amount of drainage, and/or size of hematoma giving date, time, and drawing lines around drainage on dressing for future comparison.	
Immediately apply pressure to puncture site if bleeding is noted. A sandbag may be used. Notify physician if bleeding is significant.	
Place patient in Trendelenburg position if a sudden drop in blood pressure and heart rate (vasovagal response) is noted. Notify physician. Be prepared to administer IV fluid.	A vasovagal response is caused by parasympathetic stimulation which reduces the heart rate and blood pressure, adversely affecting cardiac output and peripheral perfusion.

Nursing Interventions	Rationales
Maintain bedrest for 6–8 hr with affected extremity held straight. Prevent flexion of hip by keeping head of bed elevated at most 30° if femoral site used.	
Encourage fluids. Monitor intake and output.	Contrast medium has a diuretic effect and may cause hypovolemia and hypotension.

NURSING DIAGNOSIS: HIGH RISK FOR DECREASED PERIPHERAL TISSUE PERFUSION TO AFFECTED EXTREMITY

Risk Factors
- Edema
- Vessel occlusion
- Bleeding/hematoma

Patient Outcomes
Peripheral perfusion is adequate, as evidenced by
- palpable peripheral pulses
- circulation, movement, sensation, temperature (CMST) within normal limits with capillary refill < 3 s
- absence of pain, numbness, tingling
- absence of peripheral edema

Nursing Interventions	Rationales
Assess and mark pedal pulses prior to procedure if femoral site is used.	
Assess CMST of affected extremity and pulses every 15 min for first hour, every 30 min for 2 hr, hourly for 4 hr, and then every shift. Use Doppler if pulses are difficult to feel.	
Encourage frequent deep breathing and passive and active exercises of the unaffected extremities.	Reduces the possibility of atelectasis in the lungs and thrombus formation in the deep veins of the legs.

NURSING DIAGNOSIS: KNOWLEDGE DEFICIT—SELF-CARE AFTER CATHETERIZATION

Related To lack of previous exposure to information

Defining Characteristics

Verbalizes lack of knowledge of self-care after catheterization
Asks questions regarding heart disease and long-term management (if results are positive for heart disease)

Patient Outcomes

Patient will

- describe normal appearance and healing process of the puncture site.
- define activity restrictions.
- state what to do if bleeding occurs.
- state what to do if chest pain occurs.
- state when to notify physician.

Nursing Interventions	Rationales
Review activity restrictions of strenuous activity for 24 hr. Encourage patient to discuss return to work with physician.	
Review puncture site healing process: 1. Skin will be discolored for several weeks. 2. Tenderness and a small grape size lump in the area are normal. 3. No ointment or special care of the site is necessary.	
Instruct on what to do if bleeding occurs: 1. Lie down. 2. Apply pressure to site. 3. Call ambulance for transfer to hospital.	
Instruct patient on what to do if chest pain occurs: 1. Rest. 2. Take nitroglycerin (up to 3 tablets over 15 min) if prescribed. 3. If pain continues, call ambulance for transfer to hospital.	

Nursing Interventions

Instruct patient to notify physician
if the following occur:
1. bleeding
2. signs of infection, inflammation,
   or drainage at puncture site or
   body temperature > 100°F.
3. changes in color, temperature,
   or sensation of extremities
4. chest pain or pressure.

Rationales

DISCHARGE PLANNING/CONTINUITY OF CARE

- Assure understanding of catheterization results and self-management plan.
- If the patient was found to have heart disease, discuss a referral to a cardiac rehabilitation program with physician and patient.
- Provide information about risk factor management and review plan to minimize risk factors.
- Assist in obtaining prescriptions and establishing a medication schedule and a plan for refilling prescriptions.
- Provide information on local educational programs on heart disease or risk factor management.
- Provide information on local support groups and the local chapter of the American Heart Association.

REFERENCES

Damlt, L. H., Groene, J., & Herick, R. (1992). Helping your patient through cardiac catheterization. *Nursing 92*, 22(2), 52–55.

Guzzetta, C. & Dossey, B. (1992). *Cardiovascular nursing—Body mind tapestry*. St. Louis, MO: Mosby.

Kinney, M., Packa, D., & Andreoli, K., Zipes, D. (1992). *Comprehensive cardiac care* (7th ed). St. Louis, MO: Mosby Year Book.

Perdue, B. (1990). Cardiac catheterization before and after. *Advancing Clinical Care*, 5(2), 16–19.

Thompson, J., McFarland, G., Hirsch, J., Tucker, S., Bowers, A. (1989). *Mosby's Manual Of Clinical Nursing* (2nd ed). St. Louis, MO: Mosby.

CAROTID ENDARTERECTOMY

Penny M. Bernards, RN, MS, GNP

Carotid endarterectomy is a surgical procedure used to remove athero-sclerotic plaque from the carotid artery to increase blood flow to the brain. An incision is made on the neck, and the common carotid, external carotid, and internal carotid arteries are exposed. The arteries are clamped and the internal and common carotid arteries are incised and plaque is removed. A temporary shunt is sometimes used to bypass the clamped carotid artery during its repair, especially if there are electroencephalographic changes during clamping of the carotid artery or there is inadequate blood flow through the contralateral internal carotid artery and vertebral arteries. The arteries are closed primarily or with a patch. The patch may either be a vein graft from the leg or made of synthetic material. The skin is closed with sutures or staples. Patients are often admitted on the same day of their surgery and spend the first postoperative night in the intensive care unit. The average length of stay is 3 or 4 days.

ETIOLOGIES (INDICATIONS)

- Transient ischemic attacks in carotid artery distribution
- Magnetic resonance imaging (MRI) or computerized tomography (CT) scan evidence of prior stroke in carotid artery distribution
- Patient undergoing open heart surgery with carotid stenosis >70%
- Asymptomatic unilateral or bilateral carotid stenosis >80%

CLINICAL MANIFESTATIONS

- Asymptomatic bruits over carotid arteries
- Motor or sensory abnormalities contralateral to diseased vessel
- Amaurosis fugax (monocular blindness)
- Expressive aphasia
- Stroke in evolution
- Frank stroke

CLINICAL/DIAGNOSTIC FINDINGS

- Systolic velocity and end-diastolic velocity of carotid artery blood flow >120 cm/s on duplex scan
- Sudden increase in velocity of carotid artery blood flow on duplex scan
- Visualization of plaque in carotid arteries on duplex scan
- Filling defect in carotid arteries on angiogram

OTHER PLANS OF CARE TO REFERENCE

- Arteriogram
- Basic Standards for Preoperative and Postoperative Care

NURSING DIAGNOSIS: ANXIETY

Related To
- Fear of mortality
- Morbidity from surgery or stroke

Defining Characteristics
Anger
Irritable
Indecisive
Crying

Patient Outcomes
The patient will
- state a decrease in anxiety.
- utilize methods of coping to reduce anxiety.
- identify own support systems.

Nursing Interventions	Rationales
Assess patient's level of anxiety.	
Evaluate understanding of surgery and hospitalization.	
Explore successful coping strategies in previous experiences and relevance to current situation.	Drawing on past experiences with coping with stresses may help determine which intervention will be most beneficial.
Encourage verbalization of feelings to help identify source of anxiety.	

Nursing Interventions	Rationales
Assess level of anxiety in family members and significant others and include them in patient teaching.	Patients can have increased anxiety when people around them are anxious.

NURSING DIAGNOSIS: KNOWLEDGE DEFICIT ABOUT DISEASE PROCESS, TESTS AND PROCEDURES FOR CAROTID ARTERY DISEASE, AND POSTOPERATIVE INSTRUCTIONS

Related To lack of exposure to information

Defining Characteristics

Verbalization of inadequate understanding or misconceptions
Anger
Anxiety

Patient Outcomes

The patient will
- list the risk factors for carotid artery disease and atherosclerosis.
- state rationale for preoperative tests and procedures.
- verbalize understanding of rationale of surgical intervention.
- describe incision line care.
- state postoperative activity restrictions.
- identify parameters for additional medical interventions.

Nursing Interventions	Rationales
Assess current knowledge of disease process and progression.	
Explain to patient the etiology of carotid artery disease.	Understanding the etiology of the disease may facilitate changes in health behaviors that increase atherosclerosis formation. Atherosclerosis is the most common etiology of carotid artery disease. It most commonly forms at the bifurcation of internal and external carotid arteries. Emboli from atherosclerotic lesion or total occlusion with thrombi may cause a stroke.

Nursing Interventions	Rationales
Explain how risk factors contribute to the development of atherosclerosis, including smoking, hypertension, diabetes, hyperlipidemia, radiation, and trauma.	Risk factor modification is the basis for conservative therapy and helps prevent recurrence of stenosis after surgery.
Assess patient's understanding of surgical procedure.	
Provide instructions on incision line care. The sutures are usually removed before discharge. After the sutures are removed, the neck may be washed with mild soap and water.	
Explain the signs and symptoms of infection.	
Instruct men to use an electric razor versus a straight-edge razor if there is residual numbness along their neck.	There is a potential for trauma to the greater auricular nerve by surgical manipulation which may cause some numbness on the neck and earlobe.
Explain postoperative activity restrictions, including no lifting greater than 20 lb the first few weeks; avoid driving until neck can be moved freely and avoid straining to defecate.	Activity restrictions are used to prevent disruption of sutures and elevation of intracranial pressure.

NURSING DIAGNOSIS: HIGH RISK FOR ALTERED CEREBRAL TISSUE PERFUSION

Risk Factors
- Thrombosis
- Embolus
- Hypotension
- Evidence of previous stroke

Patient Outcomes
Patient will have adequate perfusion to cerebrum, as evidenced by
- equal motor function in extremities
- peripheral sensation at baseline

- unaffected speech
- vision intact
- alertness and orientation intact

Nursing Interventions	Rationales
Perform neurological exam, including extremity strength and function, speech, swallowing, visual acuity, facial symmetry, peripheral sensation, pupil reactivity, and mentation.	Preoperative neurological exam is used to document progression of disease which may require emergency surgery. Postoperative neurological exam may indicate residual deficits from the surgery or impending stroke.
Monitor for hypertension and hypotension.	Transient hypertension is a common postoperative complication, but occasionally hypotension is also seen. The etiology is unclear but may be due to carotid sinus manipulation or changes in volume status. Monitoring blood pressure and treatment is important to avoid problems such as cerebral hemorrhage from hypertension or thrombus formation from hypoperfusion.
Monitor vital signs.	Decreased blood pressure, increased heart rate, and increased respirations may be a sign of cerebral ischemia, whereas increased blood pressure, decrease heart rate and Cheyne-Stokes respiration may be a sign of increased intracranial pressure due to hemorrhage.
Keep patients well hydrated to prevent hypoperfusion from dehydration and concomitant thrombus formation.	
Monitor prescribed antiplatelet medication. This may include aspirin, which is often started preoperatively and continued postoperatively, indefinitely.	Used to prevent carotid thrombosis postoperatively.

Nursing Interventions	Rationales
Intravenous low molecular weight dextran may be used before incision is closed until the following day.	Used to prevent carotid thrombosis postoperatively.

NURSING DIAGNOSIS: HIGH RISK FOR IMPAIRED SWALLOWING

Risk Factor
Cranial nerve trauma

Patient Outcomes
Patient will not experience signs of cranial nerve trauma, as evidenced by
- clear speech
- tongue in midline
- facial symmetry
- ability to swallow
- equal shoulder alignment

Nursing Interventions	Rationales
Assess for hoarse voice and cough.	Manipulation of vagus nerve (cranial nerve 10) during surgery may cause some trauma to the nerve and its branches. The symptoms are usually transient but may last as long as six months.
Monitor for tongue deviation toward operative side and difficulty with speech.	Indicates trauma to hypoglossal nerve (cranial nerve 12).
Assess ability to swallow.	Inability to swallow may indicate trauma to glossopharyngeal nerve (cranial nerve 9), making patient at risk for aspiration and inability to maintain own hydration.
Observe for drooping of corner of mouth on operative side.	It may indicate injury to marginal mandibular branch of facial nerve (cranial nerve 7). This should not be confused with a stroke which affects the opposite side of diseased carotid.

NURSING DIAGNOSIS: IMPAIRED SKIN INTEGRITY

Related To surgical procedure

Defining Characteristics
Surgical incision

Patient Outcomes
The patient will have
- intact skin over incision with suture removal within the first postoperative week
- no erythema, warmth, or purulent drainage along incision

Nursing Interventions	Rationales
Keep the incision line clear of crusts to prevent separation of incision line.	
Monitor incision for signs of infection, that is, erythema, warmth, swelling, tenderness, and purulent drainage. Risk increases if reoperation is needed.	
Monitor for numbness along the incision and earlobe.	Patients may be at risk to trauma to neck or incision due to lack of sensation, especially while shaving.
Monitor for swelling and ecchymosis along the incision.	It may indicate an arterial leak or hemorrhage.

NURSING DIAGNOSIS: HIGH RISK FOR ALTERED CARDIAC TISSUE PERFUSION

Risk Factors
- Coronary artery disease
- Arrhythmia
- Heart valvular disease

Patient Outcomes

The patient will have
- controlled angina
- baseline electrocardiogram (ECG)
- controlled blood pressure and heart rate

Nursing Interventions	Rationales
Assess for presence or risk of coronary artery disease (CAD) preoperatively.	Surgical morbidity and mortality are linked with CAD.
Explain to patient the importance of cardiac assessment prior to carotid endarterectomy.	Some patients have a more extensive work-up for a carotid endarterectomy than for open heart surgery due to combined risk of CAD and stroke.
Monitor patients postoperatively with telemetry and routine ECG to evaluate for signs of cardiac ischemia.	
Monitor for complaints of angina and treat as prescribed.	Patients with known CAD may have prescribed nitroglycerin.

DISCHARGE PLANNING/CONTINUITY OF CARE

- Assure understanding of activity restrictions and ability to perform incision line care.
- Instruct patient and family to contact physician if there are any changes in neurological status such as changes in mentation, restlessness, facial asymmetry, numbness, or weakness in extremities; expressive aphasia or sudden monocular blindness; and signs and symptoms of infection or increased swelling noted in neck.
- Coordinate outpatient follow-up appointments.
- Assure understanding of medication regimen and obtaining refills.
- Instruct patient to continue blood pressure monitoring and provide equipment if needed.

REFERENCES

Fahey, V. A. (1988). Cerebrovascular insufficiency. *Journal of the Society for Vascular Nursing, 6,* 8–12.

Fode, N. C. (1990). Carotid endarterectomy: Nursing care and controversies. *Journal of Neuroscience Nursing, 22,* 25–31.

Hertzer, N. R. (1989). Postoperative management and complications following carotid endarterectomy. In R. B. Rutherford (Ed.), *Vascular surgery*. Philadelphia, PA: Saunders.

Patt, A., Marsch, J. G., & Pearce, W. H. (1988). Extracranial cerebrovascular disease. In V. Fahey (Ed.), *Vascular nursing*. Philadelphia, PA: Saunders.

▼

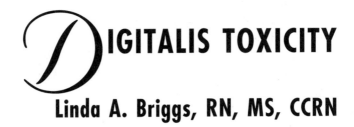IGITALIS TOXICITY

Linda A. Briggs, RN, MS, CCRN

As one of the most common cardiac medications, digitalis is prescribed to increase myocardial contractility and decrease heart rate. It is indicated for a wide variety of cardiac disorders, given for extended periods of time, and commonly administered to the elderly. The therapeutic-to-toxic dose is very narrow, thus creating a frequent clinical phenomenon of overdose or toxicity.

ETIOLOGIES

- Advanced or long-standing cardiac disease
- Electrolyte imbalance, specifically potassium and magnesium
- Decreased renal function
- Coadministration of other drugs (calcium antagonists, quinidine, beta blockers, diuretics, laxatives, antacids)
- Acid-base imbalances
- Hypoxia
- Hypothyroidism
- Altered drug absorbency

CLINICAL MANIFESTATIONS

- Gastrointestinal
  - anorexia
  - nausea
  - vomiting
  - diarrhea
- Central nervous system
  - visual disturbances (difficulty with red and green color perception, halos around objects)
  - fatigue
  - confusion

96

- depression
- psychosis
• Cardiac
  - any dysrhythmia
  - atrial tachycardia with block
  - accelerated junctional rhythms
  - sinus tachycardia and bradycardia
  - atrioventricular (AV) blocks, progressive
  - atrial fibrillation
  - ventricular dysrhythmias

CLINICAL/DIAGNOSTIC FINDINGS

• Serum digoxin level
  - usually elevated above therapeutic range (0.5–2.0 ng/mL)
  - patients with risk factors may show signs of toxicity at low or normal serum levels
• Electrolytes
  - hypokalemia, hypomagnesemia, hypocalcemia
  - may aggravate digitalis toxicity
• Electrocardiogram
  - variety of rhythm disturbances which may not be specific

NURSING DIAGNOSIS: HIGH RISK FOR DECREASED CARDIAC OUTPUT

Risk Factors
• Preexisting, advanced cardiac disease
• Electrolyte imbalance
• Decreased renal function
• Increased sensitivity with other drugs

Patient Outcomes
Patient will
• have heart rate and rhythm within acceptable range.
• have rhythm status within normal limits or controlled.
• have normal renal status [blood urea nitrogen (BUN), creatinine].
• have normal electrolytes.

Nursing Interventions	Rationales
Assess patient hemodynamic status to include 1. blood pressure 2. heart rate, including apical assessment 3. heart rhythm: • Monitor and document rhythm status (if monitored). • Investigate new rhythm disturbances; monitor on telemetry or obtain 12-lead ECG.	Rhythm disturbances frequently accompany digitalis toxicity. However, rhythm disturbances are not uncommon in the patient population requiring digitalis treatment. New dysrhythmias should be investigated. Many digitalis-related dysrhythmias may decrease cardiac output and result in decreased peripheral organ perfusion. Other dysrhythmias may lead to more lethal, life-threatening situations.
Assess for other signs of heart failure.	Digitalis toxicity may aggravate preexisting cardiac conditions.
Monitor electrolyte status and treat imbalances.	Hypokalemia will increase the potential for digitalis toxicity. Potassium and digitalis compete for similar cellular binding sites. Less potassium allows digitalis to bind with greater sites. Hypomagnesium causes refractory hypokalemia, and hypercalcemia potentials cause digitalis toxicity.
Monitor serum digoxin levels.	
Monitor renal function to include urine output, BUN, and creatinine values.	Digitalis is excreted through the kidneys, and altered renal function will potentiate digitalis toxicity.
Assess other prescribed or over-the-counter medications for potential drug interactions to include 1. antacids, neomycin 2. drugs containing calcium (quinidine, verapamil) 3. drugs that cause potassium wasting (steroids, diuretics) 4. beta blockers	Drugs such as antacids, laxatives, and neomycin may alter bowel absorption and decrease digitalis effectiveness. Calcium preparations and hypokalemia enhance digitalis toxicity. Beta blockers may decrease heart rate and potentiate digitalis-induced bradycardias

Nursing Interventions	Rationales
Prepare patient for treatment of dysrhythmias that may include temporary pacing and antiar-rhythmic drug therapy and transfer to critical care unit.	
Administer digoxin-immune Fab (antigen-binding fragments) as pre-scribed. During administration, monitor potassium levels.	The digoxin-immune Fab binds antibodies with digoxin binding sites, thus minimizing the effects of existing digitalis. A 13-year multicenter trial has proved the drug's effectiveness. Serum digoxin levels will rise and will not be a reliable indicator. Potassium levels will elevate during administration and may need to be treated with other measures temporarily.

NURSING DIAGNOSIS: HIGH RISK FOR FLUID VOLUME DEFICIT

Risk Factors
- Gastrointestinal side effects of digitalis toxicity
- Diuretic therapy
- Malnutrition

Patient Outcomes
Patient will
- verbalize relief from nausea, vomiting, and diarrhea.
- have balanced intake and output.

Nursing Interventions	Rationales
Monitor closely for gastrointestinal symptoms of nausea, vomiting, an-orexia, and diarrhea.	Gastrointestinal side effects occur in approximately 80% of patients with digitalis toxicity. These symptoms may often be over-looked and related to other fac-tors such as the underlying dis-ease process or medications. The appearance of one new symptom should be investigated.

Nursing Interventions	Rationales
Monitor fluid status to include intake, output, and daily weights.	
Provide adequate fluids and foods as tolerated.	
Administer antiemetics as prescribed.	

NURSING DIAGNOSIS: HIGH RISK FOR ALTERED THOUGHT PROCESSES

Risk Factors
- Age
- Underlying cardiac disease
- Underlying altered mental status

Patient Outcomes
Patient will demonstrate
- return to baseline mental status
- usual visual acuity

Nursing Interventions	Rationales
Obtain baseline mental status, incorporating information from family as appropriate.	Understanding patient baseline mentation is important in evaluating any observed changes. Many underlying conditions, including advancing age, may render the normal exam.
Assess patient closely for mentation changes to include fatigue, confusion, and depression.	
Protect the patient from harm by frequent orientation, monitoring closely, or assisting with ambulation.	
Provide emotional support to patient and family.	Many digitalis-induced changes in mentation completely resolve once the body is cleared of high digitalis levels.

NURSING DIAGNOSIS: KNOWLEDGE DEFICIT—DIGITALIS USE

Related To
- Lack of information
- Misinformation

Defining Characteristics

Lack of knowledge regarding digitalis and risk factors for toxicity
Does not follow prescribed treatment
Unable to identify side effects of toxicity

Patient Outcomes

Patient will
- verbalize risk factors for toxicity.
- follow recommendations for drug administration.
- verbalize side effects of toxicity.

Nursing Interventions	Rationales
Provide information on purpose of digitalis and administration guidelines.	Knowledge may increase compliance with treatment and avoid the potential for side effects.
Instruct patient to adhere to medication schedule and the importance of not omitting doses or taking extra doses.	
Instruct in pulse taking and to notify physician if pulse is less than the physician's predetermined rate.	Digitalis and associated drug combinations may cause bradycardias. Although a heart rate below 60 bpm may indicate toxicity, the physician may prescribe other heart rate guidelines.
Encourage patient to check with physician or pharmacist before taking any over-the-counter medications.	To avoid drug interactions with digitalis.

Nursing Interventions	Rationales
Inform of the following side effects to report to the physician: 1. nausea 2. vomiting 3. diarrhea 4. change in heart rate 5. visual disturbances 6. change in mentation	

DISCHARGE PLANNING/CONTINUITY OF CARE

- Assure understanding of self-management plan, including medication schedule, pulse taking, and symptoms to report.
- Refer to a home health agency for medication monitoring, compliance with treatment plan, and further education.
- Arrange follow-up with physician for continued management.
- Assist in obtaining prescriptions, devising medication schedule, and establishing a plan for refilling prescriptions.

REFERENCES

Bayer, M., (1992). When drugs turn against the heart. *Emergency Medicine*, August 15, 1992, pp. 119–136.

Guzzetta, C. & Dossey, B. (1992). *Cardiovascular nursing*. St. Louis, MO: Mosby Year Book.

McDonnell-Cooke, D. (1992). Shielding your patient from digitalis toxicity. *Nursing 92, 7*, 44–47.

FEMORAL-POPLITEAL BYPASS

Linda Wonoski, RN, MSN

Femoral-popliteal bypass is performed to treat peripheral artery insufficiency that has not responded to medical management. The impaired blood flow can occur secondary to acute conditions such as trauma or embolization but more often is due to atherosclerotic changes. Surgical intervention is necessary when intermittent claudication becomes disabling, pain is present at rest, and lower extremity ischemic ulcers or gangrene is present.

ETIOLOGIES

- Trauma
- Embolus
- Atherosclerosis factors: smoking, obesity, hypertension, diabetes, hyperlipidemia, family history

CLINICAL MANIFESTATIONS

- Intermittent claudication
- Pain in the extremity at rest
- Diminished or absent pulses
- Sluggish capillary refill
- Muscle atrophy of affected extremity
- Thick, brittle nails
- Hair loss distal to the occlusion
- Numbness, tingling
- Skin that is cool, shiny, dry, thin, pallor when elevated, rubor when extremity dependent
- Necrosis, ulceration, and gangrene in extremity

CLINICAL/DIAGNOSTIC FINDINGS

- Sound waves diminished with Doppler ultrasound
- Pain and flattening of waveforms with stress testing
- Decreased ankle brachial pressure measurements
- Stenotic lesion visualized with arteriography
- Decreased blood volume and blood flow measured by plethysmography

OTHER PLANS OF CARE TO REFERENCE

- Basic Standards for Preoperative and Postoperative Care
- Pain Management: Patient-Controlled Analgesia

NURSING DIAGNOSIS: KNOWLEDGE DEFICIT ABOUT FEMORAL POPLITEAL BYPASS PRE- AND POSTOPERATIVE PROCEDURE

Related To lack of exposure to information

Defining Characteristics
Expression of anxiety about the procedure
Verbalization of a lack of knowledge
Verbalization of a need for information
Procedure new for patient

Patient Outcomes
Patient/family will
- state reason for procedure.
- describe pre- and postoperative routine.
- state decreased anxiety about the procedure.

Nursing Interventions	Rationales
Assess patient's/family's understanding of the procedure and readiness to learn.	
Provide available teaching materials to supplement teaching.	Written materials enhance learning.
Explain preoperative routine. Mark peripheral pulses.	

Nursing Interventions	Rationales
Explain postoperative routine: 1. frequent coughing and deep-breathing exercises and incentive spirometry to enhance optimal lung expansion and gas exchange 2. frequent assessments, including vital signs, pulses, dressing checks, and circulation, movement, sensation, temperature (CMST) 3. avoiding acute knee or hip flexion or crossing of legs, which may predispose to graft kinking and thrombosis 4. leg and foot exercises (quadricep setting and ankle flexion and extension) while in bed to promote venous return 5. bedrest initially, then short, frequent walks to limit the time the operative leg is in the dependent position 6. that patient may experience discomfort postoperatively; pain management options of patient-controlled analgesia (PCA) and importance of early reporting to nurse; that sudden severe pain in extremity may indicate graft occlusion 7. that prophylactic antibiotics usually administered to help prevent wound infection; fewer doses required for patients with autogenous grafts than for patients with synthetic grafts	

▼

NURSING DIAGNOSIS: HIGH RISK FOR ALTERED PERIPHERAL TISSUE PERFUSION

Risk Factors
- Edema

- Inflammation
- Graft occlusion
- Venous stasis

Patient Outcomes

Peripheral perfusion is adequate, as evidenced by
- palpable peripheral pulses
- absence of pain in extremity
- CMST within normal limits (capillary refill <3 s)
- absence of numbness and tingling
- no signs of inflammation
- no edema present

Nursing Interventions	Rationales
Assess vital signs, peripheral pulses, and CMST every 15 min for first hour, every 30 min for second hour, hourly for 4 hr, then every 4 hr. Use Doppler if pulses are difficult to locate.	
Assess patient's level of pain at the surgical site and distally at least every 4 hr.	Increase in pain level could indicate graft occlusion.
Assess for potential deep-vein thrombosis by checking Homan's sign every 4 hr.	
Avoid 90° flexion of hip and use of knee gatch to prevent graft kinking and thrombosis. Maintain knee in neutral or slightly flexed position.	
Instruct patient not to cross legs or ankles.	
Instruct/assist patient to perform active foot and leg exercises every 1–2 hr while awake.	
Place bed cradle over lower extremities to minimize pressure from bed linens.	
Maintain adequate fluid intake of at least 2500 mL/day, unless contraindicated.	Prevents fluid volume deficit and resulting increased blood viscosity.

Nursing Interventions	Rationales
Maintain comfortable room temperature and provide patient with adequate clothing and blankets.	Exposure to cold promotes generalized vasoconstriction.

NURSING DIAGNOSIS: KNOWLEDGE DEFICIT ABOUT SELF-CARE MANAGEMENT

Related To lack of exposure to information

Defining Characteristics

Verbalizes lack of knowledge about care at home
Asking questions about atherosclerotic disease progression and risk factor
management

Patient Outcomes

Patient will
- describe normal healing process and signs of infection.
- define expected activity progression.
- describe ways to maintain and enhance lower extremity blood flow.
- state ways to prevent or slow the atherosclerotic process.
- list signs and symptoms of further circulatory problems.

Nursing Interventions	Rationales
Review normal healing process and signs of infection (i.e., reddened incisional site, drainage from incision, elevated temperature), emphasizing importance of notifying surgeon if infection occurs to receive prompt treatment.	
Review prescribed activity level and progressive walking program.	Regular exercise stimulates collateral circulation and improves circulation through muscle contraction and relaxation.

Nursing Interventions	Rationales
Review ways to promote peripheral blood flow and minimize future peripheral vascular problems: 1. Instruct to avoid crossing legs and long periods of sitting or standing, which places pressure on the arteries of the legs and impedes arterial blood flow. 2. Do active foot and leg exercises for 5 min every hour while awake to improve circulation through muscle contraction and relaxation. 3. Stop smoking to minimize the effects of vasoconstriction and spasms of the arteries, resulting in decreased blood flow to the arteries. 4. Establish a regular exercise program to improve and promote collateral circulation. 5. Avoid chronic constipation, which decreases venous return secondary to straining and increased intra-abdominal pressure. 6. Avoid constrictive clothing (i.e., knee-high stockings, girdles), which has a tourniquet effect on circulation, inhibiting flow and resulting in pooling of blood and edema in the extremity.	

Nursing Interventions

Review risk factors and their effect on promoting disease progression:
1. Smoking promotes vasoconstriction and spasms of the arteries, resulting in decreased blood flow to the arteries.
2. Obesity: Excess fat compromises blood vessels and contributes to increased venous congestion. Obese individuals are also more prone to diabetes, hypertension, and hyperlipidemia.
3. High-saturated-fat and high-cholesterol diet contributes to the development of atherosclerotic plaques.
4. Sedentary life-style: Regular exercise improves and promotes collateral circulation.
5. Hypertension causes the elastic tissue in the arteries to be replaced by fibrous collagen tissue. This contributes to the arterial wall becoming less distensible and increases the resistance to blood flow.
6. High blood sugar: Changes in glucose and fat metabolism are thought to contribute to the atherosclerotic process.
7. Stress stimulates the sympathetic nervous system and causes peripheral vasoconstriction and contributes to hypertension.

Review signs and symptoms of further circulatory problems:
1. sudden or gradual increase in extremity pain
2. CMST changes
3. significant increase in swelling of the extremity

Rationales

▼

DISCHARGE PLANNING/CONTINUITY OF CARE

- Assure understanding of self-management plan.
- Assure understanding of signs and symptoms of infection, decreased circulation, and who to contact if problems occur.
- Identify patient's plan to enhance peripheral blood flow and decrease risk factors.
- Provide information on classes and services available to assist with life-style changes, to decrease risk factors, including stress management, cardiovascular fitness, smoking cessation, dietary instruction, and weight loss.

REFERENCES

Alspach, J. (1991). *Core curriculum for critical care nursing* (4th ed.). Philadelphia, PA: Saunders.

Blank, C. A. & Irwin, G. H. (1990). Peripheral vascular disorders assessment and intervention. *Nursing Clinics of North America*, 25(4), 777–794).

Bright, L. D. & Georgi, S. (1992). Peripheral vascular disease. Is it arterial or venous? *American Journal of Nursing*, 92(9), 34–43.

Ting, M. (1991). Wound healing and peripheral vascular disease. *Critical Care Nursing Clinics of North America*, 3(3), 515–523.

▼

THROMBOPHLEBITIS/DEEP-VEIN THROMBOSIS

Penny M. Bernards, RN, MS, GNP

Thrombophlebitis is an inflammation of a vein involving formation of a clot. It may occur in superficial veins or deep veins. Superficial thrombophlebitis is rarely life threatening but may lead to a deep-vein thrombosis (DVT). Patients with a DVT are at risk for a pulmonary embolus which is life threatening. Deep-vein thrombosis may also cause damage to valves resulting in postphlebitic syndrome. Postphlebitic syndrome consists of chronic leg edema, tenderness, hyperpigmentation, stasis dermatitis, scaling, and possibly ulcerations. Thus the most important nursing intervention for DVT is prevention. If a DVT occurs, the key nursing interventions include prevention of progression of the clot, maintaining viability of involved extremity, and monitoring anticoagulation therapy.

ETIOLOGIES

- Venous stasis
- Venous trauma
- Increased blood coagulability
- Hypofibrinolysis

CLINICAL MANIFESTATIONS

Superficial
- Erythema
- Warmth
- Tenderness
- Swelling
- Ecchymosis
- Palpable hard cord

Deep
- Asymptomatic
- Swelling starting distally and progressing proximally

- Dilatation of superficial veins
- Hemosiderin pigment deposition
- Pain in calf on dorsiflexion of foot (Homan's sign)
- Malaise
- Fever
- Phlegmasia cerulea dolens (acute DVT) of the iliofemoral segment resulting in edema, severe pain, cyanosis, blisters, and diminished arterial flow which may lead to ischemia.

CLINICAL/DIAGNOSTIC FINDINGS

- Filling defects or abrupt termination of flow on venogram
- Absence of phasic changes of venous Doppler signal with respirations
- Decreased or absent augmentation of venous Doppler signal with manual compression
- Positive 125I-fibrinogen uptake test
- Congenital or acquired clotting deficits such as antithrombin III, protein C, or protein S deficiencies

NURSING DIAGNOSIS: HIGH RISK FOR ALTERED PERIPHERAL TISSUE PERFUSION

Risk Factors
Venous stasis
- Immobilization
- Obesity
- Age >40
- Congestive heart failure
- Varicose veins
- Estrogen therapy
- Spinal cord injury
- Stroke
- Pregnancy
- Myocardial infarction

Venous trauma
- Intravenous therapy
- Prior incidence of DVT
- Surgical procedures involving the abdomen, pelvis, or extremities
- Lower limb fractures
- Trauma

Hypercoagulability
- Polycythemia
- Leukemia
- Malignancies
- Sickle cell anemia

- Antithrombin III deficiency
- Protein C or S deficiency
- Puerperium
- Nephrotic syndrome
- Polycythemia vera

Patient Outcomes
The patient will
- have no sudden onset of edema or pain in an extremity.
- verbalize and demonstrate preventative measures for DVT.
- have appropriate anticoagulant therapy.

Nursing Interventions	Rationales
Assess for conditions which increase risk for DVT.	Identification of patients at risk is important to increase awareness among nursing staff.
Apply antiembolism stockings and/or intermittent pneumatic compression stockings, as prescribed, for patients who are unable to ambulate.	Stockings are used to reduce venous stasis in lower extremities.
Encourage patients to do dorsiflexion, plantar flexion, and ankle-rolling exercises while in bed or in chair. Perform passive range-of-motion exercises for patients unable to do active exercises.	Exercises help reduce venous statis in lower extremities.
Elevate foot of bed if tolerated. Use caution if pillows are used so veins are not compressed, causing further venous stasis.	Ten degree elevation increases venous blood flow 30%.
Instruct patients to do deep-breathing exercises with or without an incentive spirometer and monitor frequency.	The mechanics of breathing act as a pump which helps with venous return.
Ambulate patients as soon as medically possible.	No mechanical pump works as efficiently as the calf muscles to promote venous return.
Observe intravenous (IV) sites and change at least every 72 hr. (Each practice setting may have its own protocol.)	Rotating IV sites helps reduce venous trauma from direct injury or overuse.

Nursing Interventions	Rationales
Monitor intake and output to maintain proper fluid balance.	Overhydration and underhydration can decrease venous return and cause venous stasis.
Monitor anticoagulant therapy as prescribed by physician:	
1. Heparin is used subcutaneously for prophylactic treatment in the perioperative period and for other high-risk patients.	Heparin neutralizes factor X of the coagulation system which prevents formation of thrombin, which is necessary for formation of a clot.
2. Warfarin is also used for prophylactic treatment although it is usually used postoperatively due to risk of bleeding. An exception is made for orthopaedic patients with hip/knee fractures who are often given warfarin preoperatively as well.	Warfarin inhibits vitamin K, which is necessary to make the clotting factors VII, IX, and X and prothrombin II, which are involved with formation of thrombin.

NURSING DIAGNOSIS: ALTERED PERIPHERAL TISSUE PERFUSION

Related To reduced or disrupted venous flow due to DVT

Defining Characteristics
Edema
Pain
Dilatation of superficial veins
Malaise
Fever

Patient Outcomes
The patient will have
- decreased edema in involved extremity
- decreased pain
- intact skin

Nursing Interventions	Rationales
Maintain bedrest for several days to prevent plaque from breaking off and forming an embolus.	

Nursing Interventions	Rationales
Measure arm or leg circumference at several specific locations to document changes in edema.	
Monitor heparin IV infusions as prescribed. A heparin bolus may be used to establish a therapeutic dose more quickly.	
Monitor the activated partial thromboplastin time (PTT) and platelet count during administration of heparin. The therapeutic range is 1.5–2.0 times the control value.	The laboratory value PTT measures alterations in clotting factors which are used to regulate heparin dose. Patients on heparin are at risk for heparin-induced thrombocytopenia; thus platelet levels are monitored daily.
Monitor PTT every 4–6 hr after changes in heparin drip dose until therapeutic range and then at least twice daily.	It may take several days for the therapeutic range, requiring frequent adjustments. Patients have different tolerances to anticoagulants and require individual dosing.
Apply elastic ace bandages to affected extremity to decrease edema and prevent venous dilatation. Rewrap bandage when loose or at least twice a day to assess skin integrity.	
Elevate affected extremity above the level of the heart if tolerated.	
Apply prescription-strength compression stockings when patients are ambulatory. Stockings are worn during the day and are taken off at night.	Compression stockings are used to prevent venous dilatation. Venous dilatation may cause incompetent valves because they are unable to close completely. This results in backflow of venous blood, which increases venous pressure and may lead to leakage of fluid into interstitial spaces with subsequent venous stasis ulcerations.

Nursing Interventions	Rationales
Warfarin is initiated either with heparin or when heparin is therapeutic depending on physician preference. Instruct patient that warfarin may be continued for at least 3–6 months.	To prevent extension or recurrence of clot.
Monitor prothrombin time (PT) daily while patients are on warfarin. Changes in PT are usually not seen until 48 hr after initiating warfarin. Therapeutic range is 1.5–2.0 times the control.	The PT evaluates defects in prothrombin and factors V, VII, and X.
Monitor any changes in medications or medical condition while on warfarin.	There are numerous medications and medical conditions which can either enhance or inhibit the anticoagulation effect of warfarin.
Observe for signs of bleeding while on anticoagulation therapy. Signs may include hematuria, guaiac positive stools, nosebleeds, coffee ground emesis, coughing up frank blood, unexplained pain, drop in hematocrit and hemoglobin, bleeding gums, and excessive bleeding from incisions.	Bleeding may occur even when patients are subtherapeutic on anticoagulants.

NURSING DIAGNOSIS: HIGH RISK FOR IMPAIRED GAS EXCHANGE

Risk Factors
- Deep-vein thrombosis
- Venous stasis
- Cardiovascular disease
- Previous history of DVT or pulmonary embolus (PE)

Patient Outcomes
The patient will have adequate perfusion to the lung, as evidenced by
- regular unlabored respirations
- absence of chest discomfort
- absence of restlessness

Nursing Interventions	Rationales
Monitor vital signs and report any sudden drop in blood pressure, tachycardia, and tachypnea.	Changes in vital signs are potential signs for PE.
Monitor for signs and symptoms of PE such as shortness of breath, chest pain, fever, cough, hemoptysis, hypotension, syncope, restlessness, and hypoxemia and report them immediately to physician.	
Implement preventative measures for DVT.	The best treatment of pulmonary embolism is prevention.
Instruct patient regarding diagnostic studies used to detect pulmonary emboli, which include ventilation-perfusion scan, chest x-ray, electrocardiogram (ECG), arterial blood gas measurements, and possibly pulmonary arteriogram.	
If a pulmonary embolus is suspected, IV heparin therapy is usually initiated until diagnosis is ruled out or confirmed.	

NURSING DIAGNOSIS: KNOWLEDGE DEFICIT—DIAGNOSIS AND TREATMENT OF DVT

Related To lack of exposure to information

Defining Characteristics
Verbalization of inadequate understanding or misconceptions
Anxiety
Inaccurate demonstration of desired behaviors

Patient Outcomes
The patient will
- describe thrombophlebitis and the DVT healing process, diagnostic tests, and possible complications.
- describe anticoagulation medications regimen and plan for monitoring.
- list precautions to take while on anticoagulation therapy.
- apply and wear compression stockings.
- describe planned walking program.

Nursing Interventions	Rationales
Assess current knowledge of disease process.	Assessment of knowledge base is used to develop teaching plan.
Explain the etiology of DVT and how the identified risk factors contribute to the formation of clot.	Understanding of etiology and risk factors may facilitate changes in behavior that help prevent venous stasis and trauma.
Inform about noninvasive diagnostic tests used to detect DVT, which include	
1. Doppler ultrasound	Doppler ultrasound involves an ultrasonic beam which records an audible signal as moving blood cells pass beneath. The flow characteristics are assessed for patency. No sound is heard over occluded veins and an abnormal signal may be heard over partially occluded veins.
2. impedance plethysmography	Impedance plethysmography is used to detect more proximal DVT. A pneumatic thigh cuff is placed over the thigh, and four electrodes are placed around the calf. The thigh cuff is inflated and then rapidly deflated while the electrodes measure the venous capacitance and outflow. The outflow is decreased when a venous thrombosis is present.
3. duplex imaging	A duplex scan involves use of an ultrasound probe over the skin which provides colored imaging of venous flow and abnormalities such as thrombus.
4. venogram (considered an invasive procedure)	A venogram involves injection of contrast material through a vein in the dorsum of the foot and subsequent filming of venous flow. A filling defect in the vein indicates a thrombus.

Nursing Interventions	Rationales
Instruct regarding potential complications of DVT, especially if left untreated, including extension of clot which increases risk of pulmonary embolus and an ischemic limb if iliofemoral segment is involved and postphlebitic syndrome.	Patients need to be aware of how serious their condition is so that an informed decision can be made regarding treatment.
Assess understanding of anticoagulation therapy, including indications, dosage, target protime levels and frequency of blood draws, regulation of warfarin from protime levels, risks of therapy, and lack of therapy.	
Instruct to take warfarin at the same time daily and to not take an additional dosage, if one is missed, without consultation with their physician.	
Caution about avoiding over-the-counter products which contain aspirin while on warfarin unless directed by physician.	Aspirin enhances the anticoagulation effect of warfarin.
Instruct to wear compression stockings daily even when feeling better to prevent venous dilatation. Stockings are applied in the morning and removed before going to bed. Stockings should be replaced after they lose their elasticity at approximately 3–6 months.	Patients who have had a DVT are at increased risk for development of additional thrombosis.
Emphasize importance of a regular exercise program using leg muscles to promote venous return.	

DISCHARGE PLANNING/CONTINUITY OF CARE

- Coordinate plan for obtaining regular protime levels for regulation of warfarin dose.
- Emphasize importance of monitoring protime levels.

- Review signs and symptoms of bleeding.
- Instruct patient to contact physician if signs and symptoms of recurrent DVT develops.
- Inform patient to seek immediate medical attention if sudden shortness of breath or chest pain occurs.
- Coordinate outpatient follow-up clinic visits and testing to evaluate for reconstitution of vein.
- Assist in obtaining prescriptions and establishing medication time schedule and plan for refilling prescriptions.

REFERENCES

Coffman, J. D. (1989). Deep venous thrombosis and pulmonary emboli: Etiology, medical treatment and prophylaxis. *Journal of Thoracic Imaging, 4*, 4–7.

Fahey, V. A. (1988). Venous thromboembolism. In V. A. Fahey (Ed.), *Vascular nursing.* Philadelphia, PA: Saunders.

Herzog, J. A. (1992). Deep vein thrombosis in the rehabilitation client. *Rehabilitation Nursing, 17,* 196–198.

Nunnelee, J. D. (1988). Medications used in vascular patients. In V. A. Fahey (Ed.), *Vascular nursing.* Philadelphia, PA: Saunders.

Ogston, D. (1987). *Venous thrombosis causation and prediction.* Chichester: Wiley Medical.

▼

Common Respiratory Conditions and Procedures

▼

$\mathcal{C}$HEST TUBES

Linda Wonoski, RN, MSN

$\mathcal{C}$hest tubes with an attached drainage system are placed in the pleural cavity to drain fluid, blood, or air and reestablish a negative pressure that facilitates expansion of the lung. To drain air, which rises in the pleural space, the chest tube is frequently inserted in the second, third, or fourth intercostal space at the midclavicular line. To drain blood or fluid, which gravity forces to the base of the lung, the chest tube is placed in the fifth or sixth intercostal space at the midaxillary line.

ETIOLOGIES (INDICATIONS)

- Pneumothorax
- Hemothorax
- Pleural effusion
- Empyema
- Postthoracotomy
- Post–heart surgery

CLINICAL MANIFESTATIONS

- Respiratory distress
- Dyspnea
- Tachypnea
- Use of accessory muscles
- Paradoxical chest movement
- Trachea deviated to unaffected side
- Lungs: hyperresonant over air-filled area, dull over fluid filled area; breath sounds diminished or absent in affected area
- Cyanosis or pallor
- Pain
- Anxiety

CLINICAL/DIAGNOSTIC FINDINGS

- Chest x-ray reveals air and/or fluid accumulation; shift of mediastinal structures.
- Arterial blood gases (ABGs) deviate from patient's baseline but are variable depending on the degree of compromised lung function, altered breathing pattern, and ability to compensate.

NURSING DIAGNOSIS: ANXIETY

Related To
- Respiratory distress
- Lack of knowledge about chest tube insertion

Defining Characteristics

Patient expresses fear about inability to breathe and chest tube insertion.
Patient asks questions and verbalizes a lack of knowledge regarding chest tube insertion procedure.

Patient Outcomes

Patient will
- describe awareness of chest tube insertion.
- verbalize a decreased level of anxiety and fear.

Nursing Interventions	Rationales
Stay with patient. Maintain calm, confident reassuring approach.	
Explain the specific reason why the chest tubes are needed (e.g., to remove air or fluid or reexpand the lung).	
Review insertion procedure with patient, including	Knowledge of what to expect can decrease anxiety.
1. type of drainage system to be used (e.g., how it looks, basic function)	
2. positioning during insertion— sitting up and bending forward or lying on unaffected side	Scapula is moved out of the way for easier insertion.

Nursing Interventions	**Rationales**
3. area of chest tube insertion:—intercostal space used	Chest tube is placed high for air removal (second, third, or fourth intercostal space) or low for removal of fluid (fifth or sixth intercostal space).
4. local anesthetic injected at insertion site	
5. small incision made at insertion site	
6. chest tube inserted using several techniques, either a trocar or hemostat, and connected to the drainage system	
7. chest tube sutured in place and a sterile dressing applied	
8. chest tube and drainage system monitored closely for bleeding and leakage of air and fluid	
9. follow-up chest x-ray performed to confirm chest tube placement and reexpansion of the lung	

NURSING DIAGNOSIS: IMPAIRED GAS EXCHANGE/ INEFFECTIVE BREATHING PATTERN

Related To decreased lung expansion
- Ventilation
- Perfusion imbalance
- Pain and fatigue

Defining Characteristics
Dyspnea
Tachypnea
Hypoxemia
Restlessness
Use of accessory muscles for breathing
Splinted or guarded respirations
Abnormal ABGs: deviate from patient's baseline
Breath sounds diminished or absent

Patient Outcomes

Patient will demonstrate
- normal rate, rhythm, and depth of respirations
- ABGs within normal limits or patient's baseline
- reexpansion of the lung
- breath sounds bilaterally equal and clear

Nursing Interventions	Rationales
Auscultate lungs and assess respiratory rate, depth, and quality. Immediately report signs of increased respiratory distress (rapid, shallow breathing, cyanosis, or pressure in the chest).	Early detection of respiratory distress may indicate a tension pneumothorax which can develop when air leaks into the pleura and cannot escape.
Monitor level of consciousness and vital signs frequently.	
Monitor ABG's and pulse oximetry.	
Administer oxygen as prescribed.	
Assess and maintain patency of closed chest drainage system:	Promotes reexpansion of the lungs by draining fluid and air from the pleural space.
1. Tape all tube connections and check periodically to ensure a closed system and patency of tubes.	An air-tight closed system is required to reexpand lung.
2. Keep chest drainage system below level of patient's chest.	Gravity will aid in drainage and prevent backflow into the chest.
3. Mark original drainage fluid level (immediately postinsertion) on the outside of the drainage system; then mark hourly/shift increments (date and time).	Drainage usually declines progressively after the first 24 hr.
4. Notify physician if drainage is greater than 100 mL/hr for two consecutive hours or if there is a sudden outpouring of bright red blood.	May indicate new bleeding requiring surgical intervention or fluid replacement.

Nursing Interventions

5. Keep tubing free of kinks and prevent dependent loops. Do not let patient lie on tubing.

6. Milk/squeeze tubing gently in the direction of the drainage container only if necessary to move drainage along. Do not *strip* tubing or use heavy pressure to tubing.

7. Check fluid level in water seal chamber and maintain patient at level prescribed.

8. Monitor water seal for fluctuation (tidaling). Absence of fluctuation indicates lung reexpansion or that there is an obstruction which must be corrected (clots, kinking, or tubing).

9. Monitor for air leaks in the drainage system as indicated by constant bubbling in the water seal chamber. Report any sudden increase in bubbling; determine location of and correct any inappropriate air leak (e.g., tighten connection).

Rationales

Kinking, looping, or pressure on the drainage tubing can create back pressure, possibly forcing drainage back into the pleural space or impeding removal of air or fluid.

Gently milking/squeezing the tubing is generally enough to prevent it from becoming plugged with clots and fibrin. Chest tube stripping can create transient negative pressure on the pleural space possibly causing lung entrapment in the chest tube eyelets and tissue infarction. This results in less efficient air/fluid drainage.

Water in the water seal chamber serves as a barrier which prevents atmospheric air from entering the pleural space. The greater the fluid level in the water seal chamber, the more positive pressure is required to push air out of the drainage unit, which makes breathing more difficult.

Fluctuation of 2–6 cm during inspiration generally indicates that the chest tube and collection tube are patent.

Bubbling in the water seal chamber indicates an air leak which may be present because the lung has not yet reexpanded or there may be a leak in the system before the water seal drainage, such as a loose tubing connection or air leak around the entrance site of the chest tube.

Nursing Interventions	Rationales
10. Monitor patient for development of subcutaneous emphysema.	Subcutaneous emphysema indicates air is leaking into the tissues faster than it is being removed by the tube. The physician may change the chest tube to a larger one and/or additional suction may be applied to the chest tube in an attempt to remove air more rapidly.
11. Check suction control chamber for correct fluid level.	Amount of suction being applied to the pleural space is regulated by the amount of fluid in the suction control chamber, not the amount dialed on the wall suction.
12. Keep two hemostats at the bedside. Clamp only if the closed chest drainage system is being changed to a new system, the physician ordered clamping to verify the patient's readiness to have the chest tube removed, or to locate the source of an air leak. If the system becomes accidently disconnected, reconnect it as quickly as possible, clamping is not recommended.	Clamping chest tubes is dangerous because no air or fluid can escape and a tension pneumothorax can occur.
Encourage patient to change positions frequently. Recommended positions include semi-Fowler's and lateral with a rolled towel placed under the chest tubing to protect it from the weight of the patient's body.	Promotes drainage from the chest tube. Moves abdominal contents away from the diaphragm, enhancing chest expansion and movement of the diaphragm. Promotes patient comfort and prevents the chest tube from being compressed when the patient turns that way.
Assist patient to cough, deep breath, and use the incentive spirometer every 2–4 hr.	

NURSING DIAGNOSIS: PAIN

Related To pleural tissue trauma associated with the chest tubes

Defining Characteristics

Complaints of pain: around chest tubes, on moving, with coughing, and
  deep breathing
Hesitation to move, cough, and deep breath
Facial grimaces
Rigid posture

Patient Outcomes

Patient will
- verbalize a decrease in pain.
- increase participation in moving, coughing, and deep breathing.
- display a relaxed facial expression and body sphere.

Nursing Interventions	Rationales
Assess for pain, using a rating scale from 1–10.	
Administer prescribed analgesics at regular intervals, especially prior to coughing, turning, and/or mobility exercises.	Pain will interfere with coughing, turning, and progressive mobility. Patient may attempt rapid, shallow breathing to splint the lower chest and avoid movement of the chest tubes, which will impair ventilation.
Provide splinting to chest tube area when encouraging patient to cough and deep breath to lessen muscle pull and pain as patient coughs.	
Encourage abdominal breathing.	
Place rolled towel around chest tube to prevent pulling when assisting patient to turn or move.	
Make sure chest tubes are adequately taped to patient's chest.	

NURSING DIAGNOSIS: IMPAIRED PHYSICAL MOBILITY

Related To
- Chest tubes
- Pain
- Fatigue

Defining Characteristics
Reluctance to move
Requests for assistance to move
Limited range of motion in arm and shoulder on the side of the chest tubes
Complaints of pain with movement

Patient Outcomes
Patient will
- exhibit full range of motion
- require minimal or no assistance
- state minimal pain with movement

Nursing Interventions	Rationales
Medicate for pain 20–30 min prior to repositioning, exercise, and/or ambulation.	
Assist with passive range-of-motion exercises to the arm and shoulder on the side of the chest tubes, beginning the evening of chest tube insertion.	
Encourage active range-of-motion exercises two to three times daily beginning the first day after chest tube insertion (e.g., rotate shoulder 360°, hunch shoulder).	
Assist with repositioning every 2 hr and ambulate as ordered. Patient may ambulate with chest tubes in place as long as the water seal remains below the level of the chest.	
Promote rest periods between exercises and ambulation.	

NURSING DIAGNOSIS: KNOWLEDGE DEFICIT—CHEST TUBE REMOVAL AND HOME CARE

Related To lack of exposure to information

Defining Characteristics

Expressions of fear and lack of knowledge regarding chest tube removal
 and home care management
Asking questions about chest tube removal and home care management

Patient Outcomes

Patient will
- verbalize an understanding of the chest tube removal procedure.
- describe care at home.

Nursing Interventions	Rationales
Explain chest tube removal procedure:	
1. Patient placed in semi-Fowler's or side position.	
2. Instruct to take a deep breath and hold or perform a gentle Valsalva maneuver. Do not inhale; inspiration may result in pneumothorax.	
3. Chest tube suture is clipped and chest tube quickly removed.	
4. May experience burning, pain, and/or pulling on removal. Medication for pain is usually given prior to removal of tubes.	
5. Pressure dressing with petroleum gauze or antibiotic ointment is placed over site and sealed with tape.	
6. Rate of respirations, quality of breath sounds, and chest tube dressing are assessed frequently.	
Explain the need to continue to do coughing and deep breathing and range-of-motion exercises after discharge.	

Nursing Interventions	Rationales
Encourage to avoid exposure to smoke and air pollution. If patient smokes, explain the importance of not smoking. Provide information on smoking cessation as needed.	Irritation to the lungs can cause bronchoconstriction resulting in an irritating cough with a rapid shallow respiratory rate.
Encourage to increase activity level gradually avoiding strenuous activity or exercise until recommended by physician.	
Instruct to report the following to the physician: 1. upper respiratory infection 2. elevated temperature 3. cough 4. difficulty breathing 5. sudden sharp chest pain 6. any redness, pain, swelling, or tenderness at the puncture site	

DISCHARGE PLANNING/CONTINUITY OF CARE

- Assure understanding of self-management plan.
- Arrange follow-up with physicians for continued management postdischarge.
- Assist patient in obtaining prescriptions and establishing a plan for refilling prescriptions.
- Refer patient to a home health agency if continued nursing care, teaching, or assistance with activities of daily living is needed.
- Arrange for home respiratory equipment from vendor if needed.

REFERENCES

Erickson, R. (1989). Chest drainage—Part two. *Nursing, 19*(6), 46–49.

Suddarth, D. (1991). *Manual of nursing practice* (5th ed). Philadelphia, PA: Lippincott.

Teplitz, L. (1991). Update: Are milking and stripping chest tubes necessary? *Focus on Critical Care, 18*(60), 506–511.

Thompson, J., McFarland, G., Hirsch, J., Tucker, S., & Bowers, A. (1989). *Mosby's manual of clinical nursing* (2nd ed). St. Louis, MO: Mosby.

Wilson, S. & Thompson, J. (1990). *Respiratory disorders.* St. Louis, MO: Mosby Year Book.

LARYNGECTOMY

Linda Wonoski, RN, MSN

Laryngectomy is performed for treatment of cancer of the larynx. Treatment of carcinoma of the larynx depends on the extent of the tumor involvement. A partial laryngectomy is usually performed when the tumor has not involved surrounding muscles and there is minimal vocal cord involvement. The patient will have a temporary tracheostomy tube and may have return of some voice, but it usually remains hoarse. A total laryngectomy is performed when the cancer is advanced. The entire larynx and preepiglottic region may be removed and a permanent stoma created.

ETIOLOGIES (INDICATIONS)

Cancer of larynx

CLINICAL MANIFESTATIONS

- Tickling sensation in the throat
- Fullness (lump) in throat
- Painful swallowing
- Coughing on swallowing
- Pain radiating to the ear
- Hoarseness/voice change
- Aphonia (loss of voice)
- Dyspnea
- Hemoptysis
- Pain

CLINICAL/DIAGNOSTIC FINDINGS

- Tumor/mass detected on direct and indirect laryngoscopy, x-ray, and computerized tomography (CT) scan

- Biopsy positive for cancer
- Abnormal barium swallow

OTHER PLANS OF CARE TO REFERENCE

- Basic Standards for Preoperative and Postoperative Care
- Tracheostomy
- Nutrition Support: Enteral Nutrition
- Pain Management: Patient-Controlled Analgesia

NURSING DIAGNOSIS: ANXIETY

Related To
- Lack of knowledge regarding the surgical procedure (laryngectomy)
- Threat of death
- Changes as a result of surgery

Defining Characteristics

Asking many questions
Verbalizing lack of knowledge of the surgery and postoperative course
Expressing anxiety/fear about the surgery and resulting changes and threat
   of death

Patient Outcomes

Patient/caregiver will
- state reason for and type of laryngectomy.
- explain
   - routine pre- and postoperative care
   - reason for suctioning and feeding tube
   - pain management methods
- discuss plan for communication postoperatively.

Nursing Interventions	Rationales
Assess anxiety and readiness to learn.	A high anxiety level can decrease learning. Motivation is one of the most important variables affecting learning.
Provide written or audiovisual teaching materials to supplement teaching.	

Nursing Interventions	Rationales
Review patient's individual reason for the laryngectomy and type of procedure to be done (i.e., partial vs. total laryngectomy).	
Review pre- and postoperative procedures specific to laryngectomy: 1. vital signs 2. suctioning to maintain airway free of secretions 3. pain management methods 4. feeding tubes utilized to maintain adequate nutritional level	
Explain reason for suctioning the tracheostomy/laryngectomy tube and how each functions. Show and encourage patient to handle the tube and suctioning equipment.	
Explain inability to speak postoperatively (temporary loss of speech with partial laryngectomy vs. permanent loss of speech with a total laryngectomy). Discuss and plan for an alternative form of communication postoperatively.	After a partial laryngectomy scar/tissue fills the defect where the diseased cord was removed and becomes a vibrating surface within the larynx. This permits husky but acceptable speech. After a total laryngectomy there is no voice because of removal of the larynx.
Explain that the sense of smell is affected after the laryngectomy.	Breathing through the nose is impossible; therefore the patient does not receive olfactory sensations.
Explain that swallowing difficulty, postoperatively, may occur due to the surgical alteration of the pharynx and larynx, laryngeal edema, and pain.	

▼

NURSING DIAGNOSIS: INEFFECTIVE AIRWAY CLEARANCE

Related To
- Thick secretions
- Fatigue

Defining Characteristics
Changes in rate or depth of respirations
Dyspnea
Tachypnea
Increased work of breathing: use of accessory muscles
Pallor, cyanosis
Adventitious breath sounds (rales, rhonchi)
Ineffective cough, inability to manage secretions

Patient Outcomes
Patient will
- demonstrate a patent airway.
- demonstrate breath sounds, bilaterally, equal and clear.
- exhibit normal rate, rhythm, and depth of respirations.
- demonstrate the ability to cough out/manage secretions.

Nursing Interventions	Rationales
Assess respiratory rate and depth and quality of respirations and auscultate lungs every 2–4 hr and prn.	
Encourage patient to deep breathe and cough out secretions every 2–4 hr and prn.	
Regularly assess for patency of the tracheostomy/laryngectomy tube. Suction secretions as they accumulate (see Tracheostomy for procedure).	A tracheostomy tube is usually used with a partial laryngectomy and removed when edema in the surrounding tissue subsides. A laryngectomy tube is used with a total laryngectomy and is shorter and has a less acute angle than the tracheostomy tube. The manner in which the trachea is brought to the neck surface during a laryngectomy results in a less acute tracheal angle than that of a temporary tracheostomy. The laryngectomy tube usually remains in 2–3 weeks until the wound has healed and a permanent fistula is formed.

Nursing Interventions	Rationales
Administer humidified oxygen as prescribed.	The normal mechanism of warming, moistening, and filtering the air is bypassed when an altered airway is present. Without humidification there is a greater incidence of obstruction caused by drying of secretions.
Maintain adequate hydration for the patient: 2–3 L/day, unless contraindicated by the patient's condition.	Helps to prevent thick tenacious secretions from collecting in the patient's airway.

NURSING DIAGNOSIS: HIGH RISK FOR IMPAIRED GAS EXCHANGE

Risk Factors
- Tracheal secretions
- Possible tracheostomy/laryngectomy
- Cuff leak

Patient Outcomes
Patient will exhibit
- a patent airway
- minimal secretions
- arterial blood gases (ABGs) within normal limits
- no change in mental status
- only a minimal air leak heard on exhalation

Nursing Interventions	Rationales
Assess heart rate, temperature, respiratory rate, and depth and quality of respirations and auscultate lungs every 2–4 hr and prn.	
Assess for changes in mental status, including increasing lethargy, confusion, restlessness, and irritability, every 2–4 hr as needed.	Changes may indicate hypoxemia and/or hypercapnea and a need for suctioning.
Place patient in semi- to high Fowler's position to promote full-lung expansion.	

Nursing Interventions	Rationales
Administer humidified oxygen as prescribed.	
Monitor oxygen saturation (SaO_2) and ABGs to assess adequacy of respiratory function and to determine acid-base balance and need for oxygenation.	
Suction as needed when abnormal breath sounds are present and/or patient is unable to handle secretions.	
Ensure that tracheostomy/laryngectomy ties are secured at all times.	This prevents tube from falling out or becoming dislocated and creating a hypoxic event.
Keep a replacement tracheostomy or laryngectomy tube of the same size and type, obturator, and hemostat at the bedside at all times. In case of accidental extubation the tracheal opening should be held open with the hemostat. This will allow the patient to breathe until the replacement tube is inserted. Insert the new tube with the obturator in place which has a tapered end to provide a smooth system for entering the trachea.	
Check tracheostomy or laryngectomy cuff for inflation and/or leak every shift and as needed (see Tracheostomy for procedure).	
If the patient had a partial laryngectomy and is to be weaned from the tracheostomy tube, see Tracheostomy.	

NURSING DIAGNOSIS: HIGH RISK FOR INFECTION

Risk Factors
- Tracheostomy/laryngectomy incision, stoma

- Suctioning
- Stagnated secretions
- Decreased ability to fight infection

Patient Outcomes
The patient will
- exhibit no redness, warmth, or tenderness at the tracheostomy/ laryngectomy site.
- demonstrate a normal temperature and white blood cell (WBC) count.
- exhibit no abnormal drainage around the tracheostomy/laryngecotmy site.
- demonstrate the ability to manage secretions.

Nursing Interventions	Rationales
Assess vital signs and temperature every 4 hr.	
Assess laboratory values of WBC count and differential.	The usual response to an infection, especially to a pulmonary infection, is to mobilize increased numbers of WBCs from the bone marrow and other storage areas.
Assess tracheostomy/laryngectomy incision (stoma) for redness, warmth, tenderness, and exudate.	
Suction as needed using sterile technique.	
Provide routine tracheostomy/laryngectomy care every shift and as needed. (See Tracheostomy for procedure.)	

NURSING DIAGNOSIS: ALTERED NUTRITION—LESS THAN BODY REQUIREMENTS

Related To difficulty or inability to ingest sufficient food or nutrients

Defining Characteristics
Inability to tolerate oral feedings
Loss of weight
Caloric intake less than minimum daily requirements
Decreased serum albumin
Muscle weakness
Fatigue

Patient Outcomes

Patient will
- ingest caloric intake adequate for disease/metabolic state.
- demonstrate serum albumin within normal limits.
- resume oral intake, swallowing without coughing, or aspiration.
- maintain or increase weight.
- continue to regain strength.

Nursing Interventions	Rationales
Assess daily intake of parenteral, enteral, and oral food and fluids and output.	
Weigh daily.	
Monitor serum albumin levels.	
Monitor enteral feedings closely for aspiration. Check for tube placement in stomach and residual before each tube feeding (see Nutrition Support: Enteral Nutrition).	Swallowing is impaired initially from postoperative edema of the lower pharynx. Tube feedings provide more adequate nutrients than intravenous (IV) fluids and minimize contamination of the pharyngeal and esophageal suture lines.
Begin oral feedings approximately 7–10 days postoperatively to allow for suture line healing. Start with fluids until patient is swallowing well. Then advance diet as tolerated by patient.	
To ease patient's fear of choking, explain the postsurgical anatomic changes of no longer having a connection between the esophagus and tracheostomy.	
Stay with the patient during meals for the first few days. Have suction equipment ready.	
Use measures to encourage eating. Allow patient to select desired foods. Provide small frequent meals. Consult with dietitian about high-calorie supplements. Provide mouth care before meals. Provide attractive, clean environment at meals.	

Nursing Interventions	Rationales
Provide for adequate rest periods between meals.	

NURSING DIAGNOSIS: PAIN

Related To tissue trauma associated with the laryngectomy surgical procedure

Defining Characteristics
Communicates pain by prearranged signal or in writing
Facial grimaces
Reluctant to move, deep breathe, and cough
Rigid posture

Patient Outcomes
Patient will
- indicate a decrease in pain to tolerable levels.
- increase participation in moving and coughing and deep breathing.
- display a relaxed facial expression and body posture.

Nursing Interventions	Rationales
Assess patient for pain using a rating scale from 1 to 10.	
Administer prescribed pain medication as needed for patient complaints of discomfort.	
Monitor edema at incision site.	An increase in tissue edema can cause an increase in perceived pain.
Log roll head and chest. Teach patient self-support of head and neck when up by interlocking hands behind head to provide support when moving to a sitting position.	
Encourage patient to use alternate pain-relieving measures such as relaxation or distraction.	

NURSING DIAGNOSIS: IMPAIRED VERBAL COMMUNICATION

Related To
- Removal of vocal cords (larynx)
- Presence of tracheostomy tube

(Patients who have had a partial laryngectomy will have their speech abilities maintained with relatively minor limitations once the tracheostomy is removed.)

Defining Characteristics

Cannot speak
Gesturing to make needs known
Difficulty in making self understood

Patient Outcomes

Patient will demonstrate ability to communicate needs using alternative methods of communication.

Nursing Interventions	Rationales
Assess patient's/family's understanding of his or her inability to communicate. Clarify information as needed.	
Speak to the patient in a normal manner and tone. Although the patient can not talk, he or she usually can hear. If you use overly simplistic language or talk too loud, you may frustrate the patient even more.	
Provide patient with alternative forms of communication. Identify which form is best for the patient. Examples include pad and pencil, magic slate, and communication board with pictures or alphabet.	A magic slate ensures privacy because what is written can be erased. If writing is difficult, a communication board with common needs and equipment on it can be utilized by the patient.
Allow patient ample time to respond in writing. Avoid asking two questions at once.	Writing takes longer than speaking. Anticipating and interrupting the patient trying to communicate in writing can cause further frustration for the patient and he or she may attempt to communicate less often.

Nursing Interventions	Rationales
Provide the call light within easy reach at all times and let the patient know it will be answered immediately. Devise a system for marking the intercom to alert the staff that the patient is unable to talk.	
Consult with speech therapy to assist the patient to learn use of voice prosthesis, electrolarynx, or esophageal speech.	Speech therapists can assist the patient in learning alternate forms of speech. Until patient's esophageal speech is perfected, mechanical devices can help the patient communicate verbally.

NURSING DIAGNOSIS: BODY IMAGE DISTURBANCE

Related To
- Changes in body structure from surgery
- Laryngectomy tube/tracheostoma
- Inability to vocalize

Defining Characteristics
Change in structure and function of body part (laryngectomy tube/tracheostoma) and inability to speak
Withdrawal from social contact
Refusal to look at tracheostoma and participate in care of laryngectomy tube or tracheostoma

Patient Outcomes
Patient will begin to formulate and accept a new body image as evidenced by
- beginning to socialize with others
- looking at and touching the laryngectomy tube/tracheostoma
- participating in self-care
- accepting rehabilitation assistance (e.g., speech)

Nursing Interventions	Rationales
Assess preoperative body image.	

Nursing Interventions	Rationales
Assess for readiness to view and touch the laryngectomy tube/tracheostoma. Provide support and encouragement to do so.	
Encourage support from family members and friends to demonstrate acceptance of the patient by others.	
Encourage communication of feelings about body image.	
Encourage participation in self-care, including laryngectomy or tracheostoma care.	This allows patient to have some control and incorporate body changes and needs into life-styles.
Provide information available to support changes experienced, such as support groups, laryngectomy visitor program and speech therapist.	

NURSING DIAGNOSIS: KNOWLEDGE DEFICIT ABOUT SELF-CARE AT HOME

Related To lack of exposure to information

Defining Characteristics
Asking questions
Expressing anxiety about discharge and caring for self at home

Patient Outcomes
Patient/caregiver will
- verbalize appropriate self-care at home.
- demonstrate ability to independently perform laryngectomy tube care/tracheostoma care and suctioning if needed.
- state when and how to contact the physician.
- state resources available for support.
- demonstrate a decreased level of anxiety.

Nursing Interventions	Rationales
Assess patient/family understanding of the laryngectomy and review information as necessary (e.g., anatomy and physiology, purpose).	
Review and demonstrate laryngectomy care (see Tracheostomy) and tracheostoma care and suctioning if needed. Assist patient/caregiver until they can perform care independently.	At time of discharge most patients can cough up secretions and do not need to be suctioned.
Explain process of weaning from laryngectomy tube: 1. Usually a laryngectomy tube is worn until the stoma heals. 2. After stoma heals, a gradual process of weaning starts, leaving the tube out 1 hr at a time, to create the permanent stoma.	
Encourage patient to do a return demonstration of skills taught.	
Instruct to: 1. prevent environmental irritants from entering the laryngectomy tube/tracheostoma by wearing a scarf or shirt with a closed collar that covers the opening, yet is of porous material, thin enough to allow airflow. 2. keep products such as powders, aerosol sprays, after shave, shaving cream, soap, and so on, away from the laryngectomy tube/tracheostoma. 3. keep excessive water from entering the laryngectomy tube/tracheostoma to prevent aspiration (may bathe and shower as long as the spray and water are kept away from the stoma; may place a protective shield over stoma; swimming not recommended).	

Nursing Interventions	Rationales
4. maintain proper humidification of the environment using a room humidifier, pans of water near heat sources, and drinking 2–3 quarts of liquid daily, unless physician has restricted intake.	
Review potential problems that should be reported to the physician, including 1. unexplained dyspnea 2. severe coughing 3. bleeding around the laryngectomy tube 4. hemoptysis 5. change in color or consistency of secretions (yellow, green, brown, foul smelling, thick, and difficult to remove) 6. temperature of 101°F or more 7. lump in throat 8. dysphagia	
Provide information about wearing a Medic-Alert bracelet and developing a means of communicating at home in case of an emergency.	Patient is a neck breather and must wear a Medic-Alert bracelet providing information on the proper way to resuscitate should respiratory arrest occur.
Recommend and discuss high-fiber diet and use of stool softener.	Patient with a tracheostoma is usually not able to hold breath to "bear down" for a bowel movement.
Review resources available and make appropriate contacts: 1. visiting nurse for home care assistance 2. American Cancer Society 3. American Speech and Hearing Association 4. Lost Chord Club/New Voice Club	

▼

DISCHARGE PLANNING/CONTINUITY OF CARE

- Assure understanding of self-management plan.
- Assure understanding of what should be reported to the physician.
- Arrange follow-up with physician for continued management after discharge.
- Provide information on how and where to obtain appropriate supplies (laryngectomy and suctioning equipment).
- Assist with obtaining a Medic-Alert bracelet.
- Arrange visiting nurse follow-up if continued assistance with laryngectomy or tracheostoma care is needed.
- Provide information on local support groups (Lost Chord Club, New Voice Club) and educational programs.
- Refer to the local chapter of the American Cancer Society and the American Speech and Hearing Association.

REFERENCES

Lewis, S. & Collier, I. (1992). *Medical surgical nursing* (3rd ed). St. Louis, MO: Mosby Year Book.

Lockhart, J., Traff, J., & Artin, L. (1992). Total laryngectomy and radical neck dissection: A case study. *AORN J 55*(5), 458–479.

Martin, L. (1989). Management of the altered airway in the head and neck cancer patient. *Seminars In Oncology Nursing, 5*(3), 182–190.

Sawyer, D. & Bruya, M. (1990). Care of the patient having radical neck surgery or permanent laryngostomy: A nursing diagnostic approach. *Focus On Critical Care, 17*(2), 166–173.

▼

$\mathcal{P}$LEURAL EFFUSION

Ellen M. Jovle, RN, MS

Pleural effusion is the accumulation of excess fluid in the pleural space. Normally the space between the parietal and visceral pleurae contains less than 10 mL of serous fluid. The balance between hydrostatic and colloidal osmotic pressure maintains the rate of pleural fluid production and rate of its removal in balance. Pleural effusion occurs when the rate of fluid production exceeds the rate of its removal. Pleural effusion is rarely a primary disease. It occurs as a secondary problem when one of the following mechanisms is present: increased systemic hydrostatic pressure, as in congestive heart failure; increased capillary permeability, as with trauma or inflammation; decreased rate of removal because of lymphatic obstruction, as in malignancy; decreased colloid osmotic pressure, as in hypoalbuminemia which occurs in liver disease; and increased intrapleural negative pressure, as in atelectasis.

ETIOLOGIES

- Pulmonary infections or infarction
- Malignancies
- Rheumatoid arthritis
- Cardiac or chest surgery
- Systemic lupus erythematous
- Subphrenic infection
- Lung abscess
- Congestive heart failure
- Renal failure
- Liver failure
- Myxedema
- Chest trauma
- Atelectasis
- Peritoneal dialysis
- Pancreatitis
- Esophageal perforation

CLINICAL MANIFESTATIONS

- Dyspnea
- Dry, nonproductive cough
- Reduced chest wall movement on affected side
- Mediastinal shift toward contralateral side
- Pleuritic pain when inflammation present
- Dullness to percussion which shifts with change in position
- Decreased or absent breath sounds over affected area
- Fever present with infection and inflammation
- Tachycardia and hypotension with loss of fluid into pleural space

CLINICAL/DIAGNOSTIC FINDINGS

- Chest x-ray: Fluid accumulation of more than 200 mL is detected on usual posteroanterior and lateral chest films. Lateral decubitus films show much smaller amounts of fluid.
- Ultrasound: if chest x-rays are inconclusive.
- Blood gases: hypoxemia.
- Pleural fluid analysis: Done to diagnose cause of effusion. Common tests include stain, culture and sensitivity, cytologic examination, protein, red and white blood cell (RBC, (WBC) counts, amylase, lactic dehydrogenase (LDH), specific gravity, glucose, cholesterol, triglycerides, antinuclear antibody (ANA) titers, and pH.

OTHER PLANS OF CARE TO REFERENCE

- Chest Tubes

NURSING DIAGNOSIS: INEFFECTIVE BREATHING PATTERN

Related To decreased expansion of lungs due to fluid accumulation and/or pleuritic pain

Defining Characteristics
Dyspnea
Tachypnea
Shallow respirations
Decreased chest wall movement
Verbalizations of pain with coughing and deep breathing

Patient Outcomes
Patient will exhibit
- decrease in dyspnea

- respiratory rate and depth within normal limits for patient
- absence of complications of atelectasis and pneumonia
- coughing and deep breathing effectively

Nursing Interventions	Rationales
Assess patient's respiratory status, including rate, depth of respirations, and chest wall movement. Note respiratory effort, including use of accessory muscle and intercostal retractions.	
Auscultate lungs. Note areas of decreased/absent airflow and adventitious breath sounds.	Decreased airflow occurs in areas compressed by effusion. Adventitious sounds detect areas of atelectasis or retained secretions.
Assess for pain.	Splinting or guarding of affected area decreases effectiveness of breathing pattern and may prevent patient from coughing and deep breathing.
Elevate head of bed and assist patient in changing positions frequently.	
Administer analgesic as prescribed. Monitor effect on respirations.	Analgesics may depress respirations.
Assist patient in cough and deep-breathing exercises. Splint chest when performing exercises.	Facilitates lung expansions. Splinting chest reduces pain.
Maintain patency of chest tubes, if present (see Chest Tubes).	Promotes removal of fluid from pleural space and expansion of lung.
Teach patient importance of regular coughing and deep breathing. Demonstrate effective techniques. Encourage use of blow bottles or incentive spirometry.	
Instruct patient/family in signs of pleural effusion and symptoms to report if pleural effusion is a recurrent problem.	

NURSING DIAGNOSIS: IMPAIRED GAS EXCHANGE

Related To
- Low ventilation to perfusion rates
- Intrapulmonary shunting
- Hypoventilation

Defining Characteristics
Dyspnea
Hypoxemia
Decreased or absent breath sounds over effusion
Tachycardia
Restlessness/changes in mentation

Patient Outcomes
Patient will demonstrate
- absence of signs and symptoms of hypoxemia
- normal breath sounds
- arterial blood gases within patients normal limits

Nursing Interventions	Rationales
Monitor arterial blood gases and arterial oxygen saturation (SaO_2) using oximetry.	Hypoxemia may be present due to areas of decreased or absent alveolar ventilation. Carbon dioxide levels may also be elevated if hypoventilation is the primary etiology.
Observe for signs and symptoms of hypoxemia. Assess mental status. Monitor heart rate and rhythm, and assess color of skin, mucous membranes, and nail beds.	
Monitor hemoglobin and hematocrit.	Determines amount of hemoglobin present to carry oxygen to the tissues. Hematocrit detects blood loss into pleural space.
Maintain decreased level of activity. Pace activities as patient tolerates. Monitor response to activity including respiratory rate, heart rate, blood pressure, and SaO_2.	Reduces oxygen demands and detects need for supplemental oxygen with activity.

Nursing Interventions	Rationales
Administer oxygen as prescribed.	Corrects hypoxemia due to low ventilation to perfusion ratio.
Anticipate possible thoracentesis or chest tube insertion as treatment methods. Explain procedure to patient. Assist physician and patient with procedure.	

NURSING DIAGNOSIS: HIGH RISK FOR DECREASED CARDIAC OUTPUT

Risk Factors
- Hypovolemia secondary to loss of blood or fluid into the pleural space
- Rapid reperfusion of pulmonary blood vessels when too much fluid is pulled out of pleural space too rapidly

Patient Outcomes
Patient will demonstrate
- normal pulses and blood pressure
- normal urine output
- normal breath sounds
- normal skin color and temperature
- normal mentation

Nursing Interventions	Rationales
Monitor blood pressure, heart rate, peripheral pulses, skin color and temperature, mental status, and urinary output.	
Monitor quantity, color, and characteristics of chest tube drainage.	
Clamp chest tube, as ordered, to avoid pulmonary edema.	Lung tissue and pulmonary blood vessels have been compressed with large pleural effusion. To ensure gradual reperfusion, the chest tube may be clamped after 1 L of fluid is drained and repeated according to patient's condition and physician preference.

Nursing Interventions	Rationales
Anticipate need for fluid volume replacement if signs and symptoms of hypovolemia are present.	

▼

NURSING DIAGNOSIS: FEAR/ANXIETY

Related To
- Change in health status
- Uncertainty of diagnosis and outcome
- Insufficient knowledge of diagnostic and therapeutic procedures

Defining Characteristics
Expressed concern about health status
Expressed fearfulness, uncertainty, apprehension
Increased muscle tension
Inability to relax
Signs and symptoms of insomnia
Sympathetic stimulation

Patient Outcomes
The patient and family will
- acknowledge and discuss fears and anxiety.
- appear relaxed.
- verbalize understanding of disease process and diagnostic and therapeutic procedures.

Nursing Interventions	Rationales
Observe physical responses indicating anxiety and fear.	
Assess current level of understanding of diagnosis, treatment plan, and potential outcomes.	
Encourage expression and discussion of fear and anxiety and assist patient/family in identifying source of anxiety. Acknowledge and validate patient's anxiety and fears.	

Nursing Interventions	Rationales
Accept patient's use of anxiety-reducing behaviors such as acting out, withdrawal, and somatizing. Do not reinforce behaviors. Understand and help patient to identify feelings and meaning behind behavior.	These are mechanisms the patient is using to cope with the situation and perceived threat.
Provide opportunity for questions. Assist patient/family in asking questions of physicians.	
Explain anticipated procedures and treatment including the purpose, process, and sensations patient will experience. Reinforce physician explanations of procedure and treatments.	
Involve patient and family in planning of care.	May decrease feeling of powerlessness and loss of control.
Assist patient and family in assessing effectiveness of current coping behavior, exploring other behaviors that may be more effective. NOTE: Other diagnosis will need to be individualized depending on the cause of the pleural effusion and medical treatments.	

DISCHARGE PLANNING/CONTINUITY OF CARE

- Assure patient understanding and ability to perform self-care at home.
- Arrange medical follow-up.
- Assist in obtaining prescriptions.
- Refer to home health care agency if ongoing nursing care is required.
- Arrange hospice care as appropriate.
- Provide information on cancer, arthritis, or lupus community resources or support groups.

REFERENCES

Connor, P., Berg, P., Flaherty, N., Klem, L., Lawton, R., & Tremblay, M. (1989). Two stages of care for pleural effusion. *RN, 52*(2), 30–34.

Light, R. W. (1992). Pleural diseases. *Disease-a-Month, 28*(5), 263–331.

Lutz, M. M. (1991). Getting the facts on pleural effusion. *Nursing 91, 21*(3), 32S–32T.

Wilson, S. F. & Thompson, J. M. (1990). *Respiratory disorders.* St. Louis, MO: Mosby.

▼

$\mathcal{P}$NEUMONECTOMY

Linda Wonoski, RN, MSN

Pneumonectomy is the surgical removal of an entire lung. It is usually performed to treat lung cancer. The main arteries, veins, and mainstem bronchus at the bifurcation are severed and sutured off. Because there is no lung left to reexpand, closed chest drainage is generally not done postoperatively. The empty thoracic cavity fills with serous exudate which eventually consolidates. The phrenic nerve is also usually severed on the affected side, which causes the diaphragm to elevate and also help fill the empty thoracic space.

ETIOLOGIES (INDICATIONS)

- Lung cancer
- Tuberculosis

CLINICAL MANIFESTATIONS

- Dyspnea, aggravated by exertion
- Tachypnea
- Cough
- Rhonchi, crackles, wheezes
- Underweight (emaciation)
- Pain
- Fatigue

CLINICAL/DIAGNOSTIC FINDINGS

- Chest x-ray may show lesion, mass, pleural effusion, atelectasis, and erosion of ribs or vertebrae.
- Cytologic examination shows abnormalities of the pleural fluid or pleural or lymph node biopsies.

- Sputum shows abnormal cells.
- Bronchoscopy reveals a malignancy.
- Lung scan identifies ischemic areas.
- Pulmonary function tests are suboptimal.
- Arterial blood gases (ABGs) are abnormal.

OTHER PLANS OF CARE TO REFERENCE

- Basic Standards for Preoperative and Postoperative Care
- Pain Management: Patient-Controlled Analgesia

NURSING DIAGNOSIS: KNOWLEDGE DEFICIT REGARDING THE SURGICAL PROCEDURE—PNEUMONECTOMY

Related To no previous experience or information

Defining Characteristics
Expressing anxiety about the surgery
Verbalizing lack of knowledge
Asking many questions

Patient Outcomes
Patient will
- state reason for surgery.
- describe pre- and postsurgical routine.

Nursing Interventions	Rationales
Assess patient/family understanding of the surgery and readiness to learn.	
Provide written and audiovisual materials to supplement teaching.	
Explain routine preoperative procedures.	

Nursing Interventions

Rationales

Explain postoperative routine:

1. Frequent coughing and deep breathing and use of incentive spirometry to keep the airway patent, prevent atelectasis, and facilitate reexpansion of the lung.
2. Oxygen therapy to promote maximum oxygenation and maintain arterial PaO_2 at desired level.
3. Frequent vital signs are taken.
4. Medication for pain is given as needed for the first 48–72 hr. Pain can impair ventilation, making coughing ineffective and causing secretions to be retained. Pain also makes the patient reluctant to turn and do arm exercises.
5. Arm exercises to prevent restriction of function, especially on the operative side.
6. Frequent dressing checks since blood on the dressing is unusual and should be reported to the surgeon.
7. Fluids are encouraged to aid in liquefying secretions, making them easier to expectorate.
8. Abdominal breathing is encouraged to improve ventilation without increasing pain. Demonstrate proper breathing technique for patient.

NURSING DIAGNOSIS: INEFFECTIVE BREATHING PATTERN

Related To
- Pain
- Fatigue

Defining Characteristics

Splinted or guarded respirations

Dyspnea, tachypnea and shallow respirations
Use of accessory muscles for breathing
Abnormal ABGs

Patient Outcomes

Patient will
- demonstrate normal rate, rhythm, and depth of respirations.
- state he or she is comfortable and rested.

Nursing Interventions	Rationales
Assess respiratory rate and depth and quality every 2–4 hr. Observe for use of accessory muscles.	
Monitor ABGs and pulse oximetry and administer oxygen as prescribed.	
Assess for pain every 2–4 hr and medicate as prescribed to enhance patient's ability to cough and deep breathe.	
Encourage abdominal breathing to improve ventilation without increasing pain.	
Promote rest periods between coughing and deep-breathing exercises.	

NURSING DIAGNOSIS: INEFFECTIVE AIRWAY CLEARANCE

Related To tracheobronchial secretions

Defining Characteristics

Dyspnea, tachypnea, shallow respirations
Ineffective cough
Cyanosis, pallor, diaphoresis
Inability to move secretions
Absence of or abnormal breath sounds (crackles, rhonchi)
Abnormal ABGs
Restlessness, irritability

Patient Outcomes

Patient will
- exhibit normal breath sounds, rate and depth of respirations, and ABGs.
- demonstrate effective coughing.

Nursing Interventions	Rationales
Assess respiratory status and auscultate lungs every 2–4 hr for adventitious sounds (rale, rhonchi) indicating secretions in alveoli and airways.	
Assist with coughing and deep breathing hourly for 24 hr, then every 2–4 hr to mobilize secretions, clear the airway, and prevent atelectasis: 1. Administer pain medication 20–30 min prior to prevent interference with cough efforts. 2. Splint incision by applying gentle pressure, which makes coughing less painful and allows for deeper inspiration and increase force in cough. 3. Use incentive spirometer. 4. Assess characteristics of secretions. Suspect an infection if secretions increase in quantity and are thick, yellow or green, and/or foul smelling.	
Suction as needed if patient is unable to cough.	
Encourage fluids up to 2,500 ml/day if not contraindicated to liquefy secretions and make them easier to expectorate.	

NURSING DIAGNOSIS: PAIN

Related To tissue trauma associated with surgical procedure

Defining Characteristics

Complaints of pain: incisional, on moving, with coughing and deep breathing
Hesitation to move, deep breathe, and cough
Facial grimace, rigid posture

Patient Outcomes

The patient will

- verbalize a decrease in pain.
- increase efforts of moving and coughing and deep breathing.
- display a relaxed facial expression and body posture.

Nursing Interventions	Rationales
Assess patient for pain using a rating scale from 1 to 10.	
Administer prescribed analgesics at regular intervals during the first 48–72 hr, especially prior to coughing, turning, and/or mobility exercises.	
Provide splinting assistance during coughing and deep-breathing exercises to make coughing less painful.	
Encourage patient to use alternate pain-relieving measures such as relaxation and distraction as appropriate.	

NURSING DIAGNOSIS: IMPAIRED PHYSICAL MOBILITY

Related To incisional pain

Defining Characteristics

Reluctance to move
Requests for assistance to move

Limited range of motion in affected arm
Complaints of pain with movement

Patient Outcomes
Patient will
- demonstrate full range of motion.
- move with minimal or no assistance.
- state minimal pain with movement.

Nursing Interventions	Rationales
Medicate for pain 20–30 min prior to repositioning, exercise, and/or ambulation.	
Assist with repositioning every 2 hr. Patient may lie on back or operative side only.	Patient should not lie with operative side uppermost, in case the sutured bronchial stump opens and fluid drains into the unoperated side, the good lung, possibly drowning the patient. Additionally, this compresses the remaining lung and restricts lung excursion and ventilation.
Beginning the evening of surgery, assist with passive range-of-motion exercises to the affected side's arm.	
Encourage active range of motion two to three times daily beginning the first postoperative day.	
Assist with ambulation. Continue all exercise and activity only to point of dyspnea.	Patients who have had a lung removed may have lowered vital capacity, and exercise and activity should be limited to that which can be done without dyspnea. The body must have time to adjust to only one lung.

NURSING DIAGNOSIS: FEAR/ANXIETY
Related To diagnosis of cancer

Defining Characteristics

Expresses fear/anxiety about cancer diagnoses
Verbalizes feelings of apprehension about future
Asks many questions about cancer and future

Patient Outcomes

The patient will
- identify ways to cope with fear/anxiety.
- state an understanding of the disease process and prognosis.

Nursing Interventions	Rationales
Encourage questions and expression of feelings.	
Provide accurate information about cancer and prognosis.	
Support preferred coping style when adaptive. Explore alternatives if maladaptive coping behaviors are used.	Maladaptive coping behaviors such as withdrawal, denial, and depression may prevent a positive emotional state and limit growth toward a realistic understanding of the disease and prognosis.
Initiate additional referrals as appropriate (e.g., social services, pastoral care). Provide information on local support groups.	

NURSING DIAGNOSIS: KNOWLEDGE DEFICIT ABOUT HOME CARE AND FOLLOW-UP

Related To no previous experience or information

Defining Characteristics

Verbalizing lack of knowledge regarding home care management
Asking many questions about home care and follow-up

Patient Outcomes

Patient and family will verbalize necessary care and follow-up, including
- coughing and deep-breathing exercises
- activity and rest schedule
- any exercise and activity restrictions
- what to report to physician

Nursing Interventions	Rationales
Explain the need to continue to cough and deep breathe at least four times a day at home.	
Encourage patient to avoid smoke and air pollution. Explain need to stop smoking because smoking causes an increase in mucous production and impairs ciliary function. Refer for assistance with smoking cessation as needed.	
Encourage to schedule alternate periods of activity and rest.	
Explain importance of exercising only to point of dyspnea daily and increase exercise gradually.	
Explain need to avoid lifting and related activities until directed by physician.	
Encourage annual influenza vaccinations to decrease risk of infection.	
Explain the need to report the following to the physician: 1. persistent dyspnea, cough, hoarseness 2. pain on swallowing 3. elevated temperature 4. upper respiratory infection 5. redness, swelling, pain, or drainage from incision	

DISCHARGE PLANNING/CONTINUITY OF CARE

- Assure understanding of self-management plan.
- Assure understanding of what should be reported to the physician.
- Arrange follow-up visit with physician.
- Provide information on local support groups and educational programs. Refer to smoking cessation program if appropriate.
- Refer to the local chapters of the American Lung Association and the American Cancer Society.

REFERENCES

Patrick, M., Woods, S., Craven, R., Rokasky, J., & Bruns, P. (1991). *Medical-surgical nursing—Pathophysiological concepts* (2nd ed). Philadelphia, PA: Lippincott.

Shapiro, B., Kacmarek, R., Cane, R., Peruzzi, W., & Hamptman, D. (1991). *Clinical application of respiratory care* (4th ed). St. Louis, MO: Mosby.

Siskind, M. (1989). A standard of care for the nursing diagnosis of ineffective airway clearance *Heart and Lung*, *18*(5): 477–482.

Thompson, J., McFarland, G., Hirsch, J., Tucker, S., & Bowers, A. (1989). *Mosby's manual of clinical nursing* (2nd ed). St. Louis, MO: Mosby.

Wilson, S. & Thompson, J. (1990). *Respiratory disorders*. St. Louis, MO: Mosby Year Book.

▼

TRACHEOSTOMY

Linda Wonoski, RN, MSN

A tracheostomy is used to provide long-term ventilatory support, to facilitate suctioning of trachobronchial secretions, and to bypass a respiratory obstruction. The tube is inserted into the trachea through an incision made at the level of the second or third tracheal ring, totally bypassing the upper airway.

ETIOLOGIES (INDICATIONS)

- Upper airway obstruction (tumor, foreign body, laryngeal spasm)
- Burns
- Infections
- Surgical edema
- Traumatic injuries (head, neck, chest wall)
- Neurological disorders
- Acute respiratory failure
- Pulmonary disorders

CLINICAL MANIFESTATIONS

- Dyspnea
- Tachypnea
- Increased work of breathing
- Decreased breath sounds
- Anxiety
- Tachycardia
- Partial airway obstruction with increasing respiratory distress: gurgling, snoring, stridorous ventilations
- Complete airway obstruction
  - conscious person: no breath sounds, signs of severe respiratory distress progressing to respiratory arrest, unable to speak
  - unconscious person: ventilation attempts that produce no chest movement, no expiratory air passing from the individual's airway

CLINICAL/DIAGNOSTIC FINDINGS

- Arterial blood gases that deviate from patient's baseline
- Abnormal chest x-ray

OTHER PLANS OF CARE TO REFERENCE

- Nutrition Support plans of care

NURSING DIAGNOSIS: ANXIETY REGARDING RESPIRATORY DISTRESS AND KNOWLEDGE DEFICIT REGARDING NEED FOR TRACHEOSTOMY

Related To new experience

Defining Characteristics

Expression of anxiety about inability to breathe effectively
Asking many questions about tracheostomy

Patient Outcomes

Patient will
- state a decreased level of anxiety.
- verbalize an understanding of a tracheostomy.

Nursing Interventions	Rationales
Assess anxiety level and readiness to learn.	
Provide written and audiovisual teaching materials to supplement teaching.	
Review patient's individual reason for the tracheostomy and its particular purpose.	
Demonstrate and encourage handling of the tube and suctioning equipment.	

Nursing Interventions

Review insertion procedure:

1. surgical/sterile procedure after consent is obtained

2. positioning: supine with head extended to bring the trachea forward

3. medicated as prescribed
4. incision made at the level of the second or third tracheal ring

5. tracheostomy tube inserted and cuff inflated

6. tracheostomy tube secured with ties to minimize chance of dislodgment

7. chest x-ray obtained to confirm proper placement

Explain that frequent assessments are made after insertion.

Inform that an extra tube, obturator, and hemostat are kept at bedside at all times in case the tube is dislodged and reinsertion of a new tube is necessary.

Explain that frequent suctioning is done often to remove secretions.

Rationales

Infection of the lower airway is a serious potential problem. Establishment of an artificial airway bypasses the normal defense mechanisms that prevent bacterial contamination of the lower airway.

Below this level the end of the tracheostomy tube can erode the innominate or right common carotid arteries and hemorrhage can occur.

Cuff is inflated with air to fill the space between the outside of the tube and trachea.

Nursing Interventions	Rationales
Explain the inability to speak after insertion. Discuss and plan for an alternative form of communication.	Tracheostomy tubes are inserted below the vocal cords, blocking normal airflow and impairing the patient's ability to speak. Often the patient can speak when the cuff is not fully inflated. However, speech is still difficult since air must be forced around the tube and up through the larynx.

NURSING DIAGNOSIS: INEFFECTIVE AIRWAY CLEARANCE

Related To
- Tracheostomy tube
- Thick secretions
- Fatigue

Defining Characteristics

Tachypnea
Increased work of breathing: use of accessory muscles
Pallor, cyanosis
Dyspnea
Adventitious breath sounds (rales, rhonchi)
Ineffective cough, inability to manage secretions

Patient Outcomes

The patient will
- experience a patent airway.
- demonstrate clear and equal breath sounds bilaterally.
- demonstrate normal rate, rhythm, and depth of respirations.
- demonstrate ability to cough out/manage secretions.

Nursing Interventions	Rationales
Assess respiratory rate, depth, and quality; auscultate lungs every 2–4 hr and prn.	
Encourage patient to deep breathe and cough out secretions every 2–4 hr and prn.	

Nursing Interventions

Suction patient as often as necessary from every 5–10 min immediately after insertion to every 3–4 hr.

1. Explain suctioning procedure to patient.

2. Wear goggles, gown, gloves, and mask while suctioning.

3. Use sterile technique throughout procedure.

4. Use a catheter that is no greater than half the diameter of the tracheostomy tube to minimize hypoxia and occlusion of the cannula.

5. Before beginning suctioning, hyperoxygenate ("bag") the patient with 100% oxygen using an ambu bag connected to oxygen. Give patient five breaths.

6. Lubricate suction catheter with water. Do not apply suction while inserting. Insert 8–12 inches, gently twisting catheter while suctioning and removing.

7. Limit suction time to 5–10 s.

8. Remove the catheter if the patient starts coughing.

9. Oxygenate the patient after suctioning by giving five breaths with the ambu bag connected to oxygen.

10. If secretions are tenacious, instill 3 to 5 mL of sterile saline into the tracheostomy tube on inspiration, oxygenate with the ambu bag and then suction.

Rationales

Hypoxemia created during suctioning can induce cardiac ectopy and bradycardia.

Suctioning on insertion would unnecessarily decrease oxygen in the airway. Failure to rotate the catheter may result in damage to the tracheal mucosa.

Suctioning removes oxygen as well as secretions and may cause vagal stimulation including ectopy and bradycardia.

The catheter obstructs the trachea and the patient must exert extra pressure to cough around it.

Instilling saline during inspiration prevents it from being blown back out of the tube. Bagging stimulates cough and distributes saline to loosen secretions.

Repeated suctioning of a patient in a short time predisposes to hypoxia and is tiring and traumatic to the patient.

Nursing Interventions	Rationales
11. Continue to make suction passes, "bagging" the patient between passes, until the patient's airway is clear of secretions. Suction passes should be limited to four during each suctioning episode.	
12. Suction the patient's oral and nasal pharnyx with the catheter after suctioning the trachea.	The oral and nasal pharynx are not sterile environments. Suctioning through the tracheostomy tube after suctioning these would predispose the patient to infection.
Administer humidified oxygen as prescribed.	Humidification is necessary because the normal mechanisms of warming, moistening, and filtering the air are bypassed when an altered airway is present. Without humidification there is a greater incidence of obstruction caused by drying of secretions.
Clean inner cannula with hydrogen peroxide and saline every 4 hr and prn to maintain a patent airway by minimizing the drying and crusting of secretions on the inner cannula.	
Maintain adequate hydration of 2–3 L/day, if not contraindicated by patient's condition.	

NURSING DIAGNOSIS: HIGH RISK FOR IMPAIRED GAS EXCHANGE

Risk Factors
- Tracheostomy
- Tracheal secretions
- Possible tracheostomy leak
- Plugging and decannulation process

Patient Outcomes
Patient will exhibit
- a patent tracheostomy tube/airway

- minimal secretions
- only minimal cuff leak on exhalation

Nursing Interventions	Rationales
Assess for changes in mental status, including increasing lethargy, confusion, restlessness, and irritability, every 2–4 hr and prn.	May indicate hypoxemia and/or hypercapnea and need for suctioning.
Place patient in semi- to high Fowler's position to promote full-lung expansion.	
Suction as needed when abnormal breath sounds are present and/or patient is unable to handle secretions.	
Ensure that tracheostomy ties are secured at all times to prevent tube from falling out or becoming dislocated, creating a hypoxic event.	
Keep a replacement tracheostomy tube of the same size and type, obturator, and hemostat at the bedside at all times. In case of accidental extubation, the tracheal opening should be held open with the hemostat. This will allow the patient to breathe until the replacement tube is inserted. Insert the new tube with the obturator in place which has a tapered end to provide a smooth system for entering the trachea.	
If the patient has a cuffed tracheostomy, check cuff for inflation and/or leak every shift and prn:	Assures optimal sealing of the airway.
1. Assess amount of air leakage around cuff by listening over the cuff area with a stethoscope for a crowing sound.	
2. Explain the procedure to patient.	

Nursing Interventions	Rationales
3. Suction the trachea and then the oral and nasal pharynx to remove the secretions around the cuff which could be aspirated into the lung when the cuff is deflated.	
4. Deflate the cuff slowly. With a new sterile catheter suction through the tracheostomy.	
5. Continually monitor patient's tolerance of the cuff deflation (e.g., respiration, color, heart rate). Provide manual ventilation, if necessary, with ambu bag.	
6. Reinflate cuff. Place stethoscope over cuff area. Slowly inflate cuff with air until no leak is heard. Aspirate about 0.1 mL of air to create a small air leak. Document amount of air injected.	The objective is to place the minimal volume of air in the cuff that will allow optimal sealing of the airway. Air leakage will be heard on exhalation. Minimal leak technique is used to avoid overinflation of the cuff which could create ischemic damage to the tracheal mucosa.

Nursing Interventions

To wean patient from tube and eventual tube removal:
1. Suction the tracheostomy tube.
2. Remove the inner cannula.
3. Deflate the cuff.
4. Insert the decannulation cannula ("plug").
5. Monitor the patient for any symptoms of distress. If respiratory distress occurs, remove the decannulation cannula and insert the inner cannula.
6. Continue to plug the tracheostomy tube intermittently and increase the length of time of occlusion as the patient tolerates.
7. Following tracheostomy removal, apply dressing or steri strips to approximate wound edges, check and cleanse wound site daily, and observe for signs of infection.

Rationales

The tube should be removed when it is firmly established that the patient can breathe adequately through the respiratory tract and effectively manage secretions.

NURSING DIAGNOSIS: HIGH RISK FOR INFECTION

Risk Factors
- Tracheostomy incision
- Suctioning
- Stagnated secretions

Patient Outcomes
Patient will exhibit
- a tracheostomy incision normal in appearance with no redness, warmth, or tenderness
- normal temperature and white blood cell (WBC) count
- no abnormal drainage around the tracheostomy site

Nursing Interventions

Assess vital signs and temperature every 4 hr.

Rationales

Nursing Interventions

Assess WBC count and differential for elevation.

Assess tracheostomy incision (stoma) for redness, warmth, tenderness, and exudate.

Suction prn using sterile technique.

Provide routine tracheostomy care every shift and as needed:
1. Explain procedure to patient.
2. Wear goggles, mask, gown, and gloves during procedure to protect from potential contamination.
3. Suction trachea and oral and nasal pharynx prior to tracheostomy.
4. With clean gloves, remove soiled tracheostomy dressing.
5. Remove inner cannula and clean it in a hydrogen peroxide and saline solution. Rinse in saline. Inspect for patency and reinsert.
6. Replace tracheostomy ties if soiled. Tie tapes at side of neck in a square knot, alternate knot from side to side to prevent irritation, and rotate pressure sites and time at which tapes are changed. Tape should be tight enough to keep tube securely in the stoma but loose enough to permit one finger between the tape and neck.

Rationales

The usual response to an infection, especially to a pulmonary infection, is to mobilize increased numbers of WBCs from the bone marrow and other storage areas.

Nursing Interventions	Rationales
7. Using sterile technique, clean tracheostomy incision with a hydrogen peroxide and saline solution using gauze sponges and sterile cotton swabs, loosen and remove any crust, repeat cleaning with saline-only solution, and apply sterile tracheostomy dressing.	

NURSING DIAGNOSIS: HIGH RISK FOR ALTERED NUTRITION—LESS THAN BODY REQUIREMENTS

Risk Factors
- Anorexia
- Fatigue
- Inability to ingest food due to the tracheostomy tube

Patient Outcomes
Patient will
- maintain or increase weight.
- demonstrate adequate caloric intake for disease/metabolic state.
- demonstrate serum albumin within normal limits.
- continue to regain strength.

Nursing Interventions	Rationales
Assess daily intake of parenteral, enteral, and oral feeding and output.	
Weigh daily.	
Monitor serum albumin levels.	
If patient is receiving enteral tube feedings, monitor closely for tube placement in stomach and presence of any residual before each tube feeding (see Nutrition Support: Enteral Nutrition).	If patient is unable to tolerate oral feeding and/or needs supplemental calories, enteral feeding may be utilized.

Nursing Interventions	Rationales
Monitor oral intake: Assess likes and dislikes, provide small frequent meals, and consult with dietitian about high-calorie supplements. If patient has a cuffed tracheostomy tube, make sure cuff is inflated while eating to prevent aspiration. Elevate head of bed while eating. Provide attractive clean environment at meals. Provide mouth care before meals.	The patient with a tracheostomy tube is usually able to swallow and have normal oral intake. Patient may experience loss of taste because of decreased sense of smell.
If there is a question of aspiration, methylene blue can be mixed with the enteral feeding or colored gelatin can be given to the patient. If the dye or color of gelatin does not appear in the tracheal secretions, it is safe to proceed with feeding.	
Provide for adequate rest periods between meals.	

NURSING DIAGNOSIS: IMPAIRED VERBAL COMMUNICATION

Related To tracheostomy

Defining Characteristics
Weak or absent voice
Gesturing to make needs known
Difficulty in making self understood
Anxiety
Frustration

Patient Outcomes
Patient will
- communicate needs using alternative methods of communication.
- exhibit decreased signs of anxiety and frustration.

Nursing Interventions	**Rationales**
Assess patient's ability to speak.	Cuffed tracheostomy tubes prevent the air that is moved during inhalation and exhalation from passing over the larynx and vocal cords, blocking adequate phonation. With uncuffed tubes the patient's voice intensity may be affected.
Assess patient's and family's understanding of his or her inability to verbally communicate. Clarify information as needed.	
Speak to the patient in a normal manner and tone.	Although the patient cannot talk, he or she usually can hear. If you use overly simplistic language or talk too loud, you may frustrate the patient even more.
Provide patient with alternative forms of communication. Identify which form is best for the patient, including pad and pencil, magic slate, and a communication board with pictures or alphabet.	A magic slate ensures privacy because what is written can be erased. If writing is difficult, a communication board with common needs and equipment on it can be utilized by the patient.
To avoid damage to vocal cords, caution patient not to routinely nod or shake head in response to questions.	
Allow patient ample time to respond in writing. Avoid asking two questions at once.	Writing takes longer than speaking. Anticipating and interrupting the patient trying to communicate in writing can cause further frustration for the patient, and he or she may attempt to communicate less often.
Provide the call light within easy reach at all times and let the patient know it will be answered immediately. Devise a system for marking the intercom to alert the staff that the patient is unable to talk.	

Nursing Interventions	Rationales
If patient has a fenestrated tracheostomy tube, discuss with physician the possibility of plugging it for short periods for communication purposes.	The fenestrated tracheostomy tube has an opening at the upper curve of its outer cannula. If you remove the inner cannula and plug the tube with a tracheostomy plug or with the patient's finger, air will be forced up through the tube and the patient will be able to make short statements.

NURSING DIAGNOSIS: KNOWLEDGE DEFICIT ABOUT SELF-CARE AT HOME

Related To lack of exposure to this information

Defining Characteristics
Verbalizing lack of knowledge regarding tracheostomy care, suctioning, when to call physician, resources available for support

Patient Outcomes
Patient/caregiver will
- state when to call the physician.
- demonstrate use and care of the suction equipment.
- state how to obtain supplies.
- list health care resources available.
- demonstrate cleaning and how to replace the tracheostomy tube.
- describe prevention of environmental irritants.

Nursing Interventions	Rationales
Assess patient/caregiver understanding of the tracheostomy and review information as necessary (e.g., anatomy and physiology, purpose).	

Nursing Interventions	Rationales
Review and demonstrate tracheostomy care, including 1. suctioning 2. tracheostomy tube care 3. skin care 4. replacing tracheostomy ties 5. care of equipment: suction machine, collection bottle, connecting tubing, suction catheters (making sure patient/family knows where to purchase these supplies) 6. inflation and deflation of cuff, if cuffed tracheostomy tube	
Observe patient's and/or caregiver's ability to perform all airway and tracheostomy site care independently before discharge. Arrange a home health care referral for assistance as needed.	
Instruct to 1. prevent environmental irritants from entering the tracheostomy airway by wearing a scarf or shirt with a closed collar that covers the opening, yet is of porous material thin enough to allow airflow. 2. keep products such as powders, aerosol sprays, after shave, shaving cream, soap, and so on, away from the tracheostomy. 3. keep excessive water from entering the tracheostomy tube (may bathe and shower as long as the spray and water are kept away from the stoma). 4. maintain proper humidification of the environment using room humidifier and pans of water near heat sources and drinking 2–3 quarts of liquid daily, unless physician has restricted intake.	

Nursing Interventions	**Rationales**
Review potential problems that should be reported to the physician, including 1. unexplained dyspnea 2. severe coughing 3. bleeding around tracheostomy site 4. hemoptysis 5. change in color or consistency of secretions to yellow, green, brown, foul smelling, thick, and difficult to remove 6. temperature of 101 °F or more	
Review signs that require immediate attention: 1. inability to pass a suction catheter down the tracheostomy tube 2. tracheostomy tube accidentally dislodged or plugged (making sure patient has an extra tracheostomy tube and instructing patient/caregiver on technique of replacing it) 3. pulsing of the tracheostomy tube.	These may be life-threatening situations. There is danger of a tube eroding into the innominate artery if pulsing of the tube is seen.
Review resources available and make appropriate contacts. 1. Visiting nurse 2. American Cancer Society 3. American Lung Association 4. community- or hospital-based tracheostomy support groups	

DISCHARGE PLANNING/CONTINUITY OF CARE

- Assure understanding of self-management plan.
- Assure understanding of what should be reported to the physician.
- Arrange follow-up with physician for continued management postdischarge.
- Provide information on how to obtain tracheostomy and suctioning supplies.

- Arrange visiting nurse follow-up if continued assistance with tracheostomy care is needed.
- Provide with information on local support groups and educational programs.
- Refer to the local chapter of the American Cancer Association and/or the American Lung Association.

REFERENCES

Mapp, S. (1988). Trach care: Are you aware of all the dangers? *Nursing*, *18*(7), 34–45.

Martin, C. (1989). Management of the altered airway in the head and neck cancer patient. *Seminars in Oncology Nursing*, *5*(3), 182–190.

Shapiro, B., Kacmarek, R., Cane, R., Peruzzi, W., & Hamptman, D. (1991). *Clinical application of respiratory care* (4th ed). St. Louis, MO: Mosby.

Wilson, E. & Malley, N. (1990). Discharge planning for the patient with a new tracheostomy. *Critical Care Nurse*, *10*(7), 73–79.

THORACOTOMY

Linda Wonoski, RN, MSN

A thoracotomy is the surgical incision of the chest wall. It is usually performed to obtain a biopsy specimen, correct a defect, or locate a source of bleeding. During the procedure the ribs are spread, the pleura is entered, and the lung is examined. Since the pleura space is entered, closed chest drainage is generally required postoperatively.

ETIOLOGIES (INDICATIONS)

- Suspected lung or chest disease (cancer)
- Chest trauma (detect bleeding)
- Obtain a biopsy specimen

CLINICAL MANIFESTATIONS

- Dyspnea
- Tachypnea
- Cough
- Hemoptysis
- Crackles
- Rhonchi
- Decreased breath sounds
- Pain with coughing/breathing
- Fatigue

CLINICAL/DIAGNOSTIC FINDINGS

- Chest x-ray indicates a lesion or mass
- Bronchoscopy reveals a malignancy
- Lung scan demonstrates ischemic areas
- Pulmonary function tests may be suboptimal

- Arterial blood gases (ABGs) may be abnormal.
- Cytologic examinations show abnormalities (pleural fluid, sputum)

OTHER PLANS OF CARE TO REFERENCE

- Basic Standards for Preoperative and Postoperative Care
- Chest Tubes
- Pain Management: Patient-Controlled Analgesia

NURSING DIAGNOSIS: KNOWLEDGE DEFICIT OF THE THORACOTOMY PROCEDURE

Related To
- Lack of previous exposure to information
- Fear and anxiety about results

Defining Characteristics

Verbalizing lack of knowledge
Asking many questions
Expressing anxiety and fear about procedure

Patient Outcomes

Patient will
- state reason for surgery.
- describe pre- and postsurgical routine.
- state ways to cope with anxiety/fear.

Nursing Interventions	Rationales
Assess patient/family understanding of the surgery and readiness to learn.	
Provide written and audiovisual materials to supplement teaching.	
Explain routine preoperative procedures (see Basic Standards for Preoperative Care).	
Explain postoperative routine: 1. frequent monitoring of vital signs	

Nursing Interventions	Rationales
2. frequent coughing and deep breathing encouraged, demonstrating use of incentive spirometry	
3. oxygen therapy	
4. frequent dressing checks	
5. pain relief	medication for pain given as needed for the first 48–72 hr (pain can impair ventilation, making coughing ineffective and causing secretions to be retained)
6. frequent arm exercises encouraged	
7. fluids encouraged to liquefy secretions making them easier to expectorate	
8. abdominal breathing encouraged, demonstrating proper technique for patient	
9. chest tubes are inserted during surgery to reexpand lung monitored closely postoperatively	

NURSING DIAGNOSIS: IMPAIRED GAS EXCHANGE

Related To decreased lung expansion

Defining Characteristics
Hypoxemia
Hypercapnea
Restlessness
Irritability
Confusion

Patient Outcomes
Patient will exhibit
• normal rate, rhythm, and depth of respirations
• ABGs within normal limits
• pulse oximetry readings > 90% saturation
• breath sounds bilaterally equal and clear

Nursing Interventions	Rationales
Auscultate lungs and assess respiratory rate, depth, and quality every 2–4 hr.	
Place patient in semi-Fowler's position.	This position moves the abdominal contents away from the diaphragm, enhancing chest expansion and movement of the diaphragm.
Monitor ABGs and pulse oximetry and administer oxygen as prescribed.	Assist patient to cough and deep breathe and use the incentive spirometer every 1–2 hr, the first postoperative day, then every 2–4 hr.
Coughing clears the airway and prevents atelectasis. Incentive spirometry facilitates deep breathing to improve gas exchange.	Assess and maintain patency of closed chest drainage system (see chest tubes plans of care).

NURSING DIAGNOSIS: INEFFECTIVE BREATHING PATTERN

Related To
- Pain
- Fatigue

Defining Characteristics
Splinted or guarded respirations
Dyspnea, tachypnea, and shallow respirations
Use of accessory muscles for breathing
Abnormal ABGs

Patient Outcomes
Patient will
- exhibit normal rate, rhythm, and depth of respirations.
- state he or she is comfortable and rested.

Nursing Interventions	Rationales
Assess respiratory rate, depth, and quality every 2–4 hr. Observe for use of accessory muscles.	

Nursing Interventions	Rationales
Assess pain level every 2–4 hr and medicate as prescribed to enhance ability to cough and deep breathe.	
Encourage abdominal breathing.	Improves ventilation without increasing pain.
Assist patient to cough and deep breathe every 2–4 hr to clear airway and prevent atelectasis. Use the incentive spirometer to facilitate deep breathing to improve gas exchange.	
Promote rest periods between coughing and deep-breathing exercises.	
Assess function of chest tubes.	

NURSING DIAGNOSIS: INEFFECTIVE AIRWAY CLEARANCE

Related To
- Tracheal and bronchial secretions
- Poor cough effort
- Pain
- Fatigue

Defining Characteristics
Dyspnea, tachypnea, shallow respirations
Cyanosis, pallor, diaphoresis
Ineffective cough
Inability to move secretions
Presence of abnormal breath sounds (crackles, rhonchi, etc.)
Abnormal ABGs

Patient Outcomes
Patient will
- exhibit normal breath sounds, normal rate, rhythm, and depth of respirations, and normal ABGs.
- demonstrate effective coughing.

Nursing Interventions	Rationales
Assess respiratory status and auscultate lungs every 2–4 hr for adventitious sounds (rales, rhonchi) indicating secretions in alveoli and airways.	
Assist with coughing and deep breathing hourly for 24 hr, then every 2–4 hr. 1. Administer pain medication 20–30 min prior to preventing interference with cough efforts. 2. Encourage abdominal breathing to improve ventilation without increasing pain. 3. Splint incision. 4. Use incentive spirometer to facilitate deep breathing. 5. Assess characteristics of secretions. Suspect infection if secretions increase in quantity and are thick, yellow, or green and/or foul smelling.	
Suction as needed if patient is unable to cough.	
Encourage fluid intake of 2500 mL/day if not contraindicated.	This liquefies secretions and makes them easier to expectorate.

NURSING DIAGNOSIS: PAIN

Related To tissue trauma associated with thoracotomy and chest tubes

Defining Characteristics

Complaints of pain at incision, around chest tubes, on moving, with coughing and deep breathing

Hesitation to move, deep breathe and cough

Facial grimaces

Rigid posture

Patient Outcomes

The patient will

• verbalize a decrease in pain.

- increase efforts to move, cough, and deep breathe.
- display a relaxed facial expression and body posture.

Nursing Interventions	Rationales
Assess patient for pain using a rating scale from 1 to 10	
Administer prescribed analgesics at regular intervals during the first 48–72 hr, especially prior to coughing, turning, and/or mobility exercises.	Patient may attempt rapid, shallow breathing to splint the lower chest and avoid movement with the chest tubes present, which will impair ventilation.
Provide splinting assistance during coughing and deep-breathing exercises to make coughing less painful and lessen muscle pull.	
Encourage patient to use alternate pain-relieving measures such as relaxation and distraction as appropriate.	

NURSING DIAGNOSIS: IMPAIRED PHYSICAL MOBILITY
Related To
- Incisional pain
- Chest tubes

Defining Characteristics
Reluctance to move
Requests for assistance to move
Limited range of motion in affected arm and shoulder
Complaints of pain with movement

Patient Outcomes
The patient will
- demonstrate full range of motion.
- move with minimal or no assistance.
- state minimal pain with movement.

Nursing Interventions	Rationales
Medicate for pain 20–30 min prior to repositioning, exercise, and/or ambulation.	

Nursing Interventions	Rationales
Assist with passive range-of-motion exercises to the arm and shoulder on the side with the chest tubes beginning the evening of surgery.	
Encourage active range of motion two to three times daily beginning the first postoperative day, for example, rotate shoulder 360° and hunch shoulder.	
Assist with repositioning every 2 hr and ambulate as ordered. Patient may ambulate with chest tubes in place as long as water seal remains below the level of the chest.	
Promote rest periods between exercises and ambulations.	

NURSING DIAGNOSIS: KNOWLEDGE DEFICIT ABOUT HOME CARE AND FOLLOW-UP

Related To
- New experience
- No previous information

Defining Characteristics
Verbalizing lack of knowledge regarding home care management
Asking many questions about home care and follow-up

Patient Outcomes
Patient/family will verbalize necessary care and follow-up plans, including
- coughing and deep-breathing exercises
- activity and rest schedule
- exercise and activity restrictions
- what to report to physician

Nursing Interventions	Rationales
Explain the need to continue to do coughing and deep breathing and range-of-motion exercises at least four times daily at home.	

Nursing Interventions	Rationales
If patient smokes, explain the importance of not smoking because smoking causes an increase in mucous production and impairs ciliary production. Refer for assistance with smoking cessation as needed.	
Encourage to avoid exposure to smoke and air pollution.	Can cause bronchoconstriction with resultant irritating cough and rapid shallow respiratory rate.
Encourage to schedule alternate periods of rest and activity.	
Explain importance of exercising to tolerance daily, increasing the amount of exercise gradually.	
Instruct to avoid lifting activities until directed by physician.	
Instruct to report the following to physician: 1. persistent dyspnea 2. cough 3. elevated temperature 4. upper respiratory infection 5. redness, swelling, pain, or drainage from incision	

DISCHARGE PLANNING/CONTINUITY OF CARE

- Assure understanding of self-management plan.
- Assure understanding of what should be reported to the physician.
- Arrange follow-up visit with physician.
- Provide information on local support groups and educational programs. Refer to smoking cessation program if available.
- Refer to local chapter of the American Lung Association and, if appropriate, the American Cancer Society.

REFERENCES

Shapiro, B., Kacmarek, R., Cane, R., Peruzzi, W., & Hamptman, D. (1991). *Clinical application of respiratory care* (4th ed). St. Louis, MO: Mosby.

Siskind, M. (1989). A standard of care for the nursing diagnosis of ineffective airway clearance. *Heart & Lung, 18*(5), 477–482.

Thompson, J., McFarland, G., Hirsch, J., Tucker, S., & Bowers, A. (1989). *Mosby's manual of clinical nursing* (2nd ed). St. Louis, MO: Mosby.

Wilson, S. & Thompson, J. (1990). *Respiratory disorders.* St. Louis, MO: Mosby Year Book.

▼

Common Gastrointestinal/ Digestive Conditions and Procedures

▼

PPENDECTOMY

Susan Murray, RN, MS

Appendicitis is the inflammation of the vermiform appendix and is one of the most common reasons for emergency abdominal surgery. A patient presenting with acute abdominal pain must be carefully assessed to assure an accurate diagnosis. An appendectomy is the surgical intervention in which the appendix is removed and is classified as a simple, gangrenous, or perforated appendectomy.

ETIOLOGIES

- Bacterial invasion of the appendix due to obstruction of the lumen of the appendix
- Incidental (done during other surgical procedures)

CLINICAL MANIFESTATIONS

- Progressively severe abdominal pain in the right lower quadrant at McBurney's point
- Rebound tenderness
- Low-grade fever
- Localized pain on palpation

CLINICAL/DIAGNOSTIC FINDINGS

- Elevated white blood cell (WBC) count with a shift to the left
- Urinalysis revealing a small number of erythrocytes and leukocytes

OTHER PLANS OF CARE TO REFERENCE

- Basic Standards for Preoperative and Postoperative Care
- Pain Management: Patient-Controlled Analgesia

NURSING DIAGNOSIS: PAIN—APPENDICITIS

Related To abdominal discomfort from appendicitis

Defining Characteristics
Verbalization of pain
Guarding behavior
Moaning
Crying
Grimacing
Impaired thought process
Diaphoresis
Changes in blood pressure
Pulse or respirations

Patient Outcomes
The patient will state pain control is adequate.

Nursing Interventions	Rationales
Assess description of the pain type, duration, changes in, and location.	These data are crucial in diagnosing appendicitis.
Assess carefully for signs of perforation and peritonitis: 1. sudden relief of pain 2. increased diffuse pain 3. increased abdominal distention 4. rapid, shallow breathing 5. fever	Once an appendix has perforated, symptoms are no longer localized.
Help reduce pain by having patient lie still and avoid sudden movements, such as coughing.	
Administer analgesics as prescribed only after the diagnosis has been established.	

NURSING DIAGNOSIS: PAIN—POSTOPERATIVE

Related To
- Abdominal distention
- Gas
- Postappendectomy

Defining Characteristics
Verbalization of abdominal fullness and gas pain
Clutching and guarding of abdomen
Reluctance to move
Grimacing
Increasing abdominal girth
Dyspnea

Patient Outcomes
The patient will
- report diminished abdominal distention and gas pain.
- state pain control is adequate.

Nursing Interventions	Rationales
Assess for nonverbal signs and verbal complaints of abdominal discomfort every 4–8 hr.	
Auscultate bowel sounds every 4–8 hr.	
Encourage and assist with frequent position changes and ambulation as soon as allowed and tolerated.	Activity stimulates peristalsis and expulsion of flatus.
Instruct to avoid chewing gum, sucking hard candy, and smoking.	Air is swallowed during these activities, increasing gas and distention.
Maintain patency of nasogastric (NG) tube, if present.	Patients with a gangrenous or perforated appendix usually have a NG tube postoperatively.
When oral intake is allowed, encourage drinking of warm liquids.	Warm liquids stimulate peristalsis.
Instruct to avoid gas-producing foods and fluids.	
Encourage to expel flatus whenever the urge is felt.	
Encourage the use of nonnarcotic analgesics once severe pain has subsided.	Narcotic analgesics depress gastrointestinal activity.
Administer gastrointestinal stimulating medications (metaclopromide, bisacodyl) as prescribed and monitor their effectiveness.	

NURSING DIAGNOSIS: IMPAIRED SKIN INTEGRITY

Related To surgical incision (open or closed)

Defining Characteristics

Presence of a closed abdominal suture line or an open wound left to heal by secondary intention

Patient Outcomes

The patient will experience normal healing of the surgical wound, as evidenced by
- intact, well-approximated wound edges if healing by primary intention
- presence of granulation tissue if healing by secondary or tertiary intention

Nursing Interventions	Rationales
Assess for and report signs and symptoms of impaired wound healing (redness, swelling, pale or necrotic tissue, separation of wound edges, fever).	
Maintain an adequate fluid and nutritional status.	Promotes normal wound healing.
Clean wound and apply dressings as ordered, utilizing meticulous aseptic technique and monitor drainage.	
Instruct patient to support the surgical wound when moving and to splint the wound when coughing.	Decreases stress on the wound area.
Apply an abdominal binder during activity.	Provides additional support.

DISCHARGE PLANNING/CONTINUITY OF CARE

- Assure understanding of self-management plan.
- Provide patient with needed supplies and prescriptions.

- Refer patient to home health care agency if continued nursing care or teaching is needed.
- Arrange follow-up with physician for continued management postdischarge.

REFERENCES

Munn, N. E. (1988). Diagnosis: Acute abdomen. *Nursing, 18*(9), 34–42.
Thompson, J., McFarland, G., Hirsch, J., Tucker, S., & Bowers A. (1989). *Mosby's manual of clinical nursing,* (2nd ed). St. Louis, MO: Mosby.

BOWEL RESECTION WITH OR WITHOUT OSTOMY

Susan Murray, RN, MS

A bowel resection is the surgical removal of any part of the small or large intestine. It is done for a variety of reasons and may involve the creation of an ostomy where the remaining bowel is brought out through the abdominal wall and forms a stoma. If an ostomy is not required, the remaining sections of bowel may be anastomosed together, resulting in no interruption of the gastrointestinal system. The specific surgery for a bowel resection depends upon the area of the bowel to be removed.

ETIOLOGIES AND TYPE OF SURGERY

- Carcinoma of the bowel: right hemicolectomy, transverse colectomy, left hemicolectomy, abdominoperineal resection
- Ulcerative colitis: total proctocolectomy with ileostomy, total proctocolectomy with ileoanal reservoir
- Crohn's disease: resection of diseased colon
- Familial polyposis: total proctocolectomy with ileostomy, subtotal resection with ileorectal anastomosis
- Diverticulitis: resection of diseased colon
- Intestinal obstructions: removal of cause (i.e., hernia, adhesions, tumor)

CLINICAL MANIFESTATIONS

- Change in bowel habits
- Bloody stools
- Abdominal cramping, pain
- Anorexia, nausea, vomiting
- Fever
- Failure to pass flatus
- Weight loss
- Anemia
- Fatigue

CLINICAL/DIAGNOSTIC FINDINGS

- Ulcerative colitis
  - barium enema: shows ulceration of mucosa, shortening of bowel, pseudopolyps
  - sigmoidoscopy: submucosal inflammation and edema
  - colonoscopy: hyperemia, mucosal friability, ulcerations, pseudopolyps
  - blood work: decreased hematocrit, decreased hemoglobin, decreased serum albumin, guaiac positive stools, biopsy revealing inflammatory changes
- Crohn's disease
  - barium enema: shows asymmetric disease, skip lesions, ulcerations, fissures, strictures, fistulas
  - sigmoidoscopy: perirectal fissures, fistulas, abscesses
  - colonoscopy: skip lesions, cobblestone mucosa
  - blood work: decreased hematocrit, decreased hemoglobin, decreased serum albumin, guaiac positive stools
- Diverticulitis
  - barium enema: demonstrates diverticulum
  - ultrasound: may demonstrate mass or abscess
  - colonoscopy: reveals orifices of diverticula
  - elevated white blood cell (WBC) count with shift to left
- Familiar polyposis
  - stool positive for occult blood
  - proctosigmoidoscopy: reveals polyps
  - air contrast barium enema: may reveal polyps above rectosigmoid area
  - Carcinoma of bowel
  - proctosigmoidoscopy or colonoscopy: reveal lesion
  - barium enema: reveals lesion
  - stool positive for occult blood
- Intestinal obstruction
  - abdominal x-ray: reveals large amounts of gas bowel
  - barium enema: stops at sit obstruction

OTHER PLANS OF CARE TO REFERENCE

- Basic Standards for Preoperative Care and Postoperative Care
- Pain Management: Patient-Controlled Analgesia

NURSING DIAGNOSIS: PAIN

Related To
- Abdominal distention
- Gas post–bowel resection

Defining Characteristics

Verbalization of abdominal fullness and gas pain
Clutching and guarding of abdomen
Reluctance to move
Grimacing
Increased abdominal girth
Dyspnea

Patient Outcomes

The patient will state abdominal distention and gas pain are diminished.

Nursing Interventions	Rationales
Assess patient every 4–8 hr for nonverbal signs and verbal complaints of abdominal discomfort.	
Auscultate bowel sounds every 4–8 hr.	
Encourage and assist patient with frequent position changes and ambulation as soon as allowed and tolerated.	Activity stimulates peristalsis and expulsion of flatus.
Instruct patient to avoid chewing gum, sucking hard candy, and smoking.	Air is swallowed due to these activities, increasing gas and distention.
Maintain patency of nasogastric (NG) tube if present.	Patients with a gangrenous or perforated appendix usually have a NG tube postoperatively.
When oral intake is allowed, encourage patient to drink warm liquids.	Warm liquids stimulate peristalsis
Instruct patient to avoid gas-producing foods and fluids.	
Encourage patient to expel flatus whenever the urge is felt.	
Encourage the use of nonnarcotic analgesics once severe pain has subsided.	Narcotic analgesics depress gastrointestinal activity.
Administer prescribed gastrointestinal stimulating medications (such as metaclopromide or bisacodyl) as ordered and monitor their effectiveness.	

Nursing Interventions	Rationales
Monitor frequency, consistency, and amount of all bowel movements.	

The remainder of this care plan deals specifically with a bowel resection requiring the creation of an ostomy. The ostomy may be either a colostomy or an ileostomy. Table 19.1 outlines the various types of ostomies and features of each.

▼

NURSING DIAGNOSIS: HIGH RISK FOR IMPAIRED SKIN INTEGRITY

Risk Factors
- Chemical irritation from intestinal drainage
- Chemical irritation from allergic reaction to ostomy appliance.
- Mechanical irritation from frequent appliance changes

Patient Outcome
Peristomal skin will remain intact.

Table 19.1 • Types of Ostomies

Ostomy	Description	Output
Ileostomy	Bringing a portion of the ileum through an opening in the abdomen	Stool is constant and watery
Ascending colostomy	Made from the ascending colon	Stool is semiliquid
Transverse colostomy	Made from the transverse colon	Stool is semiformed
Sigmoid colostomy	Made from the sigmoid colon	Similar to normal bowel movements

▼

Nursing Interventions	Rationales
Assess the peristomal skin with each appliance change.	
Always use a skin barrier under the appliance.	This protects the skin from the proteolytic enzymes in the output.
Remove hair from peristomal skin using an electric or safety razor.	This helps maintain an adequate seal and reduces irritation when the appliance is removed.
Change the appliance when it first begins to leak (an early sign is odor). Do not tape a leaking appliance.	
Change appliance when the ostomy is least active (usually 2–4 hr after eating).	This prevents the output from coming in contact with the skin.
Avoid the use of ointment or creams on peristomal skin.	These interfere with adequate appliance adherence.
Utilize an ostomy paste to fill in irregularities around the stoma site.	

NURSING DIAGNOSIS: BODY IMAGE DISTURBANCE

Related To presence of an ostomy

Defining Characteristics
Change in structure and/or function of bowel
Change in social involvement

Patient Outcomes
Patient will begin to formulate and accept new body image, as evidenced by
- participating in self-care.
- looking at ostomy.
- beginning to socialize with others.

Nursing Interventions	Rationales
Assess verbal and nonverbal responses to the presence of the stoma.	

Nursing Interventions	Rationales
Provide opportunities to express feelings regarding the ostomy.	
Include patient in selecting an appliance system.	
Arrange for a trained ostomy visitor of same age and sex.	
Determine the meaning of changes in appearance and body functioning.	
Encourage returning to all presurgical activities as soon as possible.	
Instruct in ways to reduce gas formation: 1. Avoid activities that cause air swallowing (chewing gum, sucking through a straw, smoking). 2. Eat small frequent meals. 3. Limit intake of gas-producing foods. 4. Increase intake of yogurt and buttermilk.	These reduce gas formation.
Instruct in measures to reduce odor: 1. Use odor proof appliances and/or deodorizers. 2. Empty pouch regularly, rinsing inside of pouch before closing.	
Instruct to limit foods that cause output to have a strong odor (e.g., onions, garlic, fish, eggs).	
Provide information about community agencies or support groups.	

NURSING DIAGNOSIS: KNOWLEDGE DEFICIT ABOUT OSTOMY CARE

Related To
- New diagnosis
- No exposure to information

Defining Characteristics

Anger about diagnosis
Anxiety regarding appliance change
Fear of complications
Lack of questions
Many questions

Patient Outcomes

The patient will
- demonstrate an appliance change.
- state signs and symptoms to report.
- state methods to increase adherence of appliance.
- state when to change the appliance.

Nursing Interventions	Rationales
Assess for willingness to learn, cognitive and physical abilities, and any concerns.	
Consult an enterostomal therapist for assistance, if available.	Enterostomal therapists are specialists in ostomy education.
Provide handouts and samples of equipment. Use audiovisuals and models to supplement information.	Written materials are helpful for later reference.
Discuss types of equipment available, explaining advantages of each.	Ostomy appliances are available in either a one- or two-piece system and may be open or closed end.
Demonstrate the following: 1. pouch emptying 2. appliance preparation 3. appliance removal 4. skin care 5. appliance application	
Observe performance of above skills, giving positive reinforcement.	
Discuss and provide written information about the principles of skin protection: 1. Check stoma at least once per week.	Skin breakdown could be occurring under the appliance.

Nursing Interventions	Rationales
2. Stoma shrinks for 6–8 weeks postoperatively.	A change in pattern size may be necessary.
3. Allow no greater than ⅛ inches of skin exposure around stoma.	
4. Clean skin with warm soapy water when changing appliance.	
5. Stoma may be dried with hair dryer on a cool setting.	
6. Shave belly hair with electric or safety razor if necessary.	
Discuss and provide written information about methods to increase the appliance "wearing time":	
1. Empty the pouch when it is a third full.	If the pouch is allowed to become fuller than one third, it puts excessive pressure on the wafer and may loosen it.
2. Change the appliance as a planned event.	
3. Use stomahesive paste around the stoma to assure an adequate seal.	
Instruct on common complications that may be seen with an ostomy: 1. peristomal herniation 2. prolapsed stoma 3. stenosis of stoma 4. necrosis of stoma 5. retraction of stoma 6. skin excoriation 7. folliculitis 8. *Candida* infection	

DISCHARGE PLANNING/CONTINUITY OF CARE

• Have patient/family/caregiver demonstrate ability to perform an appliance change.

- Provide with necessary supplies, equipment, and prescriptions prior to discharge.
- Refer to a home health care agency for continued nursing care and teaching.
- Arrange follow-up with physician for continued management after discharge.
- Refer to an ostomy support group if desired/available.

REFERENCES

Bryant, G. (1992). When the bowel is blocked. *RN* (1), 58–67.
Massoni, M. (1990). Nurses' GI handbook. *Nursing, 20*(11), 65–80.
Thompson, J., McFarland, G., Hirsch, J., Tucker, S., & Bowers, A. (1989). *Mosby's manual of clinical nursing* (2nd ed). St. Louis, MO: Mosby.
Van Niel, J. (1991). What's wrong with this peristomal skin? *American Journal of Nursing, 91*(12), 44–45.

▼

CHOLECYSTECTOMY

Deborah R. Johnson, RN, MS, CNSN

Cholecystectomy is the surgical removal of the gallbladder. It is most often performed to treat cholecystitis and/or cholelithiasis unresponsive to conservative medical management. The gallbladder may be removed in one of two ways, depending on the patient's condition:

Open cholecystectomy
This is the standard cholecystectomy requiring a laparotomy. If gallstones are present in the common bile duct, a choledocholithotomy will be done and a "T-tube" placed in the common bile duct to maintain adequate drainage or flow of bile until ductal edema has subsided.

Laparoscopic cholecystectomy
This surgical procedure utilizes a laparoscope to remove the gallbladder through a small incision at the navel. Several other small incisions are made in the abdomen to allow the insertion of additional instruments needed to assist with the gallbladder removal. Many patients experience minimal postoperative discomfort and are discharged the day of surgery or 24 hr after the procedure. In most cases patients are able to resume normal activities and return to work in as little as 5–7 days. This technique is not appropriate for patients with atypical biliary or vascular anatomy, bleeding disorder, extensive adhesions, or peritonitis, pregnancy is an absolute contraindication.

ETIOLOGIES

- Symptomatic cholecystitis and/or cholelithiasis unresponsive to conservative medical management
- Malignancy of the gallbladder
- Malignancy surrounding the duct system

CLINICAL MANIFESTATIONS

- Pain: moderate to severe, colicy, abrupt in onset; may or may not be associated with a heavy meal ingestion; localizes to right upper quadrant (RUQ) epigastric area; radiates to midtorso, scapular area (phrenic nerve irritation)

- Biliary colic: excruciating pain associated with tachycardia, diaphoresis, and prostration
- Abdominal guarding and rigidity
- Indigestion, nausea, vomiting
- Positive Murphy's sign: tenderness elicited at tip of ninth costal margin during inspiration
- Jaundice

CLINICAL/DIAGNOSTIC FINDINGS

- Gallbladder ultrasound: thickening of gallbladder wall and presence of gallstones
- Oral cholecystogram or intravenous (IV) cholangiogram: indicates presence of gallstones, nonfunctional gallbladder with ductal system deficits
- Abdominal x-ray may indicate gallstones
- Elevated white blood count (WBC) count
- Elevated serum amylase
- Elevated lactic dehydrogenase (LDH) and alkaline phosphatase
- Elevated liver function tests [serum glutamic oxaloacetic/pyruvic transaminase (SGOT, SGPT), direct and indirect bilirubin]
- Elevated clotting studies (potential)

OTHER PLANS OF CARE TO REFERENCE

Basic Standards for Preoperative and Postoperative Care
Pain Management: Patient Controlled Analgesia

NURSING DIAGNOSIS: HIGH RISK FOR INFECTION

Risk Factors
Obstruction or dislodgment of T-tube placed for external biliary drainage after an open cholecystectomy with choledocholithotomy

Patient Outcomes
Patient does not exhibit signs of infection, as evidenced by
- normal T-tube drainage
- normal WBC count levels
- no febrile episodes
- stable vital signs

Nursing Interventions	**Rationales**
Observe color of T-tube drainage and record amount of T-tube drainage output with each patient assessment. Notify physician if drainage suddenly increases.	This determines excess bleeding and whether bile is flowing and not backing up in the liver or leaking into the peritoneal cavity. Drainage is initially bloody and then should change to greenish brown after several hours postoperatively. Approximately 400 mL/day of tube drainage is typical amount after several days postoperatively. The output decreases in amount as ductal edema subsides because bile begins to follow its normal route. Increased bile flow after it has started to decrease indicates a possible ductal obstruction below the tube.
Implement measures to prevent stasis and reflux of T-tube drainage: 1. Keep drainage system at or below waist level unless otherwise prescribed. 2. Keep drainage system free of kinks and dependent loops. 3. Do not irrigate, clamp, or aspirate T-tube unless prescribed.	Helps maintain patency of T-tube.
Assess for signs of potential T-tube obstruction (right upper quadrant pain, external bile leakage around T-tube, nausea, vomiting, clay-colored stools, dark yellow urine, jaundice). Notify physician of significant findings.	The presence of these signs of obstruction indicates backup of bile into the common bile duct and liver with lack of patency in the external drainage system. Medical intervention is often necessary to relieve the obstruction.

Nursing Interventions	Rationales
If signs and symptoms of obstructed bile flow occur: 1. Assure intervention to maintain patency (see second intervention above). 2. Leave T-tube unclamped. 3. Assist physician with T-tube irrigation as needed. 4. Prepare the patient for the following potential interventions: T-tube cholangiogram, basket removal of stone(s) through the T-tube, or an endoscopic papillotomy to remove ductal stone(s). 5. Provide emotional support to patient/family.	
Assess for signs that the T-tube has been moved or dislodged: 1. Sudden decrease in drainage. 2. Mark the tube at the skin line postoperatively and monitor its placement with each T-tube assessment or emptying of drainage system.	Prompt detection of a dislodged tube leads to prompt treatment and reduces the risk of peritonitis from biliary leakage.
Implement measures to prevent accidental removal or dislodgment of T-tube: 1. Empty drainage system at least once or twice a shift or when bag is less than a third to half full. 2. Cautiously change T-tube dressing as needed. 3. Secure tubing to abdominal dressing in manner that avoids strain or pull on the tubing. 4. Instruct patient not to pull on T-tube drainage system. 5. Assist patient with turning or when ambulating to avoid dislodging tube.	Full bags exert tension on tube exit site.

Nursing Interventions	Rationales
Assess patient response to prescribed T-tube clamping routine (usually 1–2 hr before and after meals).	Determines if bile is aiding digestion by increasing fat absorption.
Assess for indicators that bile is flowing through normal channels: 1. decreased amount of T-tube drainage 2. brown stools 3. clear yellow urine 4. no signs of jaundice	Once bile is flowing through normal channels, T-tube removal is possible, usually 7–10 days postoperatively.

NURSING DIAGNOSIS: KNOWLEDGE DEFICIT ABOUT SELF-CARE MANAGEMENT AFTER OPEN CHOLECYSTECTOMY WITH T-TUBE PLACEMENT

Related To lack of exposure to information

Defining Characteristics
Verbalize a lack of knowledge
Inaccurate follow-through of instructions

Patient Outcomes
The patient will
- demonstrate T-tube care and maintenance.
- state dietary modifications.
- state when to call the physician.

Nursing Interventions	Rationales
Provide written individualized patient education materials on T-tube care and care of skin surrounding the T-tube.	
Instruct in specific interventions: 1. Maintain T-tube drainage system at or below insertion site.	

Nursing Interventions

2. Assess T-tube site daily for signs of infection; cleanse the T-tube site and the skin around the T-tube daily. Apply a skin protectant; cover with dry sterile dressing.

3. Avoid strain or pull on the T-tube and drainage system. Anchor the system securely.

4. Empty drainage collection bag when one-third full and record amount.

Allow time for questions, clarification, and return demonstration of self-care prior to discharge.

Collaborate with dietitian to assist with prescribed dietary modifications:
1. A low-fat/moderate-fat diet may be prescribed.
2. Avoid excessive fat intake for the first 4–6 weeks postoperatively.
3. May increase dietary fat gradually and introduce food/fluids higher in fat one at a time.

Instruct to report the following conditions to the nurse and/or physician:
1. increased yellowing of skin
2. increased itching of skin
3. clay-colored stools
4. dark amber urine
5. persistent heartburn/bloating
6. green, brown drainage around T-tube or wound site
7. more than 2 cups per day of drainage from T-tube

Rationales

A skin protectant such as Skin Prep (zinc oxide) will protect the skin from any caustic bile leakage.

NURSING DIAGNOSIS: (FOR LAPAROSCOPIC CHOLECYSTECTOMY): PAIN IN SHOULDER OR NECK AREA

Related To introduction and removal of harmless carbon dioxide gas into abdomen during laparoscopic cholecystectomy

Defining Characteristics

Guarding behavior of shoulder and neck with reluctance to move
Rubbing of shoulder and neck
Facial grimacing, moaning, crying
Diaphoresis
Blood pressure and pulse changes
Anxiety
Verbal communication of shoulder, neck pain

Patient Outcomes

- Patient states the pain is tolerable.
- Vital signs are stable.

Nursing Interventions	Rationales
Explain reason for shoulder and neck pain:	
1. Introduction and removal of harmless carbon dioxide gas is necessary to allow the surgeon(s) optimal visualization of the abdominal contents during the laparoscopic procedure.	Explanations decrease anxiety and foster understanding of unexpected situations. Anxiety often occurs because patients expect incisional discomfort (there is minimal) and do not expect shoulder pain.
2. Residuals of carbon dioxide gas irritate the diaphragm/phrenic nerve.	Shoulder and neck pain is referred phrenic nerve pain.
3. Pain will subside gradually as all residual carbon dioxide gas is reabsorbed.	
Explain analgesics typically do not eliminate all of this specific type of discomfort and the discomfort improves with time.	Patients often expect prescribed analgesics to eliminate all pain.

Nursing Interventions	Rationales
Provide nonpharmacological interventions to reduce pain, decrease anxiety, and relax muscles, for example, position changes, back rubs, and assuring an environment conducive to rest.	

DISCHARGE PLANNING/CONTINUITY OF CARE

- Assure patient/family understands self-care management plan, for example, medications, dietary modifications, incisional care/ assessments, T-tube care and maintenance, and when to call the physician.
- Refer to a home care agency if continued nursing care, teaching, or assistance with self-care management is needed.
- Arrange for follow-up visits with dietitian, physician, and nurse for continued management after discharge as needed.
- Assist with obtaining prescriptions and establish a plan for refilling prescriptions.

REFERENCES

Beck, M. & Evans, N. (1993). *SGNA—Gastroenterology nursing: A core curriculum.* St. Louis, MO: Mosby.

Doughty, D. B. & Jackson, D. B. (1993). *Gastrointestinal disorders.* St. Louis, MO: Mosby.

Gadacz, T. R., Talamini, M. A., Lillemoe, K. D., & Yeo, C. J. (1990). Laparoscopic cholecystectomy. *Surgical Clinics of North America, 70*(6), 1249–1262.

Lewis, S. M. & Collier, I. C. (1992). *Medical-surgical nursing: Assessment and management of clinical problems* (3rd ed). St. Louis, MO: Mosby.

Schirmen, B. D., Edge, S. B., Dix, J., Hyser, M. J., Hanks, J. B., & Jones, R. S. (1991). Laparoscopic cholecystectomy, treatment of choice for symptomatic cholelithiasis. *Annals of Surgery, 213*(6), 665–677.

GASTRECTOMY: BILROTH I, BILROTH II, ANTRECTOMY, VAGOTOMY

Susan Murray, RN, MS

A gastrectomy is the surgical removal of all or part of the stomach. A partial gastrectomy is performed on patients with ulcer disease who do not respond to medical management. It is done to permanently reduce the capacity of the stomach to secrete acid and pepsin. With a partial gastrectomy the remaining portion of the stomach is anastomosed either to the duodenum (gastroduodenostomy or Bilroth I procedure) or to the jejunum (gastrojejunostomy or Bilroth II procedure). An antrectomy is the surgical removal of the entire antrum of the stomach and eliminates the hormonal phase of gastric secretion. A vagotomy is the cutting of the vagus nerve, which branches to the stomach. The vagus nerve is known to stimulate acid secretion. If a total gastrectomy is performed, there is an anastomosis of the esophagus to the jejunum to reestablish gastrointestinal continuity. This surgery is done to treat cancer of the stomach.

ETIOLOGIES

- Cancer of the stomach
- Gastric ulcers
- Duodenal ulcers

CLINICAL MANIFESTATIONS

- Chronic, intermittent epigastric pain logically relieved by food or antacids
- Pain occurring 2–3 hr after a meal or at night
- Pain described as burning, gnawing, aching, or cramping

CLINICAL/DIAGNOSTIC FINDINGS

- Barium study indicating presence of an ulcer
- Endoscopy revealing presence of an ulcer
- Guaiac positive stools
- Decreased hematocrit, hemoglobin

OTHER PLANS OF CARE TO REFERENCE

- Basic Standards for Preoperative and Postoperative Care
- Pain Management: Patient-Controlled Analgesia

NURSING DIAGNOSIS: PAIN

Related To
- Postoperative abdominal distention
- Gas

Defining Characteristics
Verbalization of abdominal fullness and gas pain
Clutching and guarding of abdomen
Reluctance to move
Grimacing
Increased abdominal girth
Dyspnea
Absence of or diminished bowel sounds

Patient Outcomes
The patient will verbalize diminished abdominal distention and gas pain.

Nursing Interventions	Rationales
Assess for nonverbal signs and verbal complaints of abdominal discomfort every 4–8 hr.	
Auscultate for bowel sounds every 4–8 hr.	
Encourage and assist with frequent position changes and ambulation as soon as allowed and tolerated.	Activity stimulates peristalsis and expulsion of flatus.
Instruct to avoid chewing gum, sucking hard candy, and smoking.	Air is swallowed during these activities, increasing gas and distention.

Nursing Interventions	Rationales
Maintain patency of nasogastric (NG) tube, if present.	Patients with a gangrenous or perforated appendix usually have a NG tube postoperatively.
When oral intake is allowed, encourage drinking of warm liquids.	Warm liquids stimulate peristalsis.
Instruct to avoid gas-producing foods and fluids.	
Encourage expelling of flatus whenever the urge is felt.	
Encourage the use of nonnarcotic analgesics once severe pain has subsided.	Narcotic analgesics depress gastrointestinal activity.
Administer gastrointestinal stimulating medications (metaclopromide, bisacodyl) as prescribed and monitor their effectiveness.	

NURSING DIAGNOSIS: ALTERED NUTRITION—LESS THAN BODY REQUIREMENTS

Related To inability to digest food and/or absorb nutrients

Defining Characteristics
Weight loss
Feeling of abdominal fullness
Nausea
Vomiting
Diarrhea

Patient Outcomes
The patient will maintain an adequate nutritional status, as evidenced by a gain or maintenance in weight.

Nursing Interventions	Rationales
Assess nutritional history, noting bowel habits and any weight loss.	
Monitor intake and output.	

Nursing Interventions	Rationales
Administer antiemetics as prescribed.	
Provide six small meals a day.	Minimizes effects of dumping syndrome.
Provide meals that are low in carbohydrate and high in protein.	With dumping syndrome meals that are high in carbohydrates can cause increased insulin secretion with resulting hypoglycemia.
Restrict liquids to times other than meal times.	Minimizes effects of dumping syndrome.
Monitor for excessive diarrhea.	About 70% of patients report an increase in the frequency of daily bowel movements after a vagotomy.
Instruct on a bland diet and to avoid tea, coffee, carbonated beverages, alcohol, and hot spices.	Bland diet buffers gastric acidity. These are mucosa-irritating substances.
Encourage to eat slowly, avoiding stress during meal time.	

NURSING DIAGNOSIS: INEFFECTIVE INDIVIDUAL COPING

Related To
- Situational crises
- Personal vulnerability

Defining Characteristics
Verbalization of inability to cope or inability to ask for help
Inability to meet role expectations
Inability to problem solve
Inappropriate use of defense mechanisms
High illness rate

Patient Outcomes
The patient will
- utilize appropriate coping methods to reduce stress and tension.
- verbalize source of and methods to reduce psychosocial stress and tension.

Nursing Interventions	Rationales
Assess, with patient, life-style, work-related tension, depression, and coping skills.	Stress increases gastric secretions.
Discuss how stress and emotion are linked to ulcer disease.	
Discuss realistic methods that may be used to avoid or control stress.	

DISCHARGE PLANNING/CONTINUITY OF CARE

- Assure understanding of self-management plan.
- Provide patient with needed supplies and prescriptions.
- Refer patient to a home health care agency if continued nursing care or teaching is necessary.
- Arrange follow-up with physician for continued management postdischarge.
- Refer patient to stress reduction group if desired/available.

REFERENCES

Massoni, M. (1990). Nurses' GI handbook. *Nursing 90, 20*(11), 65–80.
Thompson, J., McFarland, G., Hirsch, J., Tucker, S., & Bowers, A. (1989). *Mosby's manual of clinical nursing* (2nd ed). St. Louis, MO: Mosby.

$\mathscr{H}$IATAL HERNIA REPAIR: NISSEN FUNDOPLICATION

Susan Murray, RN, MS

A hiatal (or diaphragmatic) hernia occurs when a portion of the stomach herniates into the chest through the esophageal hiatus of the diaphragm. A Nissen fundoplication is the surgical intervention for a hiatal hernia and involves wrapping the gastric fundus partially or completely around the portion of the esophagus that is below the level of the diaphragm. This is most often done via an abdominal approach but may also be done via a thoracic approach.

ETIOLOGIES

- Congenital defects in the diaphragm
- Abdominal trauma
- Increased intra-abdominal pressure due to obesity, pregnancy, ascites, and heavy lifting

CLINICAL MANIFESTATIONS

- Heartburn
- Painful, difficult swallowing
- Dull ache behind sternum
- Feeling of fullness
- Regurgitation

CLINICAL/DIAGNOSTIC FINDINGS

- Upper gastrointestinal (GI) x-ray revealing hiatal hernia
- Esophagoscopy finding erythematous, friable esophageal mucosa

222

OTHER PLANS OF CARE TO REFERENCE

- Basic Standards for Preoperative and Postoperative Care
- Pain Management: Patient-Controlled Analgesia

NURSING DIAGNOSIS: IMPAIRED SWALLOWING, PREOPERATIVELY

Related To
- Esophageal irritation
- Reflux of gastric contents

Defining Characteristics
Observed evidence of difficulty in swallowing
Coughing
Choking

Patient Outcomes
The patient will swallow without difficulty.

Nursing Interventions	Rationales
Assess for signs and symptoms of impaired swallowing, including poor oral intake and grimace upon swallowing.	
Place in high Fowler's position during and immediately following meals.	This facilitates passage of food/ fluids through the esophagus.
Instruct on selection of foods that are easy to swallow (e.g., custard, ground meat).	
Encourage to drink fluids with meals.	
Encourage to swallow frequently when eating.	Smaller amounts of food can pass more easily through the esophagus.
Encourage to moisten dry foods with gravy or sauces.	Moist foods are easier to swallow.
Administer antacids as prescribed.	Antacids neutralize gastric contents and decrease heartburn.

Nursing Interventions	Rationales
Elevate head of bed on wood blocks (about 10 inches high) at all times.	This will help prevent gastric reflux.

NURSING DIAGNOSIS: PAIN

Related To
- Abdominal distention
- "Gas-bloat syndrome"

Defining Characteristics
Verbalization of abdominal fullness and gas pain
Clutching and guarding of abdomen
Reluctance to move
Grimacing
Increased abdominal girth
Dyspnea

Patient Outcomes
- The patient will state pain is diminished or tolerable.
- Patient's abdomen is less distended.

Nursing Interventions	Rationales
Assess every 4–8 hr for nonverbal signs and verbal complaints of abdominal discomfort.	
Auscultate for bowel sounds every 4–8 hr.	
Encourage and assist with frequent position changes and ambulation as soon as allowed and tolerated.	Activity stimulates peristalsis and expulsion of flatus.
Instruct to avoid chewing gum, sucking hard candy, and smoking.	Air is swallowed during these activities, increasing gas and distention.
Maintain patency of nasogastric (NG) tube if present.	Patients with a gangrenous or perforated appendix usually have a NG tube postoperatively.

Nursing Interventions	Rationales
When oral intake is allowed, encourage patient to drink warm liquids.	Warm liquids stimulate peristalsis.
Instruct to avoid gas-producing foods and fluids.	
Encourage to expel flatus whenever the urge is felt.	
Encourage the use of nonnarcotic analgesics once severe pain has subsided.	Narcotic analgesics depress gastrointestinal activity.
Administer gastrointestinal stimulating medications (such as metaclopromide, bisacodyl) as prescribed and monitor their effectiveness.	
For the gas-bloat syndrome, implement measures to reduce abdominal distention and gas and in addition:	
1. Assess for signs and symptoms of gas-bloat syndrome (abdominal distention, feeling of pressure in the epigastrium).	The Nissen fundoplication creates a one-way valve between the stomach and esophagus. This can cause problems with gas buildup and difficulty belching.
2. Instruct to eat six small meals per day.	Smaller meals reduce gastric distention.
3. Instruct to drink the majority of liquids between meals.	To help decrease gastric distention.
4. Instruct to not use a straw or drink carbonated beverages.	Both encourage swallowing of air and gas buildup.
5. Instruct to avoid foods with high fat content.	Fatty foods take a long time to digest and keep the stomach full for a longer time.

DISCHARGE PLANNING/CONTINUITY OF CARE

- Assure understanding of self-management plan.
- Assure understanding of signs and symptoms to report after discharge.

- Instruct patient to avoid increasing intra-abdominal pressure.
- Provide patient with needed supplies and prescriptions.
- Refer patient to a home health care agency if continued nursing care or teaching is necessary.
- Arrange follow-up with physician for continued management after discharge.

REFERENCES

Massoni, M. (1990). Nurses' GI handbook. *Nursing, 20*(11), 65–80.
Price, S. & Wilson, L. (1992). *Pathophysiology: Clinical concepts of disease processes* (4th ed). St. Louis, MO: Mosby Year Book.

PANCREATIC SURGERY: WHIPPLE PROCEDURE

Susan Murray, RN, MS

The Whipple procedure of pancreaticoduodenectomy is a complicated and delicate surgical procedure which is usually done for chronic pancreatitis or cancer of the pancreas. The procedure entails resection of the proximal head of the pancreas, the duodenum, a portion of the jejunum, the stomach (partial or total gastrectomy) and the gallbladder with anastomosis to the pancreatic duct (pancreatojejunostomy), the common bile duct (cholidochojejunostomy), and the stomach to the jejunum (gastrojejunostomy).

ETIOLOGIES

- Pancreatic carcinoma
- Chronic pancreatitis

CLINICAL MANIFESTATIONS

- Jaundice
- Abdominal pain
- Malabsorption
- Diabetes mellitus
- Diarrhea
- Nausea and vomiting
- Hyperglycemia
- Steatorrhea
- Weight loss
- Hepatomegaly

CLINICAL/DIAGNOSTIC FINDINGS

Pancreatic carcinoma
- Elevated serum and urinary amylase levels
- Elevated alkaline phosphatase level

- Elevated bilirubin level
- Elevated carcinoembryonic antigen (CEA) level
- Computerized tomography (CT) scan showing dilatation of the bile duct and possibly revealing a mass
- Endoscopic retrograde cholangiopancreatography (ERCP) showing ductal irregularity
- Positive percutaneous aspiration biopsy of pancreatic mass

Chronic pancreatitis
- Elevated serum and urinary amylase levels
- Elevated alkaline phosphatase levels
- Elevated bilirubin levels
- Hyperglycemia
- ERCP showing ductal irregularity

OTHER PLANS OF CARE TO REFERENCE

- Basic Standards for Preoperative and Postoperative Care
- Pain Management: Patient-Controlled Analgesia
- Diabetes Mellitus plan(s) of care
- Nutrition Support: Enteral Nutrition
- Nutrition Support: Total Parenteral

NURSING DIAGNOSIS: ALTERED NUTRITION—LESS THAN BODY REQUIREMENTS

Related To
- Anorexia
- Abdominal pain

Defining Characteristics
Weight loss
Verbalization of having no appetite
Weakness and fatigue
Nausea and vomiting
Early satiety

Patient Outcomes
The patient will
- have optimal nutritional and caloric intake.
- maintain or gain weight.

Nursing Interventions	Rationales
Assess the patient regularly for signs and symptoms of malnutrition.	
Keep an accurate intake and output record, including a food diary (calorie count).	
Implement measures to reduce/control pain.	
Encourage a rest period before meals.	This will minimize fatigue.
Provide oral care before meals.	
Assess patient's food likes and dislikes.	
Initiate a dietary consult.	
Encourage patient to consume a diet high in calories, protein, vitamins, and minerals.	
Encourage patient to drink supplemental elemental formulas.	
Initiate tube feedings or total parenteral nutrition as prescribed. (See appropriate plan of care.)	
Weigh patient daily.	
Assess stools for diarrhea and steatorrhea.	Steatorrhea is a sign of malabsorption of fats.
Administer prescribed insulin for endocrine dysfunction. Monitor glucoses closely.	There is a possibility of reactive hypoglycemia to insulin therapy in these patients.

NURSING DIAGNOSIS: ANTICIPATORY GRIEVING

Related To
- Diagnosis of chronic illness (chronic pancreatitis)
- Poor prognosis (pancreatic carcinoma)

Defining Characteristics
Expression of distress at potential loss
Denial of potential loss

Quiet
Anger
Sorrow
Choked feelings
Changes in eating habits
Alteration in sleep pattern
Alteration in activity level
Altered libido
Altered communication pattern

Patient Outcomes

The patient will demonstrate progression through the grieving process.

Nursing Interventions	Rationales
Encourage verbalization of fears and concerns.	
During stage of shock and disbelief: 1. Allow for use of denial. 2. Avoid confronting patient or family when symptoms are distorted. 3. Allow patient to express emotions. 4. Encourage support from family, friends, and clergy.	The purpose of this stage is to protect oneself against the overwhelming stress.
During stage of developing awareness: 1. Encourage expression of feelings. 2. Facilitate exploration of available options. 3. Encourage visits from others experiencing similar loss. 4. Refer to appropriate resources (e.g., social worker, legal consultants, clergy, support groups).	This stage includes the acute and increasing awareness of the pain and anguish of loss.

Nursing Interventions	Rationales
During period of mourning: 1. Encourage discussion of negative aspects of loss. 2. Encourage expression of feelings. 3. Help patient accept reality of impending loss.	This is a time in which support is helpful as reality becomes more evident.

NURSING DIAGNOSIS: PAIN

Related To abdominal distention and gas postoperatively

Defining Characteristics

Verbalization of abdominal fullness and gas pain
Clutching and guarding of abdomen
Reluctance to move
Grimacing
Increased abdominal girth
Dyspnea

Patient Outcomes

- The patient will state pain is diminished or tolerated.
- Abdomen distention will be decreased.

Nursing Interventions	Rationales
Assess patient every 4–8 hr for nonverbal signs and verbal complaints of abdominal discomfort.	
Auscultate bowel sounds every 4–8 hr.	
Encourage and assist patient with frequent position changes and ambulation as soon as allowed and tolerated.	Activity stimulates peristalsis and expulsion of flatus.
Instruct patient to avoid chewing gum, sucking hard candy, and smoking.	Air is swallowed during these activities, increasing gas and distention.
Maintain patency for nasogastric tube if present.	

Nursing Interventions	Rationales
When oral intake is allowed, encourage patient to drink warm liquids.	Warm liquids stimulate peristalsis.
Instruct patient to avoid gas-producing foods and fluids.	
Encourage patient to expel flatus whenever the urge is felt.	
Encourage the use of nonnarcotic analgesics once severe pain has subsided.	Narcotic analgesics depress gastrointestinal activity.
Administer gastrointestinal stimulating medications (metaclopromide or bisacodyl) as ordered and monitor their effectiveness.	

DISCHARGE PLANNING/CONTINUITY OF CARE

- Assure understanding of and ability to perform self-care management.
- Provide with needed supplies and prescriptions.
- Refer to a home health care agency or other appropriate resources such as a hospice for continued nursing care, teaching, or support.
- Arrange follow-up with physician for continued management after discharge.

REFERENCES

Ignatavicius, D. & Bayne, M. (1991). *Medical-surgical nursing.* Philadelphia, PA: Saunders.

Price, S. & Wilson, L. (1992). *Pathophysiology: Clinical concepts of disease processes.* St. Louis, MO: Mosby Year Book.

HERNIA REPAIR: VENTRAL HERNIORRHAPHY

Susan Murray, RN, MS

A ventral (or incisional) hernia is a weakness in the abdominal muscle at an operative scar through which a segment of the bowel protrudes. A herniorrhaphy is the surgical repair of the hernia. A hernioplasty is a surgical procedure reinforcing the area with wire, mesh, or fascia.

ETIOLOGIES

- A weakened surgical incision/operative scar
- Increased intra-abdominal pressure
- Wound infection
- Wound healed by secondary intention

CLINICAL MANIFESTATIONS

- Abdominal discomfort or pressure
- Bulging at the surgical incision or operative scar site

CLINICAL/DIAGNOSTIC FINDINGS

Bulging at the surgical incision or operative scar site

OTHER PLANS OF CARE TO REFERENCE

- Basic Standards for Preoperative and Postoperative Care
- Pain Management: Patient-Controlled Analgesia

NURSING DIAGNOSIS: HIGH RISK FOR ALTERED GASTROINTESTINAL TISSUE PERFUSION PREOPERATIVELY

Risk Factors
- Increased intra-abdominal pressure
- Constipation

Patient Outcomes
The patient will not develop an intestinal obstruction or strangulated hernia as evidenced by
- normal bowel sounds
- no increased abdominal pain or distention

Nursing Interventions	Rationales
Assess patient every 4–8 hr for signs and symptoms of strangulation and/or intestinal obstruction: 1. absence of bowel sounds 2. abdominal pain 3. abdominal distention and gas 4. bulge or protrusion at hernia site 5. nausea and vomiting 6. pain of increasing severity 7. abdominal rigidity	The hernia can become strangulated when the protrusion receives an inadequate blood supply. An intestinal obstruction occurs when the intestinal contents cannot pass through the bowel affected by the hernia. Both usually require emergency surgery.
Instruct patient not to perform any activity that will increase intra-abdominal pressure: 1. straining 2. coughing 3. heavy lifting	Increasing intra-abdominal pressure may cause further protrusion of the hernia.
Auscultate abdomen for bowel sounds every 4–8 hr.	An absence of bowel sounds may indicate an intestinal obstruction.
Monitor patient for bowel movements.	Constipation and failure to pass gas are signs of obstruction.
Apply an abdominal binder or truss.	These add abdominal support and can help keep a hernia reduced.
Administer prescribed laxatives to prevent constipation.	This will help patient avoid straining when having a bowel movement.

NURSING DIAGNOSIS: PAIN

Related To abdominal distention and gas postoperatively

Defining Characteristics

Verbalization of abdominal fullness and gas pain
Clutching and guarding of abdomen
Reluctance to move
Grimacing
Increased abdominal girth
Dyspnea

Patient Outcomes

- The patient will state pain is diminished or tolerable.
- Patient's abdomen is less distended.

Nursing Interventions	Rationales
Assess patient every 4–8 hr for nonverbal signs and verbal complaints of abdominal discomfort.	
Auscultate bowel sounds every 4–8 hr.	
Encourage and assist patient with frequent position changes and ambulation as soon as allowed and tolerated.	Activity stimulates peristalsis and expulsion of flatus.
Instruct patient to avoid chewing gum, sucking hard candy, and smoking.	Air is swallowed during these activities, increasing gas and distention.
Maintain patency for nasogastric tube if present.	
When oral intake is allowed, encourage patient to drink warm liquids.	Warm liquids stimulate peristalsis.
Instruct patient to avoid gas-producing foods and fluids.	
Encourage patient to expel flatus whenever the urge is felt.	

Nursing Interventions	Rationales
Encourage the use of nonnarcotic analgesics once severe pain has subsided.	Narcotic analgesics depress gastrointestinal activity.
Administer gastrointestinal stimulating medications as prescribed and monitor their effectiveness.	

DISCHARGE PLANNING/CONTINUITY OF CARE

- Assure understanding of self-care management plan, emphasizing importance of avoiding heavy lifting.
- Provide with needed supplies and prescriptions.
- Refer to a home health care agency if continued nursing care or teaching is necessary.
- Arrange follow-up with physician for continued management after discharge.

REFERENCES

Ignatavicius, D. & Bayne, M. (1991). *Medical-surgical nursing*. Philadelphia, PA: Saunders.

Mason, M. & Bates, G. (1991). *Basic medical-surgical nursing*. New York, NY: MacMillan.

Common Endocrine Conditions and Therapies

▼

*C*ORTICOSTEROID THERAPY

Ellen M. Jovle, RN, MS

*C*orticosteroids are produced by the adrenal cortex and include several hormones: glucocorticoids, mineralocorticoids, androgens, estrogens, and progesterones. Synthetic corticosteroids include glucocorticoids and mineralcorticoids. Glucocorticoids are medications used to treat adrenocorticol disorders, produce immunosuppression, and reduce inflammation (Table 25.1). When used on a long-term basis, glucocorticoids suppress the hypothalamic-pituitary-adrenal (HPA) axis. Glucocorticoids have effects on carbohydrate, fat, and protein metabolism and also have mineralcorticoid activity, which regulates electrolyte and water balance. Examples of common steroids are cortisone acetate, dexamethasone, hydrocortisone, prednisolone, prednisone, and methylprednisolone.

CLINICAL MANIFESTATIONS/DIAGNOSTIC FINDINGS

None

ETIOLOGIES

None

OTHER PLANS OF CARE TO REFERENCE

- Diabetes Mellitus: Initiating Insulin
- Thrombophlebitis/Deep-Vein Thrombosis

NURSING DIAGNOSIS: HIGH RISK FOR INFECTION

Risk Factors
- Immune system depression
- Environmental exposure
- Invasive techniques
- Malnutrition
- Chronic disease
- Stress

Table 25.1 • Major Uses Of Glucocorticoids

Treatment of Addison's disease

Treatment of hypercalcemia as a result of breast cancer, multiple myeloma, sarcoidosis, or vitamin D intoxication.

Suppression of allergic reactions

Immunosuppression in organ and tissue transplants

Relief of cerebral edema as a result of brain tumors or neurosurgery

Emergency treatment of shock

To decrease airway inflammation in asthma and COPD

A conjunctive treatment of leukemias, lymphomas, and myelomas

Relief of inflammation in autoimmune diseases such as rheumatoid arthritis, systemic lupus erythematosus, dermatomyositis, ulcerative colitis, vasculitis, myasthenia gravis, and nephrotic syndrome

Patient Outcomes

Patient will remain free of infection, as evidenced by absence of signs and symptoms of infection.

Nursing Interventions	Rationales
Monitor and report signs and symptoms of infection, including temperature, diaphoresis, chills, mental status changes, purulent drainage, pain, and fatigue.	Steroid therapy can mask the usual signs of infection such as temperature elevation. Infections may present with subtle changes.
Monitor white blood cell (WBC) count and differential.	Elevated WBCs with shift to left may indicate infection.

Nursing Interventions	Rationales
Prevent transmission of organisms by 1. meticulous hand washing 2. maintaining closed sterile drainage systems 3. meticulous care of intravascular lines following hospital protocol 4. assessing the continued need for invasive lines and catheters 5. providing personal hygiene 6. limiting exposure to individuals (visitors, staff, or other patient) with known or exposure to infections 7. avoiding unnecessary diagnostic or therapeutic invasive procedures	
Maintain patient's defense against infection by 1. encouraging adequate nutrition 2. maintaining skin integrity 3. encouraging respiratory hygiene 4. encouraging stress management	
Teach patient and family risk factors for infection, precautions to prevent infection, signs and symptoms of infection, and importance of early recognition and reporting.	

NURSING DIAGNOSIS: HIGH RISK FOR INJURY WITH HIGH-DOSE AND/OR LONG-TERM USE OF STEROIDS

Risk Factors
- Adrenal insufficiency secondary to suppression of HPA axis
- Increased lipogenesis
- Protein catabolism
- Insulin resistance
- Increased gluconeogenesis
- Gastrointestinal irritation
- Hypercoagulopathy
- Potassium and calcium loss

Patient Outcomes

Patient will exhibit no/minimal signs and symptoms of

- adrenal insufficiency
- peptic ulcer disease
- diabetes
- osteoporosis
- thromboembolism
- hypokalemia
- hypocalcemia

Nursing Interventions	Rationales
Monitor for signs and symptoms of adrenal insufficiency, including fatigue, weight loss, vomiting, diarrhea, abdominal pain, hypotension, dehydration, tachycardia, and shock. Alert physician if symptoms occur.	Adrenal insufficiency may occur when steroids are withdrawn or tapered due to suppression of HPA axis. Adrenal insufficiency may also occur during periods of stress such as surgery or trauma.
Monitor for signs and symptoms of hyperglycemia: polyuria, polyphagia, polydypsia, and elevated blood glucose.	Steroids promote gluconeogenesis resulting in hyperglycemia.
If patient develops hyperglycemia, implement plans of care for diabetes mellitus.	
Monitor for signs and symptoms of gastrointestinal irritation and bleeding: gastric pain, positive stool guaiac test, and hematemesis.	Steroids stimulate secretion of gastric acid, thereby causing gastric irritation and ulceration.
If signs and symptoms of gastrointestinal bleeding occur, notify physician and implement plan of care for peptic ulcer disease.	
Administer oral steroid medications with food or milk to reduce gastric irritation.	
Monitor patient for signs and symptoms of thromboembolism, deep-vein thrombosis (DVT), pulmonary emboli, or cerebrovascular accident (CVA).	Steroids stimulate production of red blood cells, which increases blood viscosity and the risk of thrombus formation.

Nursing Interventions	Rationales
If signs and symptoms of thrombo-embolism develop, notify physician. Implement appropriate nursing plan of care for thrombophlebitis or stroke.	
Monitor for signs and symptoms of hypokalemia, muscular weakness, nausea, vomiting, electrocardiographic changes, and decreased serum potassium level.	Steroids increase potassium excretion.
If signs and symptoms of hypokalemia occur, notify physician and anticipate potassium replacement.	
Monitor for signs and symptoms of osteoporosis: pain, kyphosis, and evidence of pathological fractures.	Steroids increase calcium and phosphorous excretion, which leads to a reduction of bone density.

NURSING DIAGNOSIS: HIGH RISK FOR FLUID VOLUME EXCESS

Risk Factors
- Increase sodium reabsorption
- Compromised regulatory mechanism

Patient Outcomes
Patient will maintain normal fluid balance, as evidenced by
- absence of edema
- blood pressure reading within patient's baseline
- absence of weight gain

Nursing Interventions	Rationales
Monitor fluid status by measuring daily weight, intake and output, blood pressure, and presence of edema.	
Assess and review sodium and fluid intake (food, oral and IV fluids and medication). Compare to fluid output.	

Nursing Interventions

Teach patient and family:
1. importance of monitoring daily weight
2. sodium-restricted diet as appropriate
3. signs and symptoms of fluid volume excess
4. importance of early recognition and early reporting of symptoms

Rationales

NURSING DIAGNOSIS: HIGH RISK FOR IMPAIRED SKIN INTEGRITY

Risk Factors
- Nutritional deficit
- Edema
- Immobility
- Protein tissue wasting
- Capillary fragility

Patient Outcomes
The patient will maintain skin integrity, as evidenced by absence of skin breakdown or irritation.

Nursing Interventions

Inspect skin frequently; note areas of erythema, blanching, warmth, maceration, or excoriation.

Initiate appropriate protective measures, including
1. keeping skin surfaces clean and dry
2. using pressure relief measures
3. reducing shear and friction forces
4. promoting optimal circulation

Rationales

These measures are critical nursing interventions in the prevention of pressure ulcers. (See Prevention and Care of Pressure Ulcers.)

Nursing Interventions	Rationales
Implement strategies to reduce dependent edema. 1. Elevate legs. 2. Avoid pressure under knee. 3. Encourage passive/active exercise.	Areas of edema may be especially vulnerable to breakdown.
Maintain adequate nutrition.	
Teach patient/family: 1. importance of good skin hygiene 2. protecting skin from trauma 3. importance of adequate nutrition	

NURSING DIAGNOSIS: HIGH RISK FOR ALTERED NUTRITION—MORE THAN BODY REQUIREMENTS

Risk Factors
- Altered fat, protein, and carbohydrate metabolism
- Increased appetite

Patient Outcomes
Patient will maintain body weight within normal limits.

Nursing Interventions	Rationales
Monitor daily weight. Note increases.	
Assess daily intake. Note caloric and fat intake.	
Discuss patient's usual activity and exercise pattern. Assist patient in establishing progressive exercise program.	
Assist patient in identifying personal and environmental factors which contribute to excessive intake.	

Nursing Interventions

Assist patient in determining appropriate caloric intake and daily dietary plan. Consult dietitian as appropriate.

Nursing Interventions	Rationales
Discuss techniques to decrease excessive intake, such as 1. setting down utensils between bites 2. serving food on smaller plates 3. eating in only one designated place 4. eating slowly and chewing food thoroughly 5. eating only when sitting down 6. avoiding other activities when eating 7. never eating from another person's plate 8. eating low-calorie snacks 9. substituting diet soda or water for high-calorie drinks 10. decreasing intake of calorie-dense or high-fat food	Techniques that modify behavior will assist in success with weight maintenance or loss.

Instruct patient and family on
1. health hazards associated with obesity
2. effects of steroids on metabolism and appetite
3. realistic weight loss goals
4. calorie-restricted diet (if appropriate)
5. behavior modification techniques to decrease excessive intake
6. role of exercise in maintaining/reducing weight
7. beginning exercise program
8. exercise guidelines

NURSING DIAGNOSIS: HIGH RISK FOR BODY IMAGE DISTURBANCE

Risk Factors
- Cushingoid appearance
- Weight gain

Patient Outcomes
Patient will
- identify factors contributing to altered body image.
- express improved perception of body image.

Nursing Interventions	Rationales
Assess meaning of changes in appearance to patient.	Identifies if patient response to changes in appearance are negative or affecting feelings about self.
Identify behavioral cues which indicate inability to accept image changes, including 1. verbalizing negative feelings of self or appearance. 2. avoiding looking at self 3. exhibiting self-destructive behavior 4. neglecting personal grooming 5. refusing to discuss changes 6. withdrawing from social contacts	
Discuss effect of steroids on appearance.	
Discuss individualized strategies with patient and family that maintain acceptance of appearance and minimize negative response, such as 1. maintaining social contacts 2. personal grooming 3. importance of expression of feelings 4. avoiding negative self-talk and negative criticism	

NURSING DIAGNOSIS: KNOWLEDGE DEFICIT—REGARDING USE OF STEROIDS MEDICATION

Related To lack of exposure to information

Defining Characteristics
Verbalized lack of knowledge about use of steroid medication

Patient Outcomes
Patient will
- identify signs and symptoms of adrenal insufficiency.
- identify correct schedule of medication.
- identify signs and symptoms of complications.
- state measures to reduce complications of steroid therapy.
- describe when to contact health care professionals.
- verbalize intention to wear Medic-Alert ID.

Nursing Interventions	Rationales
Assess current knowledge base, readiness and ability to learn and preferred learning style, and barriers to learning.	
Provide written material for home use in addition to verbal explanations.	
Instruct patient in use of steroids, including 1. purpose and actions 2. dosages 3. schedule of tapering dosages or alternate-day dosing	Abruptly discontinuing steroids may cause adrenal insufficiency.
4. not to discontinue taking steroids without physician's instruction	Identify importance of communicating steroid use to other health professionals who may provide care.
5. administering daily dose in the morning	Timing of dosage with body's endogenous secretion decreases suppression of HPA axis.
6. administering steroid with food or milk	Decrease gastric irritation.

Nursing Interventions	Rationales
Teach patient and family signs and symptoms of serious complications (see Table 25.2).	
Discuss prevention of complications: 1. regular eye exams 2. ongoing follow-up for early detection of elevated blood sugar, electrolyte imbalance, and high blood pressure 3. infection control measures 4. weight control measures 5. need for salt restriction and potassium supplementation. 6. protection of skin 7. calcium supplementation to decrease risk of osteoporosis 8. regular exercise to control weight and minimize osteoporosis and muscle atrophy	

Table 25.2 • Possible Adverse Effects of Long-Term Glucocorticoid Therapy

Hyperglycemia
Hypertension
Osteoporosis
Peptic ulcer disease
Thromboembolism
Hypokalemia
Atherosclerosis acceleration
Cataract formation
Glaucoma
Sodium and fluid retention
Depression
Mood changes
Insomnia
Impaired wound healing
Thinning of skin, easy bruising
Muscle weakness and weight gain
Susceptibility to infection
Cushingoid appearance (moonface, acne, hirsutism, buffalo humps)

DISCHARGE PLANNING/CONTINUITY OF CARE

- Assure patient's understanding and ability to take medications as prescribed at home.
- Arrange follow-up for continued management.
- Assist patient in obtaining prescriptions and establishing plan for refilling prescriptions.
- Refer patient to a home health care agency if continued nursing care is needed.

REFERENCES

Cook, D. M. (1992). Safe use of glucocorticoids. *Postgraduate Medicine,* 91(3), 145–154.

Lewis, S. M. & Collier, I. C. (1992). *Medical-surgical nursing.* St. Louis, MO: Mosby Year Book.

Porth, C. M. (1990). *Pathophysiology—Concepts of altered health states.* Philadelphia, PA: Lippincott.

▼

IABETES MELLITUS: EFFECTS OF HOSPITALIZATION AND SURGERY

Bonnie Allbaugh, RN, MS, CDE

Diabetes mellitus is the absence or insufficient secretion of insulin by the beta cells of the pancreas, resulting in abnormal carbohydrate, protein, and fat metabolism. Diabetes is classified into two types: Type I, insulin-dependent diabetes mellitus (IDDM), and Type II, non-insulin-dependent diabetes mellitus (NIDDM). (See Table 26.1.). Impaired glucose tolerance (IGT) is a form of prediabetes characterized by intermittent, mild hyperglycemia, which if untreated could become frank diabetes. Hospitalization and surgery present particular concerns for a person with diabetes due to the required changes in eating patterns and routine and the normal physiological effects of surgery. Fasting for tests, procedures, and surgery as well as the reduced physical activity during hospitalization have a major effect on the patient's normal blood sugar control. The effects of the admitting diagnosis and/or the physiological effects of surgery also adversely affect blood sugar control. The physiological stress of surgery causes release of the catecholamines, epinephrine, and norepinephrine. Epinephrine release results in hyperglycemia since it decreases the uptake of glucose by muscles, inhibits endogenous insulin release, and causes glycogen, stored in the liver, to break down into glucose. The metabolic and hemodynamic stresses may also potentiate long-term complications of diabetes, including cardiovascular disease, renal failure, and neuropathy.

ETIOLOGIES

- Witholding or delaying food
- Reduced physical activity
- Physiological stress of surgery
- Presence of illness, inflammation, and infection
- Presence of complications of diabetes

251

Table 26.1 • Type I and Type II Diabetes Compared

Type I (IDDM), 10–15%	Type II (NIDDM), 85–90%
Usual onset before 30 years	Usual onset after 40 years
Onset sudden	Onset gradual
Severe symptoms	No or mild symptoms
Thin	Usually overweight
Must use insulin	Some use insulin; some use oral hypoglycemics
Diet and exercise needed	Diet and exercise needed
Weak hereditary	Strong hereditary
Ketones	No ketones

CLINICAL MANIFESTATIONS

- Wide variation in blood sugar values
- Hypoglycemia
- Hyperglycemia
- Slow healing process
- Decreased renal function
- Increased neuropathy symptoms (pain, tingling, especially in legs)
- Abnormal cardiac function

CLINICAL/DIAGNOSTIC FINDINGS

- Blood glucose <60 mg/dL or >180 mg/dL
- Elevated blood urea nitrogen (BUN) and creatinine
- Elevated blood pressure

OTHER PLANS OF CARE TO REFERENCE

- Diabetes Mellitus: Initiation of Insulin Therapy

NURSING DIAGNOSIS: ALTERED NUTRITION—LESS THAN BODY REQUIREMENTS

Related To
- Delaying/witholding food for diagnostic/therapeutic procedures
- Hyperglycemia
- Decreased insulin sensitivity

Defining Characteristics

- Weight loss
- Reported inadequate food intake
- Hypoglycemia
- Possible ketosis if Type I

Patient Outcomes

The patient will
- have the required intake of protein, carbohydrate, and fats.
- maintain prehospital weight.
- maintain blood sugar in own normal range.

Nursing Interventions	Rationales
Identify usual meal pattern including times and size of meals and snacks. Try to maintain or return to the patient's usual pattern as soon as possible.	If patient is in good diabetes control before admission, maintaining usual patterns of eating will prevent unexpected hypoglycemia or hyperglycemia.
Assess usual food intake and consult with dietitian, if available, to review any needed changes.	Hospitalization is a good time to update patient on new information and recommendations on the diabetic diet. Current recommendations include high complex carbohydrate (60%), moderate protein (25–30%), low fat (10–15%), low salt, and high fiber. The American Diabetes Association (ADA) diet follows the same recommendations as the American Heart Association and American Cancer Society diets.
When food and fluids must be held for a short time (1–2 hr), do not give prescribed insulin (especially regular insulin) or oral hypoglycemics until the patient is able to eat.	Regular insulin begins its hypoglycemic action within 30 min of injection. Intermediate-acting insulins (NPH, UL) begin to work within 1–2 hr.
When food and fluids are withheld for long periods of time, such as preoperatively, discuss a plan with the physician , for adjustment in insulin or oral hypoglycemic dosing and intravenous fluids.	

Nursing Interventions	**Rationales**
Consider selecting one of the following alternative insulin regimens for patients using insulin:	
1. glucose-insulin infusion regimen, which is an an insulin drip of rapid-acting insulin in normal saline at 0.5 U/mL, infused by infusion pump, with a 5% dextrose (D_5W) solution given to balance glucose levels.	This is recommended for patients having lengthy procedures when allowed nothing by mouth (NPO) for 2 days or more.
2. dividing the total dose of intermediate-acting insulin and rapid-acting insulin into four equal doses of regular insulin and giving an insulin dose every 6 hrs with a D_5W solution infusing	This is recommended for short procedures and 1 or 2 days of NPO or when total parenteral nutrition (TPN) or continuous enteral feeding is being used.
3. withholding morning rapid-acting insulin and giving one half the intermediate-acting insulin	This method, while frequently used for 1-day surgery, may lead to unpredictable glycemic excursions due to the variable absorption times of intermediate-acting insulin.
Consider selecting one of the following alternatives for patients with Type II diabetes who use oral hypoglycemics:	
1. Withhold doses until able to eat and give rapid-acting human insulin subcutaneously based upon blood sugar value.	This is acceptable for short procedures or periods of NPO of 1–2 days. If long-acting oral agent was being used, such as chlorpropamide (Diabenese), it should be discontinued 36–72 hr before surgery due to its long half-life. Second-generation oral agents, glyburide and glipizide, can be discontinued the morning of surgery.

Nursing Interventions	Rationales
2. Temporarily discontinue oral hypoglycemics and begin human insulin using a prescribed sliding scale of regular insulin.	This is recommeded for long procedures and 2 or more days of NPO. Human insulin is recommended for short-term therapy. Since it is the least immunogenic insulin, it decreases the possibility of future insulin resistance and/or allergy.
Monitor blood sugar using a bedside meter at a frequency appropriate to the insulin therapy: 1. hourly if on insulin drip 2. every 6 hr if NPO and receiving insulin every 6 hr 3. before meals (AC) and at bedtime (HS) if eating 4. Two-hour postprandial may be requested when intermittent tube feedings are being given.	
Assure accuracy of meter test results by using a sufficient drop of blood and a clean meter and following procedures recommended by the meter company and your institution or agency.	Accuracy is dependent upon the sample size, clean, dust-free meter, and proficiency of the tester. The Clinical Laboratories Improvement Act (CLIA) is a federal mandate which requires quarterly quality control testing and tester certification.
Test for urinary ketones every 8–12 hr for patients with IDDM whose blood sugars are less than 200 mg/dL on average. If blood sugar is over 250 mg/dL and/or the patient exhibits signs and symptoms of diabetic ketoacidosis, test ketones every 4 hr or with each void.	
Do not withhold insulin when the patient has a normal or low blood sugar. If it is low, consult the physician for a dose adjustment.	Withholding insulin will result in a dramatic rise in blood glucose level. The dosage should be aimed at maintaining a normal range of blood sugar.

Nursing Interventions

If a sliding scale is prescribed, consult with the physician to establish scheduled doses of insulin as soon as possible to be used with or instead of the sliding scale. Return to usual insulin regimen as soon as patient is eating normally.

Rationales

The sliding scale "chases" the blood glucose rather than preventing elevated blood glucose. A scheduled dose with an additional sliding scale results in less extremes in blood sugar.

NURSING DIAGNOSIS: HIGH RISK FOR INJURY

Risk Factors
- NPO or delayed meals
- Excess insulin dose
- Hypoglycemia
- Hypoglycemia symptom unawareness
- Dehydration
- Renal insufficiency

Patient Outcomes
The patient will
- recognize, report, and receive appropriate treatment for hypoglycemia.
- have a balanced intake and output.
- prevent low levels of blood glucose if hypoglycemia unawareness is present.
- have BUN and creatinine that are unchanged from prehospital levels.

Nursing Interventions

Regularly assess for signs of hypoglycemia. Early signs include "a funny feeling," shakiness, headache, light-headedness, hunger, weakness, and sweating. Late signs include numbness and tingling of the lips and tongue, vision changes, inability to concentrate, disorientation, confusion, mood changes, irritability, and paleness.

Rationales

Early signs typically occur when the blood sugar is dropping slowly below normal. Late signs usually occur as the blood sugar drops greatly below normal but can be initial signs if the blood sugar drops very rapidly.

Nursing Interventions	**Rationales**
Anticipate times when the patient is most at risk for hypoglycemia, for example, when food is delayed, snack or meals is skipped, or NPO, at the peak action times of the insulins used and during or after scheduled physical therapy or stress tests. At high-risk times, check blood sugar as well as assess for signs and symptoms of hypoglycemia.	Patients with long-term diabetes may no longer be able to sense early or any signs of hypoglycemia.
If patient is receiving narcotics, recovering from anesthesia, or in pain, assess for increased heart rate, decreased blood pressure, and irritability as signs of hypoglycemia. Check blood sugar to verify.	
Prevent hypoglycemia by always scheduling tests/procedures requiring NPO early in the morning and consult with physician regarding adjustment of insulin dose using options described in previous diagnosis.	
Schedule physical therapy, exercise, or stress tests ½–1 hr after meals to prevent hypoglycemia.	
Treat hypoglycemia immediately following a standard for treatment. (See Tables 26.2 and 26.3.) Institutions may have their own standard or protocol for treatment.	The goal of treatment is to bring the blood sugar to normal and eliminate the hypoglycemia symptoms. Overtreating hypoglycemia is common but should be avoided. It results in rapidly fluctuating blood sugars. Following a standard for treatment reduces the frequency of overtreatment.

Nursing Interventions

Monitor and protect renal function:

1. Maintain a balanced intake and output.
2. Report hypertension and monitor until adequately treated.
3. Monitor urine albumin, BUN, creatinine, and potassium, especially if renal function is challenged (e.g., tests using iodine-based contrast medium).
4. Assure adequate hydration before dye/contrast studies.

Rationales

Renal function may begin to decline after 10 years of IDDM.

Table 26.2 • Standard for Treating Hypoglycemia

1. If glucose is under 70 mg/dL and patient is alert:
   - Give 4–6 oz of juice or 1 fruit exchange.
   - If NPO, give 10 mL of dextrose 50% (D_{50}) if IV access is available.
   - If NPO and no IV access available, give 1 mL glucagon intramuscularly or subcutaneosly.
   - If at night or longer than 1 hr to next meal, give an additional 1 bread and 1 protein exchange. If predialysis on a protein restrictive diet, give 2 breads instead of 1 bread and 1 protein.
   - If occurs in early a.m., do not use breakface as the treatment source. The patient needs an additional fruit source. You may order breakfast early, but you must still treat the hypoglycemia with juice or 1 fruit exchange.
2. If glucose is under 70 mg/dL and patient is not alert:
   - Give 10 mL of D_{50} IV.
   - Give 20 mL of D_{50} IV if glucose is under 40 mg/dL.
   - If no IV access, give 1 mL glucagon intramuscularly or subcutaneously and establish access.
3. Recheck glucose in 15 min.
4. Recheck glucose in 15 and 30 min if IV glucose or parenteral glucagon was given.

Note: Consider Na^+, K^+, protein, or fluid restriction when determining treatment. See guidelines in the text talk with a dietitian to help determine treatment.

Table 26.3 • Suggested Foods For Treating Hypoglycemia

1 fruit = 120 mL orange juice (1)
80 mL cranberry juice
80 mL grape juice
180 mL regular Sprite

1 bread = 3 graham crackers
6 saltine crackers (2)

1 meat = ¼ cup cottage cheese (2,3)
1 oz (slice) cheese (2,3)
1 tbsp peanut butter (1,2,3)

1 fruit and 1 meat = 240 mL 2% milk (1,3)

Note: (1) = high in K^+; (2) = high in Na^+; (3) = high in protein.

NURSING DIAGNOSIS: HIGH RISK FOR INFECTION/ALTERED TISSUE PERFUSION

Risk Factors

- Hyperglycemia
- Peripheral vascular disease
- Peripheral neuropathy

Patient Outcomes

The patient will

- demonstrate normal healing of surgical wounds.
- maintain normal skin integrity.
- have palpable peripheral pulses.

Nursing Interventions	Rationales
Assess and report hyperglycemia which does not normalize with current treatment.	Hyperglycemia is associated with several problems, including decreased effectiveness of leukocytes, increased risk of platelet aggregation, and increased rigidity of red blood cells, which decreases circulation through the small vessels, depriving them of oxygen and nutrients.
Observe for signs of inflammation and infection. Also observe for hyperglycemia.	An increase in blood sugar may be an early sign of developing inflammation or infection.
Provide meticulous wound care.	

Nursing Interventions	Rationales
Assess for and promote adequate circulation in extremities by 1. encouraging active and passive range of motion 2. assisting with early ambulation 3. assuring antiemboli stockings properly applied	Diabetes increases the risk of thrombophlebitis and deep-vein thrombosis.
Protect feet and legs of patients with peripheral neuropathy by observing position and skin condition. (See Prevention and Care of Pressure Ulcers.)	

NURSING DIAGNOSIS: HIGH RISK FOR DECREASED CARDIAC OUTPUT

Risk Factors
- Hypercholesteremia
- Autonomic neuropathy
- Hypertension
- History of coronary artery disease
- Impaired renal function

Patient Outcomes
- Blood pressure will be in normal range.
- Elevated cholesterol panel will be recognized and treated.
- Intake and output will be adequate and balanced.

Nursing Interventions	Rationales
Monitor blood pressure and assess effectiveness of antihypertensive medication.	
Check orthostatic blood pressure to assess for autonomic neuropathy.	

Nursing Interventions	Rationales
Monitor cholesterol panel and consult with physician regarding possible long-term treatment measures: 1. Consult dietitian and instruct on low-cholesterol diet. 2. Encourage patient to monitor and control blood sugar to reduce triglycerides. 2. Encourage patient to begin a prescribed therapeutic exercise program to increase "good cholesterol": high-density lipoprotein (HDL).	
Assess pulse for regularity. If monitored, observe for arrhythmias. Investigate and report any complaints of chest pain, shortness of breath, or change on the ECG.	Diabetes increases the risk of myocardial infarction (MI), and patients may experience myocardial damage without pain, "the silent MI."

NURSING DIAGNOSIS: HIGH RISK FOR INEFFECTIVE MANAGEMENT OF THERAPEUTIC REGIMEN

Risk Factors
- Complex treatment regimen
- Chronic illness requiring constant management
- Difficult life changes
- Economic difficulties
- Personal/family conflicts
- Knowledge deficit
- Denial
- Psychosocial issues

Patient Outcomes
The patient will
- identify components of the regimen which are most difficult.
- agree to follow a modified treatment regimen.
- describe signs and symptoms, prevention, and correction of hypoglycemia and hyperglycemia.
- obtain regular follow-up.

Nursing Interventions	Rationales
Assess understanding and usual practices in self-management of diabetes, recognizing and respecting the current knowledge and efforts the patient has used.	Patients with a long history of diabetes may have developed unique and successful ways to manage their diabetes. However, they may not have had an opportunity to receive recent information on diabetes. Hospitalization provides an opportunity for an update.
Monitor the level of glycosylated hemoglobin (hemoglobin A_{1C}) to indicate level of control over the previous 3 months. Discuss the A_{1C} result and possible factors affecting it with the patient.	The hemoglobin A_{1C} is a measure of the amount of glycosylation (presence of sugar) on the hemoglobin molecule. Since the life-cycle of the hemoglobin molecule is 3 months, this test is an excellent way to assess overall control of diabetes for the previous 3 months.
Identify the factors or components of the regimen that are the most difficult for the patient and consult with the diabetes nurse educator or teaching service, if available. The regimen may need to be modified to be more acceptable to the patient. The patient has to live with it every day, so it has to fit his or her life-style.	There are many different insulin regimens, meal patterns, and monitoring methods available. Consider all alternatives with the patient to find a realistic regimen that works for the patient.
Assess for financial difficulties, psychosocial problems, family/relationship problems, and psychiatric disorders and assist with obtaining resources. Consult social services, if available.	Diabetes is a very expensive disease to manage. Blood glucose test strips cost approximately 50–75 cents per strip. Other supplies such as insulin and syringes all add up to a large monthly sum.
Alert patient about support groups or group education programs that may be beneficial in coping with and managing diabetes.	

▼

DISCHARGE PLANNING/CONTINUITY OF CARE

- Assure understanding of self-management plan, especially if any modifications have been made.
- Refer to a home health agency if continued assistance with care or learning is required.
- Assist in obtaining prescriptions and supplies and establishing a plan for refilling prescriptions.
- Arrange follow-up with a physician, diabetes nurse educator, and dietitian to continue management and teaching after discharge.
- Provide information on local diabetes support groups and educational programs.
- Refer to the local chapter of the American Diabetes Association for further information.

REFERENCES

Dinsmoor, R. S. (1993). Hypoglycemia without warning. *Diabetes Self-Management*, March–April, pp. 6–8.

Gutherie, D. (1988). *Diabetes education: A core curriculum for health professionals.* Chicago, IL: American Association of Diabetes Educators.

Kreines, K. (1992). Diabetes management during same-day surgery and procedures. *Clinical Diabetes*, 10(4), 52–54.

Lebovitz, H. (1991). *Therapy for diabetes mellitus and related disorders.* Alexandria, VA: American Diabetes Association.

Lorber, D., Curley, A., & Nazario, M. (1990). Discharge planning and diabetes. *Practical Diabetology*, 9(4), 18–22.

▼

DIABETES MELLITUS: INITIATING INSULIN

Bonnie Allbaugh, RN, MS, CDE

Insulin is necessary for normal carbohydrate, protein, and fat metabolism. Exogenous insulin is required for people with insulin-dependent (Type I) diabetes since they do not produce enough of this hormone to sustain life. People with non-insulin-dependent (Type II) diabetes may need supplemental exogenous insulin when they have decreased insulin production or decreased insulin sensitivity, especially during times of illness, surgery, and stress. Insulin is often required for treatment of secondary diabetes, that is, occurring with other diseases and treatments such as pancreatic disease and high doses of steroid medications.

ETIOLOGIES

- New diagnosis of insulin-dependent (Type I) diabetes
- Treatment failure of oral hypoglycemics in non-insulin-dependent (Type II) diabetes
- Illness, surgery, or other stresses in Type II diabetes
- Secondary diabetes, that is, high-dose steroids and pancreatic disease

CLINICAL MANIFESTATIONS

- Consistent hyperglycemia
- Thirst, polyuria
- Ketonuria, ketonemia
- Marked weight loss

CLINICAL/DIAGNOSTIC FINDINGS

- Blood glucose > 200 mg/dL
- Elevated hemoglobin A_1c
- Presence of ketones in urine and/or blood

OTHER PLANS OF CARE TO REFERENCE

- Diabetes Mellitus: Effects of Hospitalization and Surgery

NURSING DIAGNOSIS: KNOWLEDGE DEFICIT—INSULIN USE

Related To
- Lack of exposure to information
- New diagnosis
- New treatment method

Defining Characteristics

Anger about diagnosis
Anxiety regarding injection
Fear of complications
Lack of questions
Many questions
Previous refusal to use insulin
Myths regarding need for insulin

Patient Outcomes

The patient will
- demonstrate correct preparation, administration, and site selection of insulin injection.
- state expected effect, action times, and side effects of insulin.
- describe own action plan for storage of insulin and disposal of syringes.
- demonstrate correct technique for blood glucose monitoring.
- demonstrate understanding of blood glucose values by defining blood glucose target ranges and action plan when out of ranges.
- list the common signs of hypoglycemia and own action plan for treatment and prevention.
- demonstrate urine testing for ketones.
- define when urine ketone testing is needed and the significance of ketones in the urine.
- define plan for on-going care and names of health care providers available for questions and concerns.

Nursing Interventions	Rationales
Assess for willingness to learn, cognitive and physical abilities (especially sight), and any concerns about or previous experience with injections.	Blurred vision lasting for several weeks is common when blood sugar is normalized and will return to normal. Building on previous experience, correcting misinformation, and encouraging participation in the learning experience are key adult learning principles.
Consult a diabetes teaching service for assistance, if available.	Certified diabetes educators are specialists in diabetes education.
Provide handouts and samples of equipment. Use audiovisual aids to supplement information.	Written materials are helpful for later reference.
Explain reason insulin is needed, its action, and expected effect.	Individualizing information enhances learning and acceptance.
Discuss species and types of insulin to be used, explaining differences in action and appearance (clear/cloudy).	Human insulin is preferred for those starting insulin therapy, especially if expected to be used intermittently. Fast-acting insulin onset, 30 min; peak, 3–4 hr; duration, 6–8 hr. Intermediate acting insulin onset, 1 hr; peak, 8–10 hr; duration, 18–24 hr.
Describe and demonstrate the sizes and types of syringes available. Recommend the syringe size appropriate for the expected dose of insulin.	Awareness of differences in syringe sizes can prevent incorrect doses using unfamiliar syringes.
Demonstrate drawing up insulin, including 1. cleaning hands and injection site 2. wiping top of bottle with alcohol 3. rolling intermediate insulin 4. adding air equal to the dose 5. if mixing insulins, drawing fast insulin into syringe first	Equalizing air prevents formation of a vacuum in insulin bottle. Inadvertent mixing of fast insulin into intermediate insulin bottle is less dangerous than vice versa

Nursing Interventions	Rationales
Demonstrate injection process, including	
1. 90° angle into subcutaneous tissue and 45° angle if thin	Intramuscular injection is not recommended due to faster absorption.
2. no aspiration and no rubbing of site after injection	Rubbing speeds absorption and action time.
Demonstrate recommended injection sites, including abdomen, arms, thighs, and buttocks. Explain reason for site rotation. Encourage rotation within one area for each injection rather than random rotation.	Prevents lipohypertrophy or lipoatrophy. Absorption is fastest in the abdomen, followed by the arms, thighs, and buttocks. Using one area per injection results in more predictable absorption and action time.
Observe performance of skills and give positive reinforcement.	Performing skill is essential to learning.
Describe syringe disposal:	
1. Place in a puncture-resistant disposal container.	Firm plastic bottles such as empty detergent bottles are acceptable.
2. Dispose of two-thirds full container meeting local regulations.	Many pharmacies, hospitals, and clinics will dispose of containers.
If the patient prefers to reuse syringes, explain recommendations: 1. Recap after use. 2. Do not wipe off; soak in alcohol. 3. Stop use if syringe is dull, bent, or comes in contact with any surface other than skin.	While manufacturers do not recommend syringe reuse, studies have found no infections or other problems when patients reuse their own syringes. It is not recommended with poor hygiene, decreased resistance to infection, acute concurrent illness, or open wounds on hands.
Recommend storage of insulin at room temperature while in use and in the refrigerator prior to opening. Keep within a range of 36–86 °F. Avoid using bottle longer than 30 days.	Insulin at room temperature is more comfortable. Potency will decrease after 30 days if kept at room temperature. If stored in refrigerator, potency is good until expiration date.
Define normal blood sugar values and coordinate with physician to set blood sugar goals with patient.	

Nursing Interventions	Rationales
Discuss symptoms of hyperglycemia and hypoglycemia, significance, treatment, and prevention.	
Assist patient in establishing a plan to prevent and treat hypoglycemia with blood glucose monitoring (BGM), carrying 15 g of glucose and understanding the effect of food and activity on blood sugar.	Recommended treatment is 15 g of fast-acting carbohydrate repeated in 10 min if blood glucose is less than 80 or if symptoms remain.
Instruct family on the use of the glucagon emergency kit.	Glucagon should be given immediately if the patient is unconscious or unable or unwilling to swallow.
Demonstrate use and provide with equipment and supplies for BGM.	Blood glucose monitoring is recommended for anyone using insulin.
Observe BGM technique and assess for accuracy by comparing to a simultaneous laboratory value.	Capillary-meter results are usually higher than laboratory values and should be within 15% of laboratory value.
Demonstrate ketone testing for patients with Type I diabetes. Instruct on use when ill or when blood sugar is higher than 250 mg/dL.	Ketones normally will not form in Type II diabetes.

DISCHARGE PLANNING/CONTINUITY OF CARE

- Assure understanding and ability to inject correct dose, test blood sugar, and recognize and treat hypoglycemia and hyperglycemia.
- Provide with needed supplies and prescriptions and discuss a plan for refills. Be aware of insurance/health maintenance organization requirements for obtaining supplies and equipment.
- Consult a home health agency if assistance or ongoing teaching is required.
- Arrange follow-up physician and/or diabetes nurse educator for questions and continued management.
- Provide with information on diabetes support groups in the area, American Diabetes Association affiliate office, and publications and other ongoing diabetes assistive services.

REFERENCES

American Diabetes Association Position Statement: Insulin Administration. (1990). *Diabetes Care, 13*(Suppl. 1), 28–31.

Bante, J., Weber, M., Rao, S., Challapadhyay, M., & Robertson, R. (1990). Rotation of the anatomic regions used for insulin injections and day-to-day variability of plasma glucose in Type I diabetic subjects. *JAMA, 13*, 1802–1806.

Guthrie, D. (1988). *Diabetes education: Core curriculum for health professional.* Chicago, IL: American Association of Diabetes Educators.

Tattersall, R. B. & Gale, E. A. (1990). *Diabetes clinical management.* New York: Churchill Livingstone.

Zehrer, C., et al. (1990). Reducing blood glucose variability by use of abdominal insulin injection sites. *Diabetes Educator, 16*(6), 474–477.

Common Neurological Conditions and Procedures

▼

ALTERED CONSCIOUSNESS

Andrea Strayer, RN, MS, CNRN

Consciousness consists of arousal (alertness) and content (awareness). The reticular activating system is a physiological entity which enables a person to be aroused. The cerebral cortex enables thought, expression, and higher cortical functions. Altered consciousness indicates brain dysfunction or failure. Consciousness is the most sensitive indicator of neurological change. A change in the level of consciousness can occur rapidly or very slowly; it can be subtle or severe.

ETIOLOGIES

- Mass lesions
  - traumatic brain injury
  - destructive lesions of the thalamus
  - hemorrhage
  - infarction
  - tumor
  - abscess
- Metabolic, diffuse, or multifocal causes
  - encephalitis
  - uremia
  - hypoglycemia
  - hypoxia
  - ischemia
  - sedative drugs; barbiturates, ethanol, opiates, tranquilizers
  - electrolyte imbalance

CLINICAL MANIFESTATIONS

- Confused: requires repetition of instruction, disoriented
- Lethargy: oriented but slow to respond, slowed mental processes

- Obtundation: readily arousable with stimulation, very drowsy, can follow simple commands
- Stupor: requires vigorous stimuli to respond, requires continued stimuli to keep awake
- Coma: appears to be in sleeplike state, does not respond appropriately to stimuli
- Persistent vegetative state: has sleep-wake cycles, but at no time is aware of self or environment

CLINICAL/DIAGNOSTIC FINDINGS

- Head computerized tomography (CT) or head magnetic resonance imaging (MRI): will show a mass lesion
- Laboratory data: will delineate metabolic disorders
  - hyper/hypoglycemia
  - complete blood count: elevated white blood cell (WBC) count
  - electrolytes: hypo/hypernatremia, hypercalcemia, hypomagnesia
  - arterial blood gases: respiratory or metabolic alkalosis or acidosis, hypoxemia
  - elevated liver enzymes
  - elevated blood urea nitrogen (BUN) and creatinine
  - elevated thyroid function tests
  - toxicology screen

OTHER PLANS OF CARE TO REFERENCE

- Nutrition Support: Enteral Nutrition

NURSING DIAGNOSIS: DECREASED INTRACRANIAL ADAPTIVE CAPACITY

Related To compromised intracranial fluid compensatory mechanisms

Defining Characteristics
Increased intracranial pressure
Increased lethargy, somnolence
Decreased mental status
Pupil changes
Vital sign changes: widening pulse pressure

Patient Outcomes
The patient will
- demonstrate a decrease in intracranial pressure.
- demonstrate orientation to person, place, and time.

- demonstrate normal pupillary reaction and accommodation.
- demonstrate vital signs within their normal limits.

Nursing Interventions	Rationales
Elevate the head of bed at least 30°.	Elevating the head of the bed and maintaining the patient's head and neck promote venous drainage, decreasing intracranial pressure. Additionally, it will promote oxygenation and help prevent aspiration.
Maintain the patient's head in neutral alignment.	
Provide the patient with rest periods between cares; do not cluster patient care activities.	By not clustering stimulation to patients, it helps keep their intracranial pressure low.
Perform a neurological exam as often as is warranted. This may be hourly when the patient is unstable. Assessment of level of consciousness, mental status, cranial nerves, pupils, motor strength, reflexes, sensation, and vital signs should be included in a comprehensive exam. Routine checks should be tailored to fit the patient's needs.	
Notify physician immediately of any changes in the neurological exam.	
Maintain a quiet environment; visitors may need to be limited while the patient is unstable.	Less stimulation will help keep the intracranial pressure down. This is only necessary when the patient is unstable. For instance, a patient in a chronic vegetative state requires stimulation.

NURSING DIAGNOSIS: INEFFECTIVE AIRWAY CLEARANCE
Related To
- Increased lethargy
- Impaired airway protection
- Decreased or absent spontaneous cough

Defining Characteristics
Abnormal breath sounds
Change in rate and/or depth of respirations
Tachypnea

Patient Outcomes
The patient will maintain a patent airway, as evidenced by
- normal breath sounds
- normal rate and depth of respirations

Nursing Interventions	Rationales
Assess respiratory status, including observing rate and rhythm; auscultate breath sounds at least every 4 hr.	Provides objective data on which to base interventions.
Provide pulmonary care, including cough and deep breath, oral or nasotracheal suctioning, as warranted, at least every 4 hr.	Promotes oxygenation.
Turn the patient from side to side; do not lie flat on back.	Prevents airway occlusion and promotes drainage of secretions.

NURSING DIAGNOSIS: HIGH RISK FOR INJURY

Risk Factors
- Confusion
- Lethargy

Patient Outcomes
The patient will be free of injury.

Nursing Interventions	Rationales
Keep all side rails up, bed in low position.	
Reorient the patient frequently.	
Place the patient in a room close to the nurses' station.	

Nursing Interventions	Rationales
Ask the family to bring familiar objects to put in the room.	
Keep a light on in the patient's room and the door open.	
Make sure the call light and essential items are always within reach.	
Observe the patient frequently.	
Utilize a bed monitor that will alert you when the patient is getting out of bed.	
Consider all of the above before using soft restraints or a posey vest.	

DISCHARGE PLANNING/CONTINUITY OF CARE

- Coordinate with the discharge planning nurse or social worker, if available, to plan discharge arrangements for caregiver, home health agency, or nursing home.
- Assure care provider understands and can perform ongoing care needed.
- Assure arrangements are made to obtain supplies, equipment, and medication prescriptions.
- Arrange follow-up with physician or nurse practitioner for continued management and postdischarge care. Assure telephone numbers are provided if questions or problems develop.

ACKNOWLEDGMENT

This work was supported by the Department of Veteran Affairs.

REFERENCES

Barker, E. & Moore, K. (1992). Neurological assessment. *RN, 55*(4), 28–34.

Cammermeyer, M. & Appledorn, C. (Eds.). (1990). *Core curriculum for neuroscience nursing* (3rd ed). Chicago, IL: American Association of Neuroscience Nurses.

Hickey, J. (1992). *The clinical practice of neurological and neurosurgical nursing* (3rd ed). Philadelphia, PA: Lippincott.

Lower, J. (1992). Rapid neuroassessment. *American Journal of Nursing,* 92(6), 38–45.

Plum, F. & Posner, J. (1980). *The diagnosis of stupor and coma* (3rd ed). Philadelphia, PA: Davis.

Sullivan, J. (1990). Neurological assessment. *Nursing Clinics of North America,* 25(4), 795–806.

▼

_B_RAIN TUMORS

Andrea Strayer, RN, MS, CNRN

Brain tumors affect the brain by compressing and infiltrating normal brain tissue. This results in cerebral edema, neurological deficits, and seizures. There is no known cure for brain tumors. Brain tumors can be classified by malignancy, histological origin, primary or metastatic, location, and neuroembryonic origin. See Table 29.1 for a summary of common adult brain tumors.

ETIOLOGIES

- Unknown

CLINICAL MANIFESTATIONS

- Headache
- Seizures
- Vomiting
- Papilledema
- Mental status changes
- Visual changes
- Motor deficits
- Personality changes

CLINICAL/DIAGNOSTIC FINDINGS

Head computerized tomography (CT) scan or head magnetic resonance imaging (MRI): Visualize the mass.

OTHER PLANS OF CARE TO REFERENCE

- Craniotomy
- Alterations in Consciousness
- Basic Standard for Preoperative and Postoperative Care

Table 29.1 • Common Adult Brain Tumors

Astrocytoma (grades I and II)
- Complete surgical removal rare, but may prolong life
- Irradiation for some; possibly chemotherapy
- 6–7 years prognosis, more possible

Glioblastoma multiforme (also known as astrocytoma grades III and IV)
- Surgery and debulking to decrease intracranial pressure and relieve cerebral compression
- Irradiation for some; possibly chemotherapy also
- 1–2 years prognosis

Ependymoma (grades I–IV)
- Arises from lining of ventricles
- Causes rapid increase in intracranial pressure from cerebrospinal fluid obstruction
- Tumor of children and young adults
- Surgery, if accessible, irradiation or chemotherapy for some
- 1 month prognosis for malignant; 7–8 years for benign

Oligodendroglioma (grades I–IV)
- Surgery and irradiation treatment of choice
- 5 or more years prognosis

Meningioma
- Complete removal surgically, if possible; irradiation if complete resection not possible
- Many years prognosis, especially with complete resection

Metastatic brain tumor
- Surgery, if resectable; irradiation may be an option
- Poor prognosis

Primary cerebral lymphoma
- Irradiation
- 2 years prognosis

Pituitary adenoma
- Surgery and/or irradiation
- Will see visual problems and endocrine disorders
- Prognosis very good

▼

NURSING DIAGNOSIS: KNOWLEDGE DEFICIT—DIAGNOSIS

Related To
- New diagnosis
- Fear
- Lack of exposure to information

Defining Characteristics
Many questions
Few questions
Exaggerated behaviors

Patient Outcomes
The patient will
- verbalize his or her diagnosis and its implications.
- describe available treatment options.

Nursing Interventions	Rationales
Ask patients to describe what they have been told about the diagnosis.	This gives you a baseline of their current knowledge.
Clarify the patient's understanding of the diagnosis and treatment options.	This gives you the opportunity to clarify misconceptions and repeat things they were not sure about.
Clarify the patient's understanding of the pros and cons of the treatment options.	This gives the patient the freedom to be in control.
Encourage to ask questions and raise concerns.	It is important with the vast amounts of information that they have a system for keeping track of it all.
Encourage to keep a notebook of information received and questions they wish to ask.	

NURSING DIAGNOSIS: HIGH RISK FOR INEFFECTIVE INDIVIDUAL COPING

Risk Factors
- New diagnosis of possible terminal illness
- Potential poor prognosis
- Lack of support people

Patient Outcomes
The patient will
- develop effective coping mechanisms.
- vent fears, frustrations, questions, or concerns.

Nursing Interventions	Rationales
Allow time to vent fears and ask questions. Be reassuring.	The patient needs time to adjust to the diagnosis.
Provide emotional support.	
Consult counselor or clergy.	
Assess family support systems and their ability to cope.	At this time, the family may also need additional resources to help cope.
Provide with an address of a national support group.	American Brain Tumor Association; 3725 Talman Avenue; Chicago, IL 60618. National Brain Tumor Foundation; 323 Geary Street, Suite, 510; San Francisco, CA 94102.

DISCHARGE PLANNING/CONTINUITY OF CARE

- Coordinate follow-up with radiation oncology as indicated.
- Arrange for referral to a home health agency if continued care, monitoring, or teaching is needed.
- Provide with information on the American Cancer Society, support groups, hospice care, and I Can Cope.
- Assure follow-up appointments with physician or nurse practitioner for continued care.

REFERENCES

Adams, B., Clancey, J., & Eddy, M. (1991). Malignant glioma: Current treatment perspectives. *Journal of Neuroscience Nursing, 23*(1), 15–19.

Amato, C. (1991). Malignant glioma: Coping with a devastating illness. *Journal of Neuroscience Nursing, 23*(1), 20–22.

Cammermeyer, M. & Appeldorn, C. (Eds.). (1990). *Core curriculum for neuroscience nursing* (3rd ed). Chicago, IL: American Association of Neuroscience Nurses.

Hickey, J. (1992). *The clinical practice of neurological and neurosurgical nursing* (3rd ed). Philadelphia, PA: Lippincott.

Willis, D. (1991). Intracranial astrocytoma: Pathology, diagnosis and clinical presentation. *Journal of Neuroscience Nursing, 23*(1), 7–14.

CRANIOTOMY

Andrea Stayer RN, MS, CNRN

A craniotomy is indicated for the removal of an unwanted mass or lesion in the brain. During a craniotomy the neurosurgeon makes an incision in the scalp, making a scalp flap. Burr holes are made through the skull and then a saw is used, connecting the burr holes. The piece of skull usually stays attached to the muscle; it is pulled over to make a flap. An incision is made in the dura mater. After the dura is retracted, the brain is exposed. After the surgery, the dura is sutured closed, the bone and muscle flap are replaced, and the skin is stapled into place. Occasionally, the bone is not replaced; this is called a craniectomy. Cranioplasty is a surgical procedure to repair the skull.

ETIOLOGIES (INDICATIONS)

- Tumor
- Arteriovenous malformation
- Aneurysm
- Foreign object removal
- Epilepsy surgery

CLINICAL MANIFESTATIONS

As seen with specific etiology

CLINICAL/DIAGNOSTIC FINDINGS

- Head computerized tomography (CT) or head magnetic resonance imaging (MRI): visualize etiology
- Cerebral angiography: assists with visualization of aneurysms and arteriovenous malformations

OTHER PLANS OF CARE TO REFERENCE

- Basic Standards for Preoperative and Postoperative Care
- Brain Tumors
- Ventricular Shunts
- Altered Consciousness

NURSING DIAGNOSIS: KNOWLEDGE DEFICIT OF PRE- AND POSTOPERATIVE EXPECTATIONS

Related To
- Lack of information
- Fear
- New diagnosis
- Anxiety

Defining Characteristics

Asking no questions
Asking many questions
Exaggerated behavior

Patient Outcomes

The patient will
- describe the procedure and indications for it.
- verbalize what to expect during the postoperative period.

Nursing Interventions	Rationales
Preoperatively, review the reason for surgery and give the opportunity to vent fears and questions.	
Explain what to expect postoperatively, including 1. frequent neurological assessments 2. staying in the intensive care unit 3. when they can expect transfer to general care 4. pain they may experience and what type of pain relief will be available to them 5. areas of hair requiring shaving	

Nursing Interventions

In preparation for discharge:
1. Instruct on care of craniotomy incision.
2. Instruct on signs and symptoms of increased intracranial pressure and who to call if any of these signs develop.
3. Instruct on signs and symptoms of infection of the incision and who to call if any develop. If this develops, antibiotic therapy may be warranted. Medical attention is required to prevent the spread of infection.

Rationales

NURSING DIAGNOSIS: HIGH RISK FOR ALTERED CEREBRAL TISSUE PERFUSION

Risk Factors
- Cerebral edema
- Hemorrhage
- Vessel occlusion

Patient Outcomes
The patient will
- verbalize orientation to person, place, and time.
- demonstrate normal strength and motion of all extremities.

Nursing Interventions

Perform neurological exam every hour in the immediate postoperative period; liberalize as patient stabilizes. The comprehensive neurological exam includes assessment of
1. level of consciousness
2. mental status
3. cranial nerves
4. pupils
5. motor strength
6. reflexes
7. sensation
8. vital signs

Rationales

The patient's neurological exam, especially level of consciousness, is of primary importance. A change in level of consciousness is the first sign of increase in intracranial pressure.

Nursing Interventions	Rationales
Elevate head of bed at least 30°. Keep head in neutral position.	Facilitates venous drainage, which helps lower intracranial pressure.
Notify a physician immediately if the patient develops a deterioration in the neurological exam.	The physician may order medical interventions.
Give osmotics as prescribed. Mannitol and urea may be given to decrease cerebral edema. This is usually not necessary postoperatively.	Mannitol and urea decrease cerebral edema by osmosis. They are often administered intraoperatively to decrease the moisture of the brain tissue. If they are required postoperatively, the patient would generally be in an intensive care unit.
Anticipate diagnostic tests such as a head CT.	

NURSING DIAGNOSIS: IMPAIRED SKIN INTEGRITY

Related To craniotomy incision

Defining Characteristics
Disruption of skin surface and layers

Patient Outcome
The patient's skin will heal without complication, as evidenced by no infection at craniotomy suture line.

Nursing Interventions	Rationales
Do not remove the dressing that the neurosurgeon has applied. If it becomes loose, reinforce it.	Risk of infection is decreased by leaving the dressing in place.
After the dressing has been removed, clean the incision twice daily with normal saline.	
Observe for redness, drainage, puffiness, or fever.	
In preparation for discharge, instruct on incision care and signs and symptoms of infection.	

▼

DISCHARGE PLANNING/CONTINUITY OF CARE

- Assure understanding of postoperative care at home, symptoms to report, and who to call.
- Refer to a home health care agency if continued nursing care or teaching is needed.
- Arrange follow-up with physician or nurse practitioner for continued management and postdischarge needs.

ACKNOWLEDGMENT

This work was supported by the Department of Veteran Affairs.

REFERENCES

Cammermeyer, M. & Appeldorn, C. (1990). *Core curriculum for neuroscience nursing* (3rd ed). Chicago, IL: American Association of Neuroscience Nurses.

Hickey, J. (1992). *The clinical practice of neurological and neurosurgical nursing* (3rd ed). Philadelphia, PA: Lippincott.

Kane, D. (1991). Practical points in the postoperative error management of a craniotomy patient. *Journal of Post Anesthesia Nursing, 6*(2), 121–124.

▼

LUMBAR PUNCTURE

Rochelle M. Carlson, RN, MS, CRRN

A lumbar puncture (LP) is the introduction of a sterile needle into the subarachnoid space at either level L_3–L_4 or L_4–L_5 using strict aseptic technique. The procedure is more commonly performed for diagnostic purposes but may also be used as a therapeutic measure.

ETIOLOGIES

- Diagnostic indications
  - examination of the characteristics of the cerebrospinal fluid (CSF)
  - measurement of the pressure of CSF
  - visualization of the parts of the nervous system radiographically by injection of contrast medium
- Therapeutic indications
  - intrathecal administration of anesthetic, antibiotics, steroids, or other medications

CONTRAINDICATIONS

- Infection at the site of lumbar puncture
- Greatly increased intracranial pressure

CLINICAL MANIFESTATIONS

- Fever
- Nuchal rigidity
- Change in level of consciousness
- Muscle weakness
- Other abnormal findings on neurological examination
- Pain

CLINICAL/DIAGNOSTIC FINDINGS

See Table 31.1

NURSING DIAGNOSIS: KNOWLEDGE DEFICIT—LUMBAR PUNCTURE PROCEDURE

Related To lack of exposure to procedure

Defining Characteristics

Many questions
Lack of questions
Fear of complications
Anxiety about possible diagnostic findings

Patient Outcomes

The patient will
- explain why the procedure is necessary.
- describe preprocedure preparation.
- demonstrate correct positioning during the procedure.
- describe postprocedure plan of care.
- identify health care providers to contact if questions arise following the procedure.

Nursing Interventions	Rationales
Assess the patient's understanding and fears regarding the procedure.	
Provide written as well as oral instruction when possible.	Written materials are helpful for later reference.
Explain why the procedure is indicated for this patient.	Clear explanations can prevent misunderstandings and decrease anxiety.
Describe desired outcome: diagnostic findings or therapeutic response.	
Discuss possible complications of the procedure.	Information about complications is necessary for informed consent for procedures.
Instruct the patient to be well hydrated before the procedure.	Dehydration may contribute to a postprocedure spinal headache.

Table 31.1 • Normal and Abnormal Characteristics of Cerebrospinal Fluid

Characteristic	Normal	Abnormal
Color	Clear, colorless	Cloudy: may be due to presence of bacteria or white blood cells (WBCs).
		Yellow: xanthochronic, most often due to red blood cell (RBC) breakdown.
RBC	None	Presence could be due to a traumatic tap or subarachnoid hemorrhage.
WBC	0–5/mm^3, agranulocytes	Increased WBC count associated with meningitis, tumor, multiple sclerosis, infarct, abscess, or subarachnoid hemorrhage.
Glucose	50–80 mg/100 mL	Decreased level may be suggestive of bacteria in CSF
		Increased level: no significance.
Protein	15–45 mg/100 mL	Increased level associated with tumor, infection, hemorrhage, and demyelinating disease.
		Decreased level: no significance.
Chloride	120–130 mEq/L	Low concentration associated with meningitis
Pressure	70–180 mmH$_2$O	More than 200 mmH$_2$O often seen with tumor, cerebral edema, hydrocephalus, cerebral hemorrhage, abscess, or cyst.
		Less than 50 mmH$_2$O seen in spinal block.
Culture and sensitivity	No bacteria	Presence of bacteria or fungus seen in meningitis or abscess.
		Sensitivity used to help determine appropriate antimicrobial therapy.

▼

Nursing Interventions	Rationales
Describe the procedure and the position that the patient will assume for the procedure (fetal position with the back at the edge of the bed or sitting on the exam table leaning forward).	These positions allow for greatest access to the subarachnoid space by separating the vertebral bodies.
Explain postprocedure care (flat position, drinking plenty of fluids, vital signs, and neurological checks).	Postprocedure care is aimed at recognizing and minimizing complications.
Inform the patient of who to call if questions arise pre- or postprocedure.	

NURSING DIAGNOSIS: HIGH RISK FOR PAIN

Risk Factors
- Positioning
- Introduction of the spinal needle
- Leakage of CSF

Patient Outcomes
The patient will
- experience no pain or mild pain.
- notify a health care professional if experiencing postprocedure pain.

Nursing Interventions	Rationales
Assess pain level and location (headache when assuming an upright position, low back pain, pain radiating into the legs) pre- and postprocedure.	
Position flat for 4–24 hr following the procedure.	Post-LP headaches are thought to be caused by leakage of CSF from the LP site. A flat position is believed to decrease the chances of CSF leakage. The length of time a patient should lay flat is decided by patient history and physician preference.

Nursing Interventions	Rationales
Encourage a large intake of fluids postprocedure	Extra fluids will potentiate the body, making more CSF to replace the fluid that was withdrawn in the procedure.
Administer analgesics as prescribed when pain does occur.	Acetaminophen is used for mild pain while narcotics may be used for severe pain.
Reassure the patient that back pain and extremity pain are usually transitory.	

NURSING DIAGNOSIS: HIGH RISK FOR INFECTION/ INCREASED INTRACRANIAL PRESSURE

Risk Factors
- Break in aseptic technique during LP procedure
- Elevated CSF pressure prior to LP procedure

Patient Outcome
The patient will
- be free from infection postprocedure.
- not have a rise in intracranial pressure postprocedure

Nursing Interventions	Rationales
Assess for vital signs, neurological status (level of consciousness, orientation, sensation, movement, and strength), respiratory pattern, and presence of nuchal rigidity preprocedure.	
Assist the physician as needed during the procedure to maintain aseptic technique.	The physician will be performing the following steps: sterile draping, cleansing the site, administering local anesthesia, measuring pressure and gathering fluid into sterile containers or instilling medication.
If necessary, assist in holding the patient in position.	The patient needs to remain still during the procedure to maintain asepsis and to prevent trauma.

Nursing Interventions	Rationales
Apply a Band-Aid after removal of the needle to protect the puncture site from pathogens.	
Assess for fever, nuchal rigidity, and redness or warmth at the site of needle insertion following the procedure. 1. Notify physician if these symptoms of infection are present. 2. Teach outpatients to notify nurse or physician if these symptoms occur.	
Assess vital signs, neurological status, and respiratory patterns at least every 30 min for the first 2 hr and then every hour for the next 2 hr following the procedure or as prescribed by the physician. 1. Notify physician if symptoms of increased intracranial pressure are present 2. Teach outpatients to notify nurse or physician if change in level of consciousness or disturbances in sensation or motor function occur.	

DISCHARGE PLANNING/CONTINUITY OF CARE

- Assure that the patient understands symptoms (e.g., persistent headache, fever, and redness or warmth at site of insertion) to report to nurse or physician.
- Report assessment data and care given to next shift of nurses.
- Ensure that a driver is available for patients going home following the procedure. A LP commonly performed in outpatient as well as inpatient settings.
- Provide written information, including number of nurse or physician to call, if patient is going home after procedure.
- Arrange follow-up with physician for continued management and postdischarge care.

REFERENCES

Cammermeyer, M., & Appeldorn, C. (Eds.). (1990). *Core curriculum for neuroscience nursing.* Chicago, IL: American Association of Neuroscience Nurses.

Hickey, J. V. (1992). *The clinical practice of neurological and neurosurgical nursing* (3rd ed). Philadelphia, PA: Lippincott.

Snyder, M. (Ed.). (1991). *A guide to neurological and neurosurgical nursing* (2nd ed). Albany, NY: Delmar.

$\mathcal{V}$ENTRICULAR SHUNTS

Andrea Strayer, RN, MS, CNRN

The central nervous system (CNS) ventricular system is responsible for the production and reabsorption of cerebrospinal fluid (CSF). Approximately 500 mL of CSF is made each day. At any one time, 125–150 mL of CSF is circulating in the ventricular system. Cerebrospinal fluid is made in the choroid plexus in the third, fourth, and lateral ventricles. Acting as a cushion, CSF travels around the spinal cord and brain, being reabsorbed by the arachnoid villi. A ventricular shunt may be needed if the flow of the CSF becomes obstructed, if it is not being reabsorbed properly, or if there is overproduction of CSF. Primarily ventriculoperitoneal shunts are used. Through a burr hole, the primary catheter of the shunt is surgically placed in the lateral ventricle. The reservoir, which has a one-way valve to prevent CSF reflux, is then placed under the scalp and attached to the primary catheter. Finally, the terminal catheter, which ends in the peritoneal cavity, is attached to the reservoir.

ETIOLOGIES

- Noncommunicating hydrocephalus: an obstruction of the ventricular system
  - mass (tumor)
  - congenital malformation
  - inflammatory
- Communicating hydrocephalus: the arachnoid villi are unable to reabsorb the CSF sufficiently
  - subarachnoid hemorrhage
  - meningitis
- Normal pressure hydrocephalus: ventricular enlargement with normal CSF pressure
  - subarachnoid hemorrhage
  - thrombosis of the superior sagittal sinus
  - head trauma
  - meningitis

CLINICAL MANIFESTATIONS

- Lethargy
- Vomiting
- Mental status changes
- Decreased level of consciousness
- Change of gait
- Urinary incontinence

CLINICAL/DIAGNOSTIC FINDINGS

- Head computerized tomography (CT) shows ventricular dilatation
- Elevated CSF pressure (except with normal pressure hydrocephalus

OTHER PLANS OF CARE TO REFERENCE

- Alterations in consciousness
- Craniotomy
- Basic Standards for Preoperative and Postoperative Care

NURSING DIAGNOSIS: KNOWLEDGE DEFICIT OF PURPOSE FOR SHUNT SYSTEM, SIGNS AND SYMPTOMS OF MALFUNCTION AND INFECTION

Related To lack of exposure to information

Defining Characteristics
Fear
Asking many questions
Asking very few questions

Patient Outcomes
The patient will
- verbalize the signs and symptoms of increased intracranial pressure
- verbalize the signs and symptoms of infection of the shunt system
- verbalize the discharge plan, stating who should be contacted if problems or questions arise.

Nursing Interventions	Rationales
Assess for willingness to learn and cognitive abilities.	Postoperative pain may interfere with learning. Baseline cognitive status will structure the teaching.

Nursing Interventions	Rationales
Discuss the specific purpose for the shunt and provide the patient with written materials.	
Explain the signs and symptoms of shunt malfunction, including headache, vomiting, mental status changes, gait changes, lethargy, and when and who to notify if these occur.	These are all signs of increased intracranial pressure.
Explain the signs and symptoms of infection, including: redness, swelling, or drainage at the incision sites; abdominal tenderness or pain; nausea and vomiting; neck pain; and photophobia.	

NURSING DIAGNOSIS: DECREASED INTRACRANIAL ADAPTIVE CAPACITY

Related To compromised intracranial fluid compensatory mechanisms

Defining Characteristics
Increased intracranial pressure
Decreased level of consciousness

Patient Outcomes
The patient will
- demonstrate alertness and orientation to name, place, and time.
- demonstrate normal pupillary reaction and accommodation.
- demonstrate vital signs within their normal limits.

Nursing Interventions	Rationales
Elevate the head of bed at least 30°.	Elevating the head of bed promotes venous drainage and promotes oxygenation.

Nursing Interventions	Rationales
Perform a neurological exam as often as is warranted. This may be hourly if the patient is unstable. Assessment of level of consciousness, mental status, cranial nerves, pupils, motor strength, reflexes, sensation, and vital signs should be included in a comprehensive exam. Routine checks should be tailored to fit the patient's needs.	If the patient's neurological status declines, the shunt may need pumping or it may be malfunctioning.
Notify the physician immediately of any changes in the patient's neurological status.	

DISCHARGE PLANNING/CONTINUITY OF CARE

- Assure patient and significant other have an understanding of signs and symptoms of shunt malfunction and infection.
- Refer patient to a home health care agency if continued nursing care or teaching is needed.
- Assure that a follow-up appointment with the physician or nurse practitioner has been made.
- Give the appropriate telephone number to call if problems or questions arise.
- Provide with address of national support group: Hydrocephalus Association, 870 Market Street #955, San Francisco, CA 94102.

ACKNOWLEDGMENT

This work was supported by the Department of Veteran Affairs.

REFERENCES

Cammermeyer, M. & Appeldorn, C. (Eds.). (1990). *Core curriculum for neuroscience nursing* (3rd ed). Chicago, IL: American Association of Neuroscience Nurses.

Greif, L., & Miller, C. (1991). Shunt lengthening: A descriptive review. *Journal of Neuroscience Nursing*, 23(2), 120–124.

Hickey, J. (1992). *The clinical practice of neurological and neurosurgical nursing* (3rd ed). Philadelphia, PA: Lippincott.

Kirk, E., White, C., & Freeman, S. (1992). Effects of nursing education intervention on parents' knowledge of hydrocephalus and shunts. *The Journal of Neuroscience Nursing, 24*(2), 99–103.

Masters, J., & O'Grady, M. (1992). Normal pressure hydrocephalus: A potentially reversible form of dementia. *Journal of Psychosocial Nursing, 30*(6), 25–28.

▼

Common Renal Conditions and Procedures

▼

$\mathcal{H}$EMODIALYSIS

Lynn Schoengrund, RN, MS

Hemodialysis is one form of renal replacement therapy for patients with acute and chronic renal failure. It is the passing of blood over a semipermeable membrane to remove the excess fluids, electrolytes, and metabolites that accumulate in all body tissues when renal failure occurs. Three components must be present to perform hemodialysis. One is an access to a large blood supply that will allow blood flow up to 500 mL/min. The second component is the dialyzer, or artificial kidney, which is the semipermeable membrane over which blood is passed. Excess solutes are removed from the blood by the processes of diffusion and fluid movement and solute drag. Fluid is removed by ultrafiltration, the movement of fluid under pressure. The third component is a fluid called dialysate, which is circulated on the other side of the semipermeable membrane. Dialysate mimics normal serum, containing normal or slightly less than normal quantities of sodium, chloride, potassium, bicarbonate, and calcium. Dialysate can be altered or prescribed to add or delete electrolytes for specific patient conditions.

ETIOLOGIES

- Diabetes
- Glomerulonephritis
- Chronic hypertension
- Polycystic kidneys
- Autoimmune disorders, for example, lupus or Goodpasture's
- Progression of acute renal failure to chronic renal failure
- Chronic acetaminophen use or abuse
- Heroin use

CLINICAL MANIFESTATIONS

- Severe fatigue
- Anorexia, nausea, vomiting

- Pallor
- Signs of fluid overload

CLINICAL/DIAGNOSTIC FINDINGS

- Increased creatinine, BUN
- Decreased creatine clearance to 5–10% of normal
- Altered serum electrolytes, especially potassium

OTHER PLANS OF CARE TO REFERENCE

- Peritoneal Dialysis

NURSING DIAGNOSIS: HIGH RISK FOR INFECTION

Risk Factors
- Frequent invasive procedure
- Exposure of blood and body fluids to extracorporeal equipment
- Exposure to blood-borne pathogens, for example, hepatitis and human immunodeficiency virus (HIV)
- Chronic illness

Patient Outcomes
Patient is free from infection.

Nursing Interventions	Rationales
Discuss the need for vaccinating against hepatitis B infection with the patient and family and administer the vaccine as prescribed prior to or as the patient begins chronic dialysis.	High-risk groups should be immunized against hepatitis. During the 1970s hepatitis was epidemic in dialysis units. Generally patient's infections are benign, but spread to family members or staff is common.

Nursing Interventions	**Rationales**
Use Universal Precautions and follow OSHA guidelines to prevent the spread of blood-borne infections to self or others.	Spread of blood-borne infections is well documented in epidemiological studies of dialysis patients. Despite immunization against hepatitis B, hepatitis C and HIV remain risks as well as other unknown viral agents. The mode of transmission of hepatitis B and C and HIV requires blood-to-blood or mucous-membrane-blood contact. This mode encompasses the ingestion of the virus from contaminated surfaces, sexual activity, and blood contact with open cuts or sores.
Inspect the fistula or graft (Figures 33.1 and 33.2) daily for signs of infection, especially at needle insertion sites. Look for redness; palpate for heat. Inspect for purulent drainage or whitened areas at needle sites. Regular needle insertion into the fistula or graft increases the risk of infection.	Early diagnosis and treatment may prevent the development of septicemia. Grafts may need to be surgically removed to prevent life threatening-infection.

NURSING DIAGNOSIS: FLUID VOLUME DEFICIT

Related To excessive ultrafiltration of fluid during dialysis.

Defining Characteristics
Hypotension, orthostatic hypotension
Excessive fatigue, weakness, or dizziness
Rapid or thready pulse
Decreased weight

Patient Outcomes
- Weight, blood pressure, and pulse are stable.
- The patient does not report increased fatigue, weakness, or dizziness.

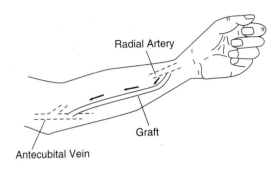

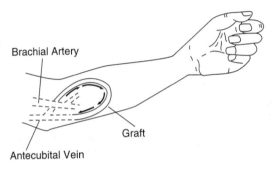

Figure 33.1 The placement of straight and curved grafts between arteries and veins. Arrows indicate the flow of blood through the grafts. From *Renal Problems in Critical Care* (p. 79) by Schoengrund and Balzer, 1985, Albany, NY: Delmar. Copyright 1985 by Delmar Publishers. Reprinted by permission.

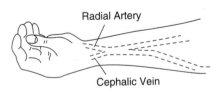

Figure 33.2 AV fistula. The radial artery is shown in a side-to-side anastomosis with the cephalic vein. After maturation, needles are placed in the vein for hemodialysis. From *Renal Problems in Critical Care* (p. 77) by Schoengrund and Balzer, 1985, Albany, NY: Delmar. Copyright 1985 by Delmar Publishers. Reprinted by permission.

Nursing Interventions

Assess the fluid status after dialysis:
1. Compare the predialysis weight to postdialysis weight.
2. Compare blood pressure values pre- and postdialysis.
3. Assess the jugular vein with the patient lying flat; the vein should be filled.

Assess for symptoms of dizziness, increased fatigue, and weakness. Assess the patient's ability to stand and ambulate.

Rationales

Hemodialysis removes fluid from vascular space. Fluid moves into the vascular space from the interstitial space and finally from the cellular space. There is a time lag in the movement of fluid from the cellular level to the vascular level; therefore patients may demonstrate hypotension while continuing to demonstrate excess total body fluids with symptoms such as edema. Control of fluid volume is based on human calculations of fluid balance and machine settings to remove fluid during dialysis. The calculations cannot always be precise. Excessive removal results in fluid volume deficit. Inadequate removal results in fluid volume excess. Therefore, assessment of fluid status after dialysis is of paramount importance.

Administer oral salt solutions (broth) for symptoms of hypotension, rapid pulse, and dizziness.

Salt solutions will move fluids quickly into the vascular space to offset hypovolemia.

Administer intravenous saline if patient is unable to drink or if hypotension is life threatening.

Severe hypotension must be treated immediately despite long-range goals of fluid removal.

Teach patients to recognize and report early symptoms of hypotension to prevent its progression.

Patients experience early symptoms of hypotension that vary by the individual. Examples may include nausea, ringing in the ears, slight apprehension, or nervous sensations.

Nursing Interventions	Rationales
Prevent need for excessive fluid removal during dialysis by assisting patients in learning their individual fluid needs. Review intake, symptoms, and dialysis treatments and assist the patients in drawing correlations.	

NURSING DIAGNOSIS: HIGH RISK FOR INJURY

Risk Factors
- Increased clotting potential of diverted or artificial vessels
- Bleeding from needle sites after dialysis
- Heparinization during dialysis with overlap effect
- Diverted circulation from distal or anastomosis on affected limb
- Presence of 100–1200 mL blood supply in fistula or graft

Patient Outcomes
- Dialysis access will be patent.
- No bleeding will occur from access site.

Nursing Interventions	Rationales
Regularly assess the patency of the fistula graft by palpating for a thrill or auscultating for a bruit.	The presence of arterial blood in the vein or graft produces a bruit or thrill. Absence of these signs indicates decreased flow.
Assess needle site dressings after dialysis and review amount of heparin used during dialysis.	
Teach patients to avoid constricting flow through the access by avoiding pressure of clothing or postures. Do not take blood pressure, draw blood, or place tourniquets on limb with access.	Flow through the access must be maintained at all times.
Communicate fistula/graft care and need to avoid constricting flow to all caregivers including lab technicians.	

NURSING DIAGNOSIS: BODY IMAGE DISTURBANCE

Related To
- Presence of atrioventricular (AV) graft or fistula
- Changed physical appearance (pallor, yellowing of skin)
- Dependence on technology for continued life

Defining Characteristics
Neglect of hygiene
Avoidance of fistula or graft
Focus on previous strengths
Function or appearance
Fear of rejection by others
Feelings of helplessness or hopelessness
Preoccupation with change or loss
Extension of body boundary to include components of dialysis
Refusal to acknowledge changes

Patient Outcomes
The patient will demonstrate acceptance of body image changes, as evidenced by discussing feelings and planning clothing selections.

Nursing Interventions	Rationales
Empower the patient to discuss feelings by validating rather than denying patient perceptions.	Patients will not discuss feelings if they are not in a safe environment. Denial of feelings perpetuates and accelerates the patient's negative emotions.
Assist the patient in exploring altered self-image by verbalizing fears and exploring reality.	Patients need to incorporate physical changes into their self-definition.
Assist patient in selecting clothing to cover access site and grooming to enhance appearance.	
Refer patient to psychotherapists if symptoms are severe or continued.	

NURSING DIAGNOSIS: INEFFECTIVE MANAGEMENT OF THERAPEUTIC REGIMEN

Related To
- Complex treatment regimes
- Difficult required changes in life-style and habits

Defining Characteristics
Verbalization of desire to manage the treatment of illness
Verbalization of difficulty with regulation or integration of any of the regimens needed to maintain health on hemodialysis.
Verbalization of no action to make changes previously.

Patient Outcomes
The patient will
- demonstrate understanding of components of treatment plan.
- set realistic priorities to meet selected components of the plan.
- identify factors which inhibit following treatment plan.

Nursing Interventions	Rationales
Provide educational resources through literature, slides, or video tapes.	
Assist the patient in talking through perceived need for behavioral changes. Help the patient set priorities. Individualize plans by reviewing the patient's life-style.	
Provide validation for patient efforts. For example, demonstrate changes in laboratory results as dietary habits change.	
Refer patients to appropriate experts (dietitian, exercise physiologist, nephrology nurses, and physicians) for assistance in individualizing treatment regimen.	

DISCHARGE PLANNING/CONTINUITY OF CARE

- Schedule outpatient dialysis treatments and provide detailed report to the dialysis caregivers.
- Assure understanding of self-management plan, especially any additional regimens added during hospitalization.
- Review symptoms that would require immediate reporting to the nephrologist.

REFERENCES

Lewis, S. M. & Collier, I. C. (1992). *Medical Surgical Nursing*. St. Louis, MO: Mosby.

Liebairt, A. (1991). Nursing management of continuous arteriovenous hemodialysis. *Heart & Lung, 20*(2), 152–160.

Patrick, M. L., Woods, S. J., Crawer, R. F., Rokoshy, J. S., & Boraine, P. (1991). *Medical surgical nursing pathophysiological concepts*. Philadelphia, PA: Lippincott.

Porth, C. M. (1990). *Pathophysiology—Concepts of altered health states*. Philadelphia, PA: Lippincott.

▼

NEPHRECTOMY

Mercy Galicia, RN, BSN
Gail Gaustad, RN, MS

Nephrectomy is a surgical removal of a kidney indicated when the kidney is extensively damaged with irreversible causes and is no longer functioning. A nephrectomy is also performed for removal of a healthy kidney for appropriate transplant purposes.

ETIOLOGIES (INDICATIONS)

- Nonfunctioning kidney due to
  - cystic disease of the kidney
  - hydronephrosis
  - chronic renal failure
  - fibrosis
  - kidney tumor
  - posttraumatic kidney injury
  - tuberculosis
  - renal carcinoma
- Functioning kidney for transplant

CLINICAL MANIFESTATIONS

Relate to etiology and vary from normal kidney function (transplantation) to signs and symptoms of kidney failure

CLINICAL/DIAGNOSTIC FINDINGS

- Increase in uric acid, creatinine, blood urea nitrogen (BUN), lactic dehydrogenase (LDH), alkaline phosphatase, serum glutamic oxaloacetic transaminase (SGOT), white blood cell (WBC) count, erythrocyte sedimentation rate (ESR), renin levels
- Anemia

- Urinalysis: positive red and white blood cells (RBCs, WBCs)
- Kidney, ureter, and bladder (KUB): x-ray enlarged kidney
- Intravenous pyelogram (IVP): decrease or absent dye excretion
- Renal arteriogram: obstruction

OTHER PLANS OF CARE TO REFERENCE

- Basic Standards for Preoperative and Postoperative Care
- Pain Management: Patient-Controlled Analgesia

NURSING DIAGNOSIS: HIGH RISK FOR ALTERED RENAL TISSUE PERFUSION

Risk Factors
- Surgical procedure (renal area is highly vascular)
- Slippage of suture in renal artery

Patient Outcomes
The patient will not develop hemorrhage, as evidenced by
- stable vital signs
- warm, dry skin
- palpable peripheral pulses
- urine output at 30 mL/hr
- baseline mental status

Nursing Interventions	Rationales
Monitor and report excessive bleeding and signs of hypovolemia: restlessness, significant blood pressure drop; resting heart rate > 100 bpm; rapid, labored respirations; cool, pale, cyanotic skin, diminished or absent peripheral pulses; and urine output < 30 mL/hr.	Early detection of complication allows early medical intervention. Hemorrhage shock is a potential complication in the early postoperative period.
Implement measures to prevent bleeding. 1. Anchor nephrostomy tube, securing it to the abdomen. 2. Review splinting to reduce strain on suture line.	Avoids tissue irritation and subsequent bleeding caused by movement of tubes.

Nursing Interventions	Rationales
Inspect dressing for excessive bleeding every 4 hr. Check back area if surgical approach is the flank.	

NURSING DIAGNOSIS: HIGH RISK FOR IMPAIRED GAS EXCHANGE

Risk Factors
- Pulmonary emboli formation
- Venous statis
- Prolonged immobility/prolonged sitting
- Hypercoagulability, varicose veins
- History of pulmonary embolism
- Dehydration
- History of smoking, cancer, diabetes, oral contraceptive use
- Obesity

Patient Outcomes
Patient will demonstrate
- stable vital signs
- skin warm and usual color
- clear breath sounds

Nursing Interventions	Rationales
Observe for signs of pulmonary embolism as described.	Renal surgery has a greater risk for development of pulmonary emboli related to the close proximation of the surgical site to the vena cava and other large vessels. The incidence for emboli formation is greatest 5–10 days after surgery.
Review the importance of regular leg exercises. Ambulate early as indicated. Avoid standing, sitting, or crossing legs for prolonged periods.	Inactivity and prolonged sitting, standing, and crossing legs can result in venous stasis.
Prevent use of knee gatches and extremity elevation above heart.	Danger of blood vessel constriction in popliteal region. Elevation can impede circulation, causing blood pooling in pelvis; potential for clot formation.

Nursing Interventions	Rationales
Review and encourage deep-breathing exercises every 1–2 walking hours and every 4 hr at night.	Produces increased negative pressure in the thorax; assists in large-vein emptying.
Avoid massaging or rubbing calves.	This prevents danger of breaking existing clot.
Maintain fluid intake of 2500 mL/ day, unless contraindicated.	Prevents dehydration, which may lead to increased stasis and increased blood viscosity, predisposing thrombus formation.
If above signs are observed, notify physician and institute the following measures: 1. Keep head of bed (HOB) elevated above 30°. 2. Initiate oxygen therapy. 3. Place intravenous line. 4. Keep patient/significant other calm and reassured.	

NURSING DIAGNOSIS: DYSFUNCTIONAL GRIEVING

Related To
- Diagnosis of cancer
- Loss of vital organ (kidney)

Defining Characteristics
Depression
General irritability
Inappropriate expressions of anger
Decreased tolerance for pain
Decreased communication
Muscular tension
Insomnia
Self-pity
Verbal attacks on staff
Rejection of significant others
Loss of appetite
Increasing fatigue
Excessive physical dependency
Inability to problem solve

Patient Outcomes

Patient will demonstrate the use of effective coping skills while going through the grieving process, as evidenced by
- verbalization of ability to cope with loss or diagnosis
- expression of grief
- willingness to participate in the treatment plan and self-care activities
- recognition and utilization of available support systems

Nursing Interventions	Rationales
Promote development of a therapeutic relationship by maintaining continuity of caregivers.	May facilitate verbalization of fears and concerns.
Allow for expression of anger and loss related to diagnosis.	Unaddressed feelings can inhibit effective coping.
Encourage maximum participation and allow patient choices, if indicated.	Enables a sense of self-control.
Provide reassurance that remaining kidney will be sufficient (provided it is a normal kidney) without compromising health.	Some harbor the unfounded fear they will be seriously incapacitated after surgery. This is a reality if the kidney removed is the only functioning one, in which case dialysis and considerable lifestyle change would be required.
If removed kidney is being transplanted: 1. Explore concern with donor and donor's family that kidney may be rejected. 2. Provide emotional support. 3. Refer to counseling, if necessary.	
Encourage utilization of support system, that is, family, friends, clergy, and so on.	Presence of loved ones may assist reaction/coping.

NURSING DIAGNOSIS: KNOWLEDGE DEFICIT REGARDING FOLLOW-UP CARE AFTER DISCHARGE

Related To lack of exposure to information

Defining Characteristics
Inability to describe treatment plan
Inability to perform desired skill
Inaccurate interpretation of information
Questions/requests for information

Patient Outcomes
Patient will
- verbalize understanding of treatment plan after discharge.
- demonstrate necessary procedures correctly.
- relate what signs and symptoms are reportable and suggestive of complications.

Nursing Interventions	Rationales
Review instructions regarding maintenance of remaining kidney, taking precautions to prevent urinary tract infection (UTI):	
1. Drink at least 8–10 glasses of fluid/day.	Unless contraindicated by coexisting medical condition.
2. Void whenever the urge is felt.	Brisk flow of dilute urine through the urinary tract discourages development of urolithiasis.
3. Avoid long periods of inactivity.	
4. Maintain acidic urine by including cranberry, prune juice, and grapes in diet.	
5. Keep perineal area clean and dry.	
Immediately report signs of UTI: chills, fever, dysuria, and flank pain.	
Inform other providers about nephrectomy so that prophylactic antibiotic therapy may be initiated before invasive procedures such as dental work and minor surgeries.	
Avoid activities that might cause trauma to remaining kidney (i.e., horseback riding).	

Nursing Interventions	Rationales
Consult physician before taking other medications that might be toxic to the remaining kidney (salicylates, sulfonamides).	
Clarify plans for subsequent treatment of underlying disorder (i.e., chemotherapy radiation) if appropriate.	
Instruct to avoid lifting heavy objects for about 6 months.	Allow for complete healing of incised muscles.

DISCHARGE PLANNING/CONTINUITY OF CARE

- Assure patient/family understands and can perform self-care management at home.
- Refer a home care agency if continued care, teaching, or assistance is needed.
- Arrange for follow-up with physician for continued management postdischarge.
- Assist with obtaining prescriptions and supplies and establish a plan for refilling prescriptions.
- Provide with information on community agencies and appropriate support groups depending upon diagnosis and reason for nephrectomy.

REFERENCES

Brunner, L. & Suddarth, D. (1992). *Textbook of Medical-Surgical Nursing* (7th ed). Philadelphia, PA: Lippincott.

Cass, A. S. (1990). Nephrectomy. A review of the surgical approaches. *Today's OR Nurse, 12*(6), 16–21.

Tucker, S., Canobbio, F., Vargo, P. E., & Wells, M. (1988). *Patient care standards—Nursing process, diagnosis and outcomes.* St. Louis, MO: Mosby.

EPHROSTOMY

Gail Gausted, RN, MS
Mercy Galicia, RN, BSN

A Nephrostomy tube insertion is performed to provide temporary or permanent renal system decompression. It is also used for external urinary diversion from the bladder or an operative site or for therapeutic medication administration to the renal collecting system.

ETIOLOGIES (INDICATIONS)

- Sepsis secondary to urethral obstruction
- Impassable ureteral obstruction related to stone, tumor, or stricture
- Diagnostic purposes: pressure perfusion studies
- Medication administration

CLINICAL MANIFESTATIONS

- Flank pain
- nausea, vomiting, fever, chills
- burning on micturation
- visible hematuria
- cloudy urine

CLINICAL/DIAGNOSTIC FINDINGS

- Low hemoglobin and hematocrit
- Leukocytosis
- Visible radiopaque calculi on kidney x-ray
- Positive intravenous urogram
- Positive Whitaker test or Pfister test

NURSING DIAGNOSIS: HIGH RISK FOR INJURY

Risk Factors
- Inadvertent severance of blood vessel(s) during placement of nephrostomy tube
- Surgical procedure on a highly vascular organ

Patient Outcomes
Patient will not develop hemorrhage, as evidenced by
- stable vital signs
- warm skin with usual color
- palpable peripheral pulses
- urine output of at least 30 mL/hr

Nursing Interventions	Rationales
Check vital signs, dressing, and nephrostomy tube every 2–4 hr for 48 hr, then every shift thereafter, if normal. Check dressing under patient's back.	Expect to observe bloody drainage initially. The color should change to a light pink within 48 hr. Drainage will flow with gravity.
Assess for hematuria.	Small amount of hematuria that ceases spontaneously within 6–36 hr is expected after insertion of nephrostomy tube.
Notify physician of persistent bright red drainage.	Persistent bright red drainage is indicative of abnormalbleeding.
Assess for swelling or bruising in the affected flank. Report changes to physician immediately.	Suggestive of internal bleeding.
Ensure the nephrostomy tube is securely taped to the patient's side.	Do not attempt to reposition a displaced tube.

NURSING DIAGNOSIS: RISK FOR INFECTION

Risk Factors
- Presence of nephrostomy tube and urethral catheter
- Noncompliance with urinary tract and wound infection precautions
- Decreased resistance to infection

Patient Outcomes

Patient will not demonstrate signs and symptoms of local or systemic infection.

Nursing Interventions	Rationales
Monitor for postprocedural infection and prevent and/or initiate management, as appropriate.	Infection is a common postnephrostomy complication.
Obtain urine or wound culture if infection is suspected.	Facilitates organism identification, so that appropriate treatment can be instituted quickly.
Prevent interruption of closed drainage system. Do not disconnect the tubing unless absolutely necessary. Avoid contamination if tubing must be disconnected.	Nephrostomy tubes go directly into the renal collecting system and pose risk of pyelonephritis, unless precautions are maintained. Once the system is open, it is potentially contaminated.
Assess tubing for kinks. If a persistent leak exists, notify physician. Change dressings when wet; do not reinforce. Cleanse area around tube with betadine solution or hydrogen peroxide.	If urine has leaked under the dressing, it acts as a wick, enabling the microorganisms to move toward the incision. It is a good medium for bacterial growth.
Encourage fluid intake to at least 8–10 glasses/day, unless contraindicated, including 3 glasses of cranberry juice.	Rapid flow of urine through the urinary tract discourages multiplication of bacteria. It also produces a good mechanical flushing and dilutes urinary particles that cause calculus formation. Cranberry juice aids in keeping urine clear and acidic, thus inhibiting bacterial growth and preventing tube encrustation by urinary sediment.
Keep collection bags below kidney level and tubing free from kinks.	Prevents reflux, promotes urine flow, and eliminates obstruction.
Do not clamp nephrostomy tube unless ordered.	Clamping will precipitate acute pyelonephritis unless the urinary tract is proven patent.
Preform catheter/meatal care twice daily or as needed.	Prevents accumulation of mucus around the meatus.

NURSING DIAGNOSIS: HIGH RISK FOR IMPAIRED SKIN INTEGRITY

Risk Factors
- Presence of nephrostomy tube
- Excessive leakage of drainage around nephrostomy tube site
- Lack of skin barrier
- Prolonged contact of skin with wet dressing.

Patient Outcomes
Patient will maintain skin integrity around the nephrostomy tube, as evidenced by absence of redness, irritation, and breakdown.

Nursing Interventions	Rationales
Keep the tube securely taped to the patient's flank. If extension tubing is used to connect the nephrostomy tube to collection device, it should be coiled and taped to abdomen as a "safety loop" or coiled and secured to bed if connected to bedside drainage.	Prevents accidental pulling or tugging of tube that may cause dislodging.
If the nephrostomy tube becomes dislodged, facilitate immediate replacement.	Dislodgement of the tube is considered an emergency. If the tube is not reinserted within 1–2 hr, the nephrostomy opening will contract, and it may be impossible to reinsert the tube through the same tract.
Report sudden onset or increase in pain in affected kidney area.	Can indicate perforation of an organ by the tube.
Report persistent gross hematuria (bright red urine, possibly with clots).	Transient hematuria can be expected for 24–48 hr after tube insertion.
Notify physician of leakage around tube and sudden decrease in urine output which can occur with blockage and/or obstruction.	Leakage should stop in about 10 days. A sudden decrease in output is a sign of tube dislodgment.

Nursing Interventions	Rationales
Hand irrigate the nephrostomy as needed as indicated with no more than 5 mL of specified irrigant using strict sterile technique.	Normal kidney pelvis holds 2–5 mL of fluid; more than this amount can cause mechanical damage to the kidney or infection from pyelorenal backflow.
Inspect skin areas that are in contact with wound drainage for signs of irritation and breakdown. Protect skin from moisture or drainage around the tube. Apply skin barrier of ostomy appliance around wound where there is prolonged or copious drainage. Change dressing when wet as soon as possible. Do not reinforce.	Drainage with urine is highly irritating to skin and can easily cause breakdown of skin integrity.

NURSING DIAGNOSIS: ALTERED URINARY ELIMINATION

Related To
- Presence of nephrostomy/urethral indwelling catheter
- Urinary retention.

Defining Characteristics
Disruption of urine flow through nephrostomy tube or urethral catheter
Inability of patient to void
Flank pain
Suprapubic distention and/or discomfort
Decreased urine output

Patient Outcomes
Patient will establish a normal pattern of urinary elimination after nephrostomy/urinary catheter removal (voidings > 100 mL.

Nursing Interventions	Rationales
Measure nephrostomy and urethral catheter outputs every hour for first 24–48 hr, then every 4–8 hr, and report any changes.	A sudden decrease could mean obstruction or loss of kidney function. An increase of more than 2,000 mL/8 hr could indicate postobstructive diuresis, which can cause fluid and electrolyte imbalance.

Nursing Interventions	Rationales
Assess for signs of reobstruction after the nephrostomy tube is clamped and removed, that is, leakage around the nephrostomy tube site, flank pain, and fever.	The nephrostomy tube remains in place until obstruction of the urinary tract is removed. Removal occurs if clamping regimen is tolerated. Expect drainage from site for up to 12 hr after removal. The tract should close completely in 2 days, leaving a small scar.
Maintain accurate record of intake and output.	

▼

NURSING DIAGNOSIS: KNOWLEDGE DEFICIT—REGARDING FOLLOW-UP CARE

Related To
- Lack of exposure to information
- New procedure

Defining Characteristics
Inability to describe treatment plan
Inability to perform desired skills
Verbalizes deficiency of knowledge or skill of information
Expresses inaccurate interpretations of information
Repeated questions/requests for information

Patient Outcomes
Patient and/or significant other will
- verbalize understanding of treatment plan after discharge.
- demonstrate necessary procedures correctly.
- relate what signs and symptoms to report.
- state measures to prevent recurrent stone formation.
- demonstrate independent maintenance of nephrostomy tube.

Nursing Interventions	Rationales
Assess the patient's/significant other's ability to care for themselves and/or provide care at home. Plan teaching sessions to include family members/significant others.	Because of the nephrostomy tube location, someone will have to help patient with dressing changes and tube management.

Nursing Interventions	Rationales
Stress importance of good hand washing before handling equipment or dressing. Review dressing removal and site cleansing using an outward circular approach. Remind not to touch the side of the dressing that touches the tube. The preferred cleansing solution preference is soap and water or antiseptic solution with an antibacterial ointment.	
Review cleansing of the bedside drainage collector and leg bag after each use and replace these bags weekly. Cleanse bags with a phosphoric acid detergent, rinse with clear water, followed by final rinse of vinegar solution (1 oz vinegar to 1 qt water). Do not use hot water.	This practice controls odor. Hot water causes odor retention.
Remind patient to keep tube taped to the flank and attached to a drainage bag. Instruct to empty the leg bag when it is two thirds full and to cleanse bag tubing tips with an alcohol or betadine solution with bag changes.	
Instruct to call if the nephrostomy tube has moved even 2–3 inches out of tract. Repositioning of the tube should never be attempted by the patient.	
Review signs and symptoms of infection. Instruct to call if redness, warmth, or drainage at the site, fever, flank pain, and bloody, cloudy, or foul-smelling urine are noticed.	Assess current knowledge regarding stone formation. Refer patient to a dietitian for prescribed diet as needed. Reinforce the importance of adequate fluid intake of at least 8–10 glasses/day.
Review activity level 1. Exercise, lifting or straining should be avoided until permitted by physician. Walking can be done without fear of tube dislodgement.	Active, strenuous physical activities can dislodge the nephrostomy tube.

Nursing Interventions	Rationales
2. Sexual activities are discouraged while the nephrostomy tube is still in place, but concerns should be discussed with physician.	
3. Sleeping on the same side as nephrostomy tube should be avoided.	This can disrupt the flow of nephrostomy tube drainage.

DISCHARGE PLANNING/CONTINUITY OF CARE

- Assure patient/family understand and can perform self-care at home.
- Refer to a home care agency if continued care, teaching, or assistance with self-care management is needed.
- Arrange for follow-up with physician.
- Assist with obtaining prescriptions and supplies and establishing a plan for refilling as needed.

REFERENCES

Barr, J. E. (1988). Standards of care for the patient with a percutaneous nephrostomy tube. *Journal of Enterostoma Therapy, 15,* 147–153.

Ghiotto, D. (1988). A full range of care for nephrostomy patient. *RN,* April, pp. 72–74.

Guidos, B. (1988). Preparing the patient for home care of the percutaneous nephrostomy tube. *Journal of Enterostoma Therapy, 15,* 187–190.

Sage, S. J. (1992). Nephrostomy dressing procedure. *Ostomy and Wound Management Journal, 32,* 32–36.

$\mathcal{P}$ERITONEAL DIALYSIS

Lynn Schoengrund, RN, MS

$\mathbf{P}$eritoneal dialysis is a form of renal replacement therapy for patients with acute and chronic renal failure. It is an intracorporeal process that utilizes the highly vascular peritoneal membrane in the abdomen as the semipermeable membrane. A soft, silastic, multilumen catheter is surgically placed in the peritoneal cavity as the access for use of the peritoneum. The peritoneal dialysis procedure is performed by the patient at home (see Tables 36.1 and 36.2). When the patient is hospitalized, it is generally performed by the bedside nurse.

ETIOLOGIES

- Diabetes
- Glomerulonephritis
- Chronic hypertension
- Polycystic kidneys
- Autoimmune disorders, for example, lupus or Goodpasture's
- Progression of acute renal failure to chronic renal failure
- Chronic acetaminophen use or abuse
- Heroin use

CLINICAL MANIFESTATIONS

- Severe fatigue
- Anorexia, nausea vomiting
- Pallor
- Signs of fluid overload

CLINICAL/DIAGNOSTIC FINDINGS

- Increased creatinine, BUN
- Decreased creatine clearance to 5–10% of normal
- Decreased hemoglobin and hematocrit
- Altered serum electrolyes, especially potassium

Table 36.1 • Steps in Peritoneal Dialysis

Inflow: Dialysate is introduced into the abdominal cavity via the dialysis catheter.

Dwell: Dialysate remains in the abdominal cavity and fluid and electrolytes are drawn in.

Outflow: Fluid is drained via the dialysis catheter.

Exchange: The preceding three steps combined. Exchanges are varied based on patient needs.

Table 36.2 • Forms of Peritoneal Dialysis

CAPD (continuous ambulatory peritoneal dialysis): Patients manually perform three or four exchanges with long dwell times at 4–6 hr. The procedure is continuous.

CCPD (continuous cycling peritoneal dialysis): Automated exchanges are performed by a machine while the patient sleeps. Six to eight exchanges are performed at home.

IPD (intermittent peritoneal dialysis): Automated exchanges are performed in a dialysis center.

OTHER PLANS OF CARE TO REFERENCE

- Hemodialysis

NURSING DIAGNOSIS: HIGH RISK FOR INFECTION

Risk Factors
- Dialysis catheter
- A foreign object which communicates to the external environment
- High dextrose concentration in dialysate
- Warm, moist environment of the peritoneal cavity
- Chronic illness

Patient Outcomes
The patient will
- not have signs and symptoms of peritonitis.
- not have signs and symptoms of catheter exit site infections.

Nursing Interventions	Rationales
Prevent introduction of bacteria during exchanges by wearing sterile gloves and masks, washing hands well, and following manufacturers' recommendations for using supplies.	Although peritonitis may occur despite perfect technique, some occurrences may be preventable if procedures are followed with painstaking care.
Assess for peritonitis at each exchange. The earliest sign is cloudy overflow. Inspect each outflow; manufacturers' print should be visible from the other side of the bag if the outflow is not cloudy. Draw samples from outflow for culture and gram stain as indicated by protocol or medical order.	Early detection can prevent rapid spread of bacteria and prevent complications. Unchecked peritonitis may scar the peritoneum and decrease its effectiveness as a semipermeable membrane.
Report the results of cultures to physicians and add antibiotics to dialysate as prescribed using aseptic technique.	Intraperitoneal antibiotics are an effective route for treatment of peritonitis and require no placement of additional venous access.
Assess the catheter exit site for signs of infection, including redness, inflammation, purulent drainage, and crust formation at exit.	The catheter exit site or tunnel may become sites of bacterial infection.
Use aseptic technique to set up and perform all exchanges.	

NURSING DIAGNOSIS: FLUID VOLUME DEFICIT

Related To
- Excessive ultrafiltration of fluid during dialysis
- Inadequate intake

Defining Characteristics
Hypotension, orthostatic hypotension
Rapid or thready pulse
Weakness, dizziness
Dry mucous membranes

Patient Outcomes
- Vital signs are within normal limits of patient.
- Mucous membranes are moist.

- Intake and output are balanced.
- Weight is stable.

Nursing Interventions	Rationales
Assess fluid balance at least daily 1. Weigh the patient at the same point in the exchange to compare weights (after drain, before inflow); when the patient is empty is recommended. 2. Compare weights over several exchanges and several days. 3. Calculate ultrafiltration by measuring or weighing outflow. 4. Assess the patient for signs and symptoms of fluid deficit.	Removal of fluid in peritoneal dialysis is based on selection of one of three concentrations of dextrose in dialysate (1.5, 2.5, or 4.25%). Some patients will ultrafiltrate significant amounts of fluid with the lowest concentration and need to drink fluids to maintain fluid balance. Calculation of the amount of fluid that needs to be removed is not as simple as it appears since it also varies with changes in body weight, accessibility of fluid to the semipermeable membrane, and variable responses with each exchange. Responses to fluid removal vary from individual to individual and in the individual by circumstances. Illness and hospitalization affect patient routines and may increase the potential for poor oral fluid intake. Peritonitis often interferes with ultrafiltration of fluid.
Adjust schedule of dextrose concentrations in exchanges and patient intake as prescribed and indicated by assessment.	Each exchange provides an opportunity to adjust patient fluid balance.
Administer oral salt solutions (broth) if the patient is symptomatic. If symptoms are severe, administer prescribed intravenous saline solutions.	Symptoms indicate a deficit in the vascular space that needs to be corrected to maintain circulation. Saline solutions pull fluid rapidly back into the vascular space.

Nursing Interventions	Rationales
Assist patients in learning about their responses to dialysis and fluid intake by reviewing the data collected in assessment.	Patients must learn to balance their life-style and treatment by trial and error. Examples are helpful in demonstrating both techniques for decision making and results. Patients who previously were on hemodialysis have to learn new routines.

NURSING DIAGNOSIS: FLUID VOLUME EXCESS

Related To inadequate ultrafiltration in peritoneal dialysis

Defining Characteristics
Hypertension
Jugular distention
Increased weight
Edema
Pulmonary congestion, rales

Patient Outcomes
- Patient will not complain of shortness of breath.
- Weight will be stable.
- Breath sounds will be normal.

Nursing Interventions	Rationales
Assess the capability of the peritoneum to ultrafiltrate fluid 1. Measure or weigh outflow fluid. 2. Time outflow of fluid. 3. Compare ultrafiltration outflow to intake, and note concentration of dextrose.	The cause of patients' fluid balance problems must be discovered so that treatment is appropriate. Loss of ultrafiltration fluid in peritoneal dialysis is associated temporarily with peritonitis. Other patients may not regularly ultrafiltrate fluid due to scarring of the peritoneum or for unknown reasons.
Assess regularly for signs of pulmonary edema and promptly report.	Patients may need temporary or permanent hemodialysis to prevent life-threatening fluid excess.

NURSING DIAGNOSIS: BODY IMAGE DISTURBANCE

Related To to presence of permanent external peritoneal dialysis catheter

Defining Characteristics
Neglect of hygiene
Avoidance of catheter or catheter care
Focus on previous functions or appearances
Fear of rejection by others
Feelings of helplessness or hopelessness
Preoccupation with changes or loss
Extension of body boundary to include components of dialysis

Patient Outcomes
The patient will
- discuss feelings and concerns about image changes.
- demonstrate acceptance of changes with effective coping mechanisms.

Nursing Interventions	Rationales
Empower the patient to discuss feelings by validating rather than denying patient perceptions.	Denial of feelings perpetuates and accelerates the patient's negative feelings. Patients can discuss these emotions if in a safe environment.
Assist in verbalizing fears and exploring reality.	Patients will need to incorporate physical changes into their self-definition.
Assist with clothing selection that minimizes appearance of catheter.	
Refer patients to psychotherapists if symptoms are severe or continued.	

NURSING DIAGNOSIS: ALTERED NUTRITION—LESS THAN BODY REQUIREMENTS

Related To
- Loss of protein across the peritoneal membrane
- Decreased appetite due to feelings of fullness of dialysate dwell

Defining Characteristics
Body weight loss
Negative nitrogen balance
Blood urea nitrogen (BUN) >15 mg/100 mL
Inadequate food intake
Muscle tone or mass less
Weakness
Complaints of fullness

Patient Outcomes
The patient will
- maintain weight.
- eat adequate diet.

Nursing Interventions	Rationales
Assess food intake, serum BUN, creatinine, and protein as well as weight comparisons.	Simple measurements such as weight changes are masked by fluid volume changes in dialysis patients. Responding to early cues may prevent severe malnutrition.
Consult dietitian to assess nutritional status.	Plan a protein intake for the patient that offsets protein loss in peritoneal dialysis.
Work with the patient to discover foods and serving sizes that are tolerated.	Ideal methods for obtaining adequate nutrition must be discovered through trial and error.
Encourage family involvement.	

NURSING DIAGNOSIS: INEFFECTIVE MANAGEMENT OF THERAPEUTIC REGIMEN

Related To
- Complexity of regimen
- Lack of knowledge
- Frustration with chronic illness

Defining Characteristics
Verbalizes desire to manage the treatment of illness
Verbalizes difficulty with regulation or integration of any of the regimens needed to maintain health on hemodialysis
Verbalization of no action to make changes previously

Patient Outcomes

The patient will
- demonstrate understanding of components of treatment plan.
- set realistic priorities to meet selected components of the plan.
- identify factors which inhibit following treatment plan.

Nursing Interventions	Rationales
Provide educational resources through literature slides or video tapes.	
Assist the patient in talking through perceived need for behavioral changes. Help the patient set priorities. Individualize plans by reviewing the patient's life-style.	
Provide validation for patient efforts. For example, demonstrate changes in laboratory results as dietary habits change.	
Refer patient to appropriate experts (dietitian, exercise physiologist, nephrology nurses, and physicians) for assistance in individualizing treatment regimen.	

DISCHARGE PLANNING/CONTINUITY OF CARE

- Assure that patient has sufficient supplies for treatment at home.
- Provide detailed report of hospitalization to dialysis caregivers.
- Assure understanding of self-management plan and any additional care regimens due to hospitalization.
- Review symptoms that require immediate reporting to the nephrologist.

REFERENCES

Covalesky, R. (1990). Myths and facts about peritoneal dialysis. *Nursing,* 20(4), 91.

Lewis, S. M. & Collier, I. C. (1992). *Medical surgical nursing.* St. Louis, MO: Mosby.

Patrick, M. L., Woods, S. J., Crawer, R. F., Rokoshy, J. S. & Boraine, P. (1991). *Medical surgical nursing pathophysiological concepts.* Philadelphia, PA: Lippincott.

Porth, C. M. (1990). *Pathophysiology—Concepts of altered health states.* Philadelphia, PA: Lippincott.

Common
Urological and
Gynecological
Conditions

▼

YSTERECTOMY

Mercy Galicia, RN, BSN
Gail Gaustad, RN, MS

Hysterectomy is the surgical removal of the uterus. This surgical procedure may be classified as total, subtotal, or radical. A total hysterectomy is the removal of the uterus including the cervix, leaving the ovaries and fallopian tubes. A subtotal hysterectomy entails removal of only a portion of the uterus, leaving the cervical stump intact. A radical hysterectomy, commonly the treatment of choice for cervical carcinoma, is the removal of all reproductive organs. The total or sutotal hysterectomy may be done through a vaginal or abdominal surgical approach. The radical hysterectomy requires an abdominal surgical approach.

ETIOLOGIES

- Fibroids
- Endometriosis
- Cancer or precancer
- Dysfunctional uterine bleeding
- Pelvic relaxation
- Irreparable rupture or perforation of the uterus

CLINICAL MANIFESTATIONS

- Sense of pelvic heaviness/pain
- Backache
- Abnormal vaginal bleeding
- Constipation/painful defecation
- Urinary retention/stress incontinence
- Infertility
- Weakness
- Weight loss

CLINICAL/DIAGNOSTIC FINDINGS

- Pelvic exam revealing palpable nodules, marked uterine prolapse, uterine enlargement
- Positive Pap smear
- Positive Schiller test
- Positive biopsy
- Abnormal colposcopic exam
- Positive cone biopsy
- Low hemoglobin and hematocrit
- Elevated erythropoietin
- Leukocytosis
- Elevated sedimentation rate
- Positive intravenous urography
- Positive pelvic sonography

OTHER PLANS OF CARE TO REFERENCE

- Basic Standards for Preoperative and Postoperative Care
- Pain Management: Patient-Controlled Analgesia

NURSING DIAGNOSIS: KNOWLEDGE DEFICIT REGARDING PREOPERATIVE AND POSTOPERATIVE EXPECTATIONS

Related To no previous exposure to information

Defining Characteristics
Asking questions
Apprehensive

Patient Outcomes
The patient will
- relate less anxiety after teaching.
- verbalize postoperative expectations.
- demonstrate postoperative exercises and respiratory regimen.

Nursing Interventions	Rationales
Inform the patient and significant other to expect the following post-operatively: drainage from the incision and dressing changes; feeling of the urge to urinate, even with the urinary catheter in place; and the presence of suprapubic catheter.	Serosanguinous drainage is expected postopertively, especially if tubes are left in the wound. The catheter can irritate the bladder wall and cause the urge to void.

NURSING DIAGNOSIS: HIGH RISK FOR INJURY

Risk Factors
- Accidental surgical tear
- Ligation to bladder and/or ureters

Patient Outcomes
- Patient will not experience injury to bladder.
- If bladder injury occurs, patient will experience resolution, as evidenced by:
  - gradual resolution of hematuria and backache
  - urine output $\geq$ 30 mL/hr

Nursing Interventions	Rationales
Monitor for and report signs and symptoms of bladder or ureteral injury: hematuria, urinary output <200 mL initial 6–8 hr postoperatively, and persistent or increasing backache.	Early detection allows for early intervention.
If signs and symptoms of bladder or ureteral injury are present: 1. Continue to monitor urine output hourly. 2. Prepare patient for surgical repair, if indicated. 3. Provide emotional support to patient and significant others.	

NURSING DIAGNOSIS: HIGH RISK FOR FLUID VOLUME DEFICIT

Risk Factors
- Bleeding postoperatively
- Inadequate fluid relacement
- NPO status
- Vomiting
- Use of anticoagulant preoperatively
- Advanced age

Patient Outcomes
Patient will demonstrate
- stable vital signs
- warm skin with usual color
- palpable peripheral pulses
- urine output > 30 mL per/h
- usual mental status

Nursing Interventions	Rationales
Monitor for and report excessive bleeding and signs and symptoms of hypovolemia: apprehension, circumoral pallor, cold, moist, pale skin, thirst, increased pulse rate (>100/min), rapid deep respirations, temperature drop, decreased cardiac output and narrow pulse pressure, decreasing blood pressure, drop in hemoglobin and hematocrit.	
Inspect abdominal wound/vagina as possible source of bleeding. Apply pressure dressing over external bleeding site if actively bleeding.	
Increase intravenous (IV) infusion rate and administer blood as prescribed.	Monitor closely for signs of increased bleeding tendencies after transfusions. Numerous rapid blood transfusions may induce coagulopathy and prolong bleeding time.

Nursing Interventions	Rationales
If evidence of hypovolemic shock, position patient properly in bed by elevating the lower extremities 20°, keeping knees straight, trunk horizontal, and head slightly elevated.	Avoid Trendelenburg position because it increases blood flow to the head, a reflex compensatory action takes place (causing vasoconstriction and decreasing blood supply to brain), and viscera tend to fall against the diaphragm, increasing resistance to breathing and ventilation.
Monitor urinary output hourly.	Output of 30 mL/h indicates adequate renal perfusion.
Provide emotional support to patient and significant others.	
Perform actions to prevent nausea and vomiting when oral intake allowed. Maintain a fluid intake of at least 2500 mL/day unless contraindicated.	

NURSING DIAGNOSIS: HIGH RISK FOR ALTERED URINARY ELIMINATION

Risk Factors
- Trauma to urethra or perineal area
- Surgical pain
- Prolonged urethral catheter placement
- Decreased activity
- Anxiety/fear
- Obesity

Patient Outcomes
Patient will demonstrate
- resolution of urgency, bladder fullness, and discomfort.
- return of preoperative bladder functioning.

Nursing Interventions	Rationales
Monitor output and/or voiding.	Small voids (30–50 mL every 15–30 min), may indicate bladder overdistention.

Nursing Interventions	Rationales
Ensure that pain is well controlled before walking and initial voiding attempts after ctheter removal.	Pain-free/relaxed state can facilitate bladder emptying.
Maintain patient fluid intake at 2500 mL/day, if not contraindicated.	
Offer sitz bath for inability to void.	
Instruct and assist to perform Credé technique, unless contraindicated.	Facilitates bladder emptying.
Consult physician regarding reinsertion of catheter or intermittent catheterization if other measures fail to alleviate retention. If prescribed, check residual voids 5–15 min after voids.	Residual urine should be 50–100 mL. Continue to check if greater than 100 mL.

NURSING DIAGNOSIS: HIGH RISK FOR ALTERED BOWEL ELIMINATION

Risk Factors
- Surgical manipulation of intestines
- Paralytic ileus development
- Anesthesia
- Narcotic use
- Immobility
- Dehydration

Patient Outcomes
Patient will demonstrate
- resolution of abdominal pain and cramping
- soft nondistended abdomen
- gradual return of bowel sounds
- passage of flatus and bowel movement prior to discharge

Nursing Interventions	Rationales
Assess and report sign and symptoms of paralytic ileus: decreased or no bowel sounds, failure to pass flatus, complaint of abdominal cramping, abdominal distention, pressure and pain, and no bowel movement.	Ileus most commonly occurs between third and fifth postoperative day. Characterized by sharp, colicky, abdominal pain, with pain-free intervals. Eating may intensify pain. Abdominal distention and hiccups may occur, and complete obstruction may cause intestinal contents to back up into the stomach and cause vomiting; however, no bowel movement will occur. If obstruction is partial or incomplete, diarrhea may occur.
Implement measures to prevent paralytic ileus: 1. Increase activity/ambulation, as allowed/tolerated. 2. Give return flow enema or insert rectal tube for reported gas, if ordered/indicated. 3. Give stool softner or mild laxative, as ordered. 4. Progress diet, as ordered, when bowel sounds are audible and passing flatus.	
If signs and symptoms of ileus occur: 1. Continue to increase activity. 2. Withhold all oral intake. 3. Replace fluids and electrolytes as ordered. 4. Insert nasogastric (NG) tube and maintain suction as ordered. 5. Monitor for and report signs of bowel necrosis [e.g., fever, increased white blood cell (WBC) count, shock]. 6. Monitor fluid, electrolytes, and acid-base balance. 7. Administer narcotic judiciously; opiates can further suppress peristalsis.	If obstruction is not relieved, vomiting continues, distention becomes more pronounced, pulse increases, hypovolemic shock develops, and if not resolved, death ensues.

Nursing Interventions	Rationales
8. Monitor and document characteristics and amount of emesis and NG drainage.	Essential for correct fluid replacement therapy.
Provide frequent reassurance to patient and significant others.	

NURSING DIAGNOSIS: SELF-ESTEEM DISTURBANCE

Related To
• Altered body image
• Sexuality
• Fertility
• Loss of reproductive organ(s)
• Alteration in hormone balance

Defining Characteristics
Depressed, sad, irritable, hopeless, anxious, angry
Loss of interest in usual activities
Loss of energy, fatigue
Low self-esteem
Feelings of worthlessness
Crying
Inability to concentrate

Patient Outcomes
Patient verbalizes concerns and indicates ways of dealing with them.

Nursing Interventions	Rationales
Assess emotional stress the patient is experiencing.	Determine and understand individual response to the surgical procedure. When hormonal balance is upset, as often occurs in disturbances of the reproductive system, the patient may exhibit depression and heightened emotional sensitivity to people and situations.

Nursing Interventions	**Rationales**
While assisting patient with self-care measures, involve in conversations that can provide further insights into her feelings and coping patterns. Reinforce correct information and provide factual information to correct any misconceptions.	Exhibiting interest, concerns, and willingness to listen to patient's fear will add immeasurably to patient's progress throughout her experience. Common misconceptions: the woman gains weight, develops facial hair, becomes wrinkled, old, and masculine, looses her mind, or becomes nervous and depressed.
Allow discussion of feelings about herself as a woman. Reassure her that her surgery will not take away her femininity. Encourage her to discuss her feelings with her significant other. Reassure her that she will not go through premature menopause if her ovaries are not removed. Discuss hormone therapy if ovaries are removed.	
If patient expresses an interest in child adoption, refer her to a social worker and provide names of appropriate community agencies.	
Discuss counseling with physician if patient requests or if she seems unable to adapt to changes resulting from surgery.	

NURSING DIAGNOSIS: KNOWLEDGE DEFICIT REGARDING FOLLOW-UP CARE AFTER DISCHARGE

Related To
- Lack of exposure to needed information
- Cognitive impairment

Defining Characteristics
Inadequate performance or demonstration of skill
Inadequate understanding
Misinterpretation/misconception of teachings
Request for information and verbalization of problem

Patient Outcomes

Patient will

- state plan for care at home.
- perform skills required to care for self.
- state signs and symptoms to report.
- describe plan for follow-up care.

Nursing Interventions	Rationales
Provide simple, specific written instructions (e.g., scheduled follow-up appointment, treatment plan, activity level, diet, medications, signs and symptoms to report) at patient's level of comprehension.	Reinforce verbal information with handouts. Giving information that is easy to understand can increase compliance.
Explain the need to avoid sexual relations, douching or use of tampons for 4–6 weeks unless otherwise specified by physician.	This can injure the incision site and cause bleeding.
Instruct to avoid lifting heavy objects for at least 1 month–6 weeks.	
Advise against sitting too long at one time, as in driving long distances. Suggest delay driving a car until third postoperative week or until advised by physician.	There is a possibility of pooling of blood in the pelvis and of thromboembolism. Pressing the brake while driving may even initiate discomfort in the abdomen.
Suggest taking showers vs. tub baths until advised by physician.	Reduces risk of infection.
If patient is discharged with suprapubic catheter, ensure understanding of use and demonstrate care of the incision and the catheter.	

Nursing Interventions	Rationales
Instruct to report the following signs and symptoms: persistent low-grade or significantly high temperature (38.3 °C, or 101 °F), increasing redness, or swelling in calf of one or both legs; urine retention, frequency, and urgency; dysuria; cloudy, foul-smelling urine; abdominal distention and/or discomfort; continued nausea and vomiting; difficulty breathing; chest pain; and productive cough of green, rust-colored, or purulent sputum.	Increasing knowledge and compliance with goals or instructions is more easily achieved. It can play an active role in the care of the patient. It will help patient to undertake self-monitoring. Patient will know when to report signs and symptoms.
Explain need to take hormones as prescribed. Explain that menstruation will no longer occur if patient had a total hysterectomy with salpingo-oophorectomy.	

DISCHARGE PLANNING/CONTINUITY OF CARE

- Assure understanding and ability to care for self at home.
- Refer to a home care agency if continued assistance with care is needed.
- Assist with obtaining prescriptions, supplies, and equipment and a plan for refilling prescriptions if necessary.
- Explain the importance of maintaining regular outpatient gynecological exams.
- Arrange follow-up appointment with physician.
- Provide information on support groups or other community agencies that may be helpful.

REFERENCES

Brunner, L. & Suddarth. D. (1992). *Textbook of medical-surgical nursing* (7th ed). Philadelphia, PA: Lippincott.

Gambone, J. C., Linch, J. B., Slesniski, M. J., Reiter, R. C., & Moore, J. G. (1989). Validation of hysterectomy indications and quality assurace process. *Obstetrics and Gynecology*, 73(6), 1045–1049.

Suddarth, D. (1991). *The Lippincott manual of nursing practice*. Philadelphia, PA: Lippincott.

PROSTATECTOMY

Gail Gaustad, RN, MS
Mercy Galicia, RN, BSN

The sole function of the prostate is to manufacture a secretion that aids the passage and nourishment of spermatozoa. The size of the prostate increases with disease processes, variably with malignancy and 100–200% larger in benign prostatic hypertrophy (BPH) causing urinary obstruction. Transurethral resection of prostate (TURP) is a surgical intervention that treats moderately enlarged prostate and prostate cancer, a palliative measure to reduce obstruction. A radical perineal prostatectomy is indicated for prostate cancer but is also performed for BPH if the prostate is too large for a TURP and the patient is no longer sexually active. Suprapubic and retropubic prostatectomies are surgical interventions also employed for BPH if the prostate is too large for a TURP and are also used for prostate cancer when total removal of the gland is necessary.

ETIOLOGIES (INDICATIONS)

- Benign prostatic hyperplasia
- Prostate adenocarcinoma

CLINICAL MANIFESTATIONS

- Decreased urinary force
- Hesitancy
- Intermittency
- Terminal dribbling
- Incomplete emptying
- Nocturia
- Frequency
- Abdominal discomfort and flank pain during voidings
- Bladder distention
- Acute urinary retention
- Uremia
- Renal failure

350

CLINICAL/DIAGNOSTIC FINDINGS

- Palpable bladder distention
- Rectal exam revealing enlarged prostate (average is 4 cm in length and width)
- Elevated blood urea nitrogen (BUN), creatinine
- Hematuria, uremia
- Cystoscopy: evaluates degree of prostate enlargement
- Postvoid residual > 150 mL
- Decreased uroflowmetry
- Abnormal retrograde urography: visualizing defects in the renal pelvis and ureter
- Elevated prostate specific antigen (normal 0–4 mg/mL)
- Positive fine-needle aspiration

OTHER PLANS OF CARE TO REFERENCE

- Basic Standards for Preoperative and Postoperative Care
- Pain Management: Patient-Controlled Analgesia

NURSING DIAGNOSIS: KNOWLEDGE DEFICIT OF PREOPERATIVE AND POSTOPERATIVE EXPECTATIONS

Related To
- Anxiety
- New experience
- No previous exposure to information

Defining Characteristics
Asking questions
Apprehension
Stating concerns and fears

Patient Outcomes
The patient will
- experience a reduction in anxiety.
- relate his understanding of the surgical procedure and postoperative course and routine care.
- demonstrate postoperative exercises and respiratory regimen.

Nursing Interventions	Rationales
Inform patient and significant others preoperatively about:	
1. red urine in drainage bag	Serosanguinous drainage is expected postoperatively.
2. blood clots in urine	May indicate bladder spasm.
3. bloody drainage around catheter	
4. drainage from incision and drain and dressing change	
5. feeling of urgent need to urinate	
Explain that symptoms such as urgency and frequency that are present before surgery may still continue after catheter removal postopratively.	This results from poor bladder tone and trauma from surgery and urinary catheter.

NURSING DIAGNOSIS: URINARY RETENTION AND URINARY INCONTINENCE AFTER CATHETER REMOVAL

Related To
- Obstruction of urinary catheter due to blood clots or possibly kinks of tubing
- Difficulty urinating following catheter removal associated with loss of bladder tone, pain, bleeding, bladder irritation
- Trauma to urinary sphincter
- Damage to urinary sphincter and perineal nerves and muscles (primarily after perineal approach or radical prostatectomy)
- Temporary loss of bladder tone associated with continued decompression of bladder while catheter was in place

Defining Characteristics
Bladder distention
Burning with micturation
Change in voiding patterns
Hematuria
Lack of control, dribbling, frequency, hesitancy, urgency
Pain or discomfort

Patient Outcomes

Patient will experience
- freely flowing urine through catheter
- balanced intake and output
- normal voiding after catheter removal

Nursing Interventions	Rationales
Monitor for and report the following:	
1. urinary retention when catheter is present, for example, c/o fullness or suprapubic discomfort, distention, and absence of fluid in drainage tubing, especially if continuous irrigation is running output that continues to be less than intake 48 hr after surgery.	Urine output is expected to be less than intake due to blood loss, vomiting, diaphoresis and, increased secretion of antidiuretic hormone (ADH) and aldosterone.
2. urinary retention following catheter removal, for example, complaints of bladder fullness or suprapubic discomfort and distention, frequent small voids (25–50 mL), and increased complaints of urgency.	
Establish adequate drainage of the bladder and maintain patency of urinary catheter:	
1. Maintain a closed sterile gravity system of drainage.	A three-way system is utilized to control bleeding. Continuous bladder irrigation reduces clot formation (does not correct the cause of bleeding).
2. Regulate flow of irrigating solution to keep urine a light pink to straw color, free of clots, and transparent in appearance.	
3. Notify physician of significant variances in total amount of irrigating solution from the total urinary output.	Accurate output is essential to obtain urinary output (subtract irrigation fluid from total output volume).

Nursing Interventions	Rationales
4. If not draining and if ordered, hand irrigate urinary catheter gently with 50 mL of isotonic solution at a time using a plunger-type syringe.	Avoids clot formation and obstruction of catheter but may increase bleeding if done unnecessarily. Isotonic solution will not cause hemolysis. Too much force may damage recently operated area.
5. Make sure that the amount of irrigant is recovered. Avoid overdistending bladder with irrigating fluid.	Overdistending the bladder can produce secondary hemorrhage by stretching coagulated vessels in the prostate capsule.
6. Rotate catheter to move drainage "eye" or catheter away from bladder wall or blood clot; then apply gentle suction.	Strong suction on a recently occluded vessel can cause bleeding.
Tell the patient the following:	
1. Urge to void is caused by the presence of the catheter or bladder spasms (painful contractions of muscles bladder neck and wall).	Watch catheter tubing; a column of urine moving between pain episodes or when patient coughs may indicate bladder spasms.
2. Catheter should be drawn back gently toward the external meatus when patient has spasms.	A frequent cause of spasm is the catheter touching (and stimulating) the posterior bladder wall.
3. Patient should refrain from pulling on catheter.	This can cause bleeding, clots, plugging of catheter, and distention.
4. Catheter should be taped to lower abdomen/or inner thigh to prevent pressure on penoscrotal junction.	Straighten the angulation of the penoscrotal junction, reducing pressure on the urethra exerted by the catheter, to minimize the risk of accidental traction and subsequent trauma to the bladder and urethra.
Be alert for obstruction of urinary drainage tube by kinking, tissue remnants, and blood clots.	Will cause bladder distention and increased pain and bleeding.

NURSING DIAGNOSIS: HIGH RISK FOR INFECTION

Risk Factors
- Advanced age
- Indwelling urinary catheter
- Frequent bladder irrigations
- Surgical procedure, wound contamination during surgery

Patient Outcomes
Patient will
- show no signs of urinary tract infection or local or systemic infection.
- verbalize knowledge of signs and symptoms of infection.

Nursing Interventions	Rationales
Check vital signs every 4 hr or following hospital policy. Report if temperature exceeds 101°F (38.5 °C).	
Maintain closed gravity drainage system.	
Perform catheter care twice daily or as needed to prevent accumulation of blood and mucus at the insertion site.	Minimizes/prevents bacterial invasion through indwelling catheter.
Keep urine drainage bag lower than level of the bladder at all times.	To prevent reflux or stasis of urine.
Monitor for and report signs and symptoms of urinary tract infection (UTI) and wound infection.	Infection is recognized and treated early.
Encourage adequate fluid intake to at least 2000–2500 mL/day when oral fluid is permitted and tolerated.	Flushes kidneys/bladder of debris and bacteria. Prevents urinary stasis.

NURSING DIAGNOSIS: HIGH RISK FOR FLUID VOLUME DEFICIT

Risk Factors
- Advanced age
- Persistent bleeding blood vessels
- Venous absorption of hypotonic irrigating solutions via open bladder sinus communicating with blood circulation
- Hyponatremia

Patient Outcomes
Patient will show no signs or symptoms of hemorrhage/shock or hyponatremia postoperative prostatectomy.

Nursing Interventions	Rationales
Be alert to signs of hemorrhage (hypotension, tachycardia, dyspnea, cool and clammy skin, syncope):	Hemorrhage can lead to hypovolemic shock and death.
1. Watch drainage for evidence of increased bleeding. Differentiate type of bleeding: bright red with bright red clots increased viscosity; dark burgundy with dark clots, less viscous.	Urine will show bright blood in the beginning, decreasing to pink and then to clear. Arterial blood (bright red) requires aggressive interventions. Venous blood (burgundy) will subside independently.
2. Apply external traction to urethral catheter to control bleeding, as directed by physician; release intermittently and reassess bleeding.	Prolonged traction may cause permanent problem with urinary control.
3. Check the drainage bag, dressings, and incision area for evidence of bleeding; report excessive bleeding.	
4. Prepare patient for blood transfusion and start replacement if indicated and as prescribed.	

Nursing Interventions	Rationales
Monitor for and report signs and symptoms of dilutional hyponatremia (low serum sodium, change in mental status, confusion, restlessness, nausea and vomiting, shortness of breath (SOB), elevated blood pressure, muscle twitching, convulsions). Administer ordered parental fluids: hypertonic saline, diuretics, or sodium bicarbonate, as prescribed.	Venous absorption of large amounts of hypotonic irrigating solution through the bladder can produce excess water relative to sodium level.

NURSING DIAGNOSIS: HIGH RISK FOR SELF-ESTEEM DISTURBANCE

Risk Factors
- Loss of body parts
- Loss or perceived loss of body function: fear of impotence, loss of male identity
- Surgery
- Urinary incontinence

Patient Outcomes
Patient will
- describe feelings related to change in body image.
- resume activities of daily living.

Nursing Interventions	Rationales
Be aware that patients undergoing this type of surgery are under considerable emotional stress. Provide openings for patients to talk about concerns of incontinence and sexual functioning.	Most patients will have anxieties and questions about the effects of surgery and may be hesitant about asking necessary questions.
Give accurate information about expectation of return of sexual function.	Physiological impotence occurs when the perineal nerves are cut during radical procedures. In other procedures, sexual activity can usually be resumed in 6–8 weeks.

Nursing Interventions	Rationales
If the patient had a TURP or suprapubic or retropubic prostatectomy, inform him that retrograde ejaculation may occur when he has an orgasm but that ejaculatory pattern should return to normal within a few months. If permanent sterility is expected after a perineal approach or radical prostatectomy, discuss alternative methods of becoming a parent if this is a concern.	Seminal fluid goes into the bladder and is excreted with the urine but does not interfere with sexual functioning.
Alert physician if a disturbance in self-concept is identified.	Appropriate interventions or referral can be initiated.
If incontinence of urine is a problem:	
1. Reinforce the importance of continuing to do perineal exercises.	To improve bladder control.
2. Instruct patient in ways to minimize incontinence so that social interaction is possible (e.g., use of collection device, disposable liners, etc.).	
3. Include spouse or significant others in teaching.	Provides opportunity to enhance support system.

NURSING DIAGNOSIS: KNOWLEDGE DEFICIT REGARDING FOLLOW-UP CARE AFTER DISCHARGE

Related To
- Lack of exposure to information
- Cognitive impairment

Defining Characteristics
Clinical evidence of cognitive impairment
Inappropriate behavior, for example, apathetic, agitation
Inadequate performance or demonstration of skill
Inadequate understanding, misinterpretation, misconception of teachings
Request for information
Verbalization of problem

Patient Outcomes

Patient and significant others will

- state awareness about current health status.
- perform skills required for care at home.

Nursing Interventions	Rationales
Provide simple, specific written instructions (e.g., follow-up appointments, treatment plan, activity level, dietary modification, prescribed medications, signs and symptoms to report) at patient's level of comprehension.	Reinforces verbal instructions and serves as a reminder. Giving information that is easy to understand can increase compliance.
Instruct in ways to prevent pressure on the surgical area in order to prevent bleeding: 1. Avoid straining during bowel movements by increasing fluid intake and intake of high-fiber foods. 2. Avoid prolonged sitting or standing, long walks, long car rides, running, strenuous exercises, sexual intercourse, and lifting objects over 10 lb for 6–8 weeks after discharge.	
Instruct in ways to regain or maintain control of bladder emptying: 1. Try to urinate every 2–3 hr and whenever urge is felt.	
2. Avoid drinking large quantities of liquid (especially alcohol) over a short period of time.	Spacing the kind and amount of liquid intake will help prevent frequency.
3. Avoid drinking caffeine-containing beverages.	Caffeine is a mild diuretic and may make urinary control more difficult.
4. Abstain from liquids 2 hr before bedtime.	Reduces risk of urine retention and night incontinence.
5. Avoid activities that make it difficult to empty bladder as soon as urge is felt (e.g., long car rides, lengthy meetings).	

Nursing Interventions	Rationales
6. Perform perineal exercises while awake until urinary control is regained.	
Demonstrate catheter care, emptying of collection bag, changing from nighttime drainage to a leg bag, and clamping the collection devices.	
Stress the importance of keeping drainage bag below bladder level.	To prevent backflow of urine to minimize occurrence of UTI.
Instruct patient to report the following signs and symptoms: persistent low-grade fever (38.3 °C, or 101 °F), difficulty breathing, chest pain, increasing redness, warmth, swelling around wound, unusual excessive drainage from wound site, pain, redness and swelling in calf, urine retention, frequency, urgency, burning on urination, cloudy, foul-smelling urine, persistent bright red urine, continued persistent bright red clots, decrease in urine output, and persistent or increased bladder pain or spasms.	Same blood is expected intermitently for 2–4 weeks after surgery, but this should diminish with rest and fluid intake.
Explain the side effects of medications and the importance of taking as prescribed.	

DISCHARGE PLANNING/CONTINUITY OF CARE

- Assure that patient and/or significant other can perform skills required for care at home.
- Refer to a home care agency if continued care or teaching is required.
- Arrange follow-up visits with physician.
- Assist with obtaining prescriptions and supplies and establishing a plan for refilling prescriptions.
- Provide with information on support groups of information available (American Cancer Society).

REFERENCES

Moore, S. (1992). Nerve Sparing prostatectomy. *American Journal of Nursing, 92*(4), 59–64.

Suddarth, D. (1991). *The Lippincott manual of nursing practice.* Philadelphia, PA: Lippincott.

Tanagho, E. A. & McAninch, J. W. (1992). *Smith's general urology* (13th ed). Norwalk, CT: Appleton & Lange.

Common Breast Conditions and Procedures

▼

*B*REAST *B*RECONSTRUCTION

Gail Gaustad, RN, MS
Mercy Galicia, RN, BSN

Breast reconstruction is available for women following a mastectomy without evidence of further active disease processes. Reconstruction offers choices of varying complexity. The techniques employed can be divided into two functional categories: (1) the use of locally available tissue and/or implant and (2) the use of tissue from a distant site.

ETIOLOGIES (INDICATIONS)

Status postmastectomy without invasive disease

CLINICAL MANIFESTATIONS

- Expressed concern regarding body image and sexual identity
- Contraindications: previous radiation therapy, radical mastectomy, obesity, smoking, impaired healing, patient expresses unrealistic expectations.

CLINICAL/DIAGNOSTIC FINDINGS

Refer to Mastectomy diagnostic findings.

OTHER PLANS OF CARE TO REFERENCE

- Basic Standards for Preoperative and Postoperative Care
- Pain Management: Patient-Controlled Analgesia
- Mastectomy

NURSING DIAGNOSIS: ANXIETY

Related To
- Surgery
- Anticipated pain
- Perceived significance of procedure
- Unfamiliarity with pre- and postoperative care

Defining Characteristics

Apprehension
Facial tension
Accelerated speech and motor activity
Inability to concentrate and relax
Increased breathing
Pacing
Crying and trembling

Patient Outcomes

Patient will
- demonstrate the postoperative activities she will be required to perform.
- state pre- and postoperative procedures and expectations.
- identify coping mechanism to decrease anxiety.

Nursing Interventions	Rationales
Explain what to expect postoperatively: 1. bulky halter breast dressing 2. presence of tubes and suction device which will remove blood drainage to minimize the potential for hematoma formation	This drainage system is usually removed when drainage is less than 10–20 mL over 24 hr. Drains are commonly removed after 48 hr.

Nursing Interventions	Rationales
Explain that movement and activity may be restricted following surgery, depending on the procedure used. When an implant is placed under ample tissue, recovery is rapid and hospitalization is usually 1–3 days. Flap reconstruction is more involved, and movement and activity may be more restricted. Patients having a latissimus flap reconstruction are usually discharged after 4–5 days, when the drains are removed. A rectus abdominis procedure is more extensive, and because of the lipectomy, the patient usually is on bedrest for a little longer and is discharged a few days later.	

NURSING DIAGNOSIS: PAIN

Related To
- Surgical incision
- Tissue trauma

Defining Characteristics
Complaints of pain in operated site
Facial expression of pain
Guarding behavior
Anxiety
Lack of participation in activities

Patient Outcomes
Patient will experience diminished pain, as evidenced by
- verbalization of decreased pain or relief of pain
- relaxed facial expression and body positioning
- increased participation in activities

Nursing Interventions	Rationales
Assess level of pain by rating the intensity of pain from 0 to 10 prior to analgesic administration and again after analgesic has taken effect.	Accurate, thorough assessment is the most important component in pain control.
Provide optimal pain relief with prescribed analgesic. Use a preventive approach by medicating prior to an activity but evaluate the hazard of sedation. Instruct to request pain medication before the pain becomes severe.	It is easier to prevent pain than it is to relieve it once the intensity is severe. Medicating before an activity maintains comfort level and allows patient to participate with patient care activities without pain hindering her efforts; it also facilitates rest.
Provide diversionary activities based on patient's interest and preference.	Distraction focuses attention away from the pain. Relaxation helps to decrease anxiety, increase control, and prevent muscle contraction and fatigue.
Employ basic comfort measures, for example, comfortable and quiet environment and soothing massage to pressure points.	This helps to increase relaxation, reduce stress, and relieve muscle tension.

NURSING DIAGNOSIS: INEFFECTIVE BREATHING PATTERN

Related To reluctance to breathe deeply associated with chest wall incisional pain, effects of anesthesia, narcotics, restrictive chest dressings, fear, and anxiety

Defining Characteristics
Shallow, slow respirations
Fear and inability to cough
Diminished or absent breath sounds
Dyspnea
Hyperventilation

Patient Outcomes
Patient will maintain an effective breathing pattern, as evidenced by
- normal rate, rhythm, and depth of respirations
- absence of adventitious sounds

Nursing Interventions	Rationales
Encourage deep breathing every 2 hr during waking hours and every 4 hr during the night.	To correct ineffective breathing exercises. If not done properly, it can overly exhaust patient with minimal result.
Assist to support incision during pulmonary exercises.	This reduces pain and aids in expanding lungs during breathing exercises.
Monitor vital signs and breath sounds every 4 hr as needed.	To evaluate pulmonary status and detect accumulations of secretions.
Assess and relieve pain.	Pain interferes with breathing exercises.
Assess compression of chest dressing. Refer to physician if it is too restrictive.	
Ambulate patient as soon as allowed and tolerated.	Allows good lung expansion and helps to mobilize secretions.
Instruct and assist in the use of incentive spirometer if ordered.	

NURSING DIAGNOSIS: HIGH RISK FOR INFECTION

Risk Factors
- Surgical procedure
- Presence of drainage tube
- Decreased resistance to infection
- Wound contamination

Patient Outcomes
Patient will remain free of wound or arm infection, as evidenced by
- absence of redness, warmth, and inflammation of wound area or arm of the operative side
- absence of foul-smelling wound drainage
- normal white blood cell (WBC) count and normal wound culture

Nursing Interventions	Rationales
Monitor temperature every 4 hr or following hospital standard and report elevation.	Elevation of body temperature and an increase in pain are strong indications of presence of infection.

Nursing Interventions	Rationales
Instruct patient to avoid touching intravenous (IV) lines, dressings, drainage tubing, and incision.	
Do not use affected arm for blood draws, IV infusions, and injections. Review care of the affected arm with the patient and family following National Cancer Institute guidelines.	

NURSING DIAGNOSIS: HIGH RISK FOR ALTERED TISSUE PERFUSION

Risk Factors
- Hematoma formation
- Tension on surgical incision
- Malfunction of drainage system
- Necrosis of skin graft or grafted nipple

Patient Outcomes
The patient will
- not develop a hematoma at the surgical site, as evidenced by absence of
  - undue swelling
  - increased skin discoloration of surgical area
- not develop necrosis of the skin flap or grafted nipple, as evidenced by
  - warm and normal color of flap and nipple
  - approximated wound edges
  - absence of foul odor from site

Nursing Interventions	Rationales
Assess for and report signs of impaired blood flow to skin flap, nipple, and donor site 1. increased swelling and discoloration, temperature of operative site 2. drainage output > 50 mL/hr 3. lack of suction in drainage	Swelling and mottling should be reported immediately as possible signs that circulation is impaired.

Nursing Interventions	Rationales
Check dressing and drainage system every 2 hr for the first 24 hr, every 4 hr on the first postoperative day, then every shift, unless abnormal drainage is observed.	Ensure suction and patency of the suction device by "charging" the device every 2–4 hr, or as often as necessary. "Milk" or strip tubing, as directed, and keep tubing free of kinks.
Check for bleeding, especially under axilla of operative site and in area in which patient is lying.	Drainage flows with gravity.
Instruct to keep elbow at the side for 3–7 days after surgery. With arm at side, encourage patient to use lower arm to cradle reconstructed breast while being assisted with turns or when ambulating.	To avoid tension on the surgical site, thus preventing subsequent bleeding.
Keep supine with head of bed elevated 30° and foot of bed slightly elevated with knee gatched.	This position results in adequate circulation and comfort and will relieve strain on the abdominal incision with the rectus abdominis procedure.
Keep nausea and vomiting under control by administering antiemetics.	This prevents tension on the abdominal incision.
Place needed items within reach to prevent excessive arm and shoulder movements immediately after surgery.	
Ascertain that dressings are not too tight.	
Instruct patient to refrain from smoking, if at all possible, during the healing process. Institute measures to help patient control urge to smoke, for example, offer hard candies and vegetable sticks and provide diversionary activities according to patient's interest and preference.	Nicotine causes vasoconstriction and therefore impairs healing and has direct detrimental effect on tissue healing of the flap.

NURSING DIAGNOSIS: HIGH RISK FOR INJURY

Risk Factors
- Scar tissue formation around implant
- Capsular contraction or ingestion

Patient Outcomes
Patient will not develop
- capsular contraction around the breast implant, as evidenced by absence of increased firmness and breast mound deformity.
- migration or deflation of breast implant, as evidenced by maintenance of implant under skin flap.

Nursing Interventions	Rationales
Teach the patient to massage the breast implant as prescribed, usually three times a day for the first year after surgery. The procedure involves a gentle rotary motion to squeeze and flatten the breast implant.	Massage will decrease capsular formation around implant and keeps it mobile. It will stretch the spherical scar formation around the implant to create more space for the implant.
Instruct to wear compressive and supportive garment or bra for 4–8 weeks.	
Instruct to minimize breast motions for 4–8 weeks by avoiding jarring forces on breast, refraining from doing high-impact aerobic and jogging. Walking is permissible.	
Recommend use of different sexual positions that avoid pressure on chest wall and operative area or alternate forms of sexual expression during the initial healing process and while surgical site is still tender.	This maintains position and integrity of breast implant while enabling the patient to promote her own femininity.

NURSING DIAGNOSIS: BODY IMAGE DISTURBANCE

Related To
- Mastectomy
- Breast reconstruction surgery

Defining Characteristics

Angry, hostile
Quiet, withdrawn
Worries about physical changes excessively
Increased dependency
Not looking at reconstructed breast
Loss of interest in personal appearance
Nonparticipation in therapy plan and self-care

Patient Outcomes

Patient will
- relate realistic expectations of the appearance of the reconstructed breast.
- demonstrate movement toward acceptance of body image after surgery.
- describe a positive body image.

Nursing Interventions	Rationales
Reinforce physician's explanation that the goal of reconstructive surgery after mastectomy is to achieve a normal appearance under the clothing. Emphasize that it is not possible to exactly duplicate the size, shape, and contour of a natural breast.	
Explain that breast will be swollen and discolored in the immediate postoperative period and will appear usually high on the chest wall if a subpectoral implant has been done; assure the patient and significant other that this is temporary.	

Nursing Interventions	Rationales
Explain that when one breast is reconstructed, symmetry does not usually occur until the tissue surrounding the implant or muscle flap has stretched.	
Explain that a loss of sensitivity in the grafted nipple and skin around the suture lines is a common occurrence.	
Discuss the emotional responses that women often have following breast reconstruction, such as elation during the early postoperative period followed by depression or confusion.	
Explain that some of the depression and confusion may be a result of the memory of the mastectomy and fear of cancer. Reassure patient that these feelings are normal and usually disappear after a short time.	
Provide emotional support by being with the patient when the first dressing is removed. Explain that the reconstructed breast will not look like the other breast at first but that the molding process will begin during the recovery period and continue for 3–6 months.	
Collaborate with other professionals to assist patient toward acceptance of body image post–breast reconstruction, as needed.	
Consult physician if the patient has unrealistic expectations about the post-operative appearance of the breast.	

NURSING DIAGNOSIS: SELF-CARE DEFICIT

Related To impaired physical mobility associated with restricted arm movement, pain, and fear of injury

Defining Characteristics

Limited range of motion of the affected arm
Self-bathing deficits
Self-dressing deficits
Feeling of helplessness

Patient Outcomes

Patient will perform self-care activities within physical limitations of the affected arm and postoperative activity restrictions.

Nursing Interventions	Rationales
Medicate for pain as needed, especially before activity.	Intense pain affects patient's motor performance.
Assist patient with personal hygiene tasks that require extensive abduction of arm on the operative side (e.g., bathing, washing, and combing of hair), and encourage patient to gradually increase her own participation in self-care activities with the affected arm.	Encourage to participate in planning her care, reduce her feelings of powerlessness, and promote her feelings of control and self-worth. Inability to care for self produces feelings of dependency and poor self-concept. With increased ability for self-care, self-esteem increases.
Include significant others in providing assistance with activities of daily living (ADLs) until the patient can resume previous activities.	To provide support to the patient.
Anticipate patient needs. Leave needed items within reach.	Prevent excessive affected arm and shoulder movements while promoting some sense of independence.

NURSING DIAGNOSIS: KNOWLEDGE DEFICIT REGARDING CARE AFTER DISCHARGE

Related To lack of exposure to information

Defining Characteristics

Inability to describe treatment plan
Inaccurate interpretation of information
Repeated questions/requests for information

Patient Outcomes

Patient will
- describe plan for care after discharge.
- demonstrate dressing and activity procedures correctly.
- relate the signs and symptoms to be reported.

Nursing Interventions	Rationales
Provide patient/significant others with information on the care of the incision. Instruct to report the following: 1. persistent redness, pain, swelling, drainage at the incision site 2. implant thinning 3. change of color or breakdown of skin over implant or flap site 4. sudden change in position, size, and appearance of breast implant	
Review activity restrictions for the first 6–8 weeks or as prescribed by physician, including strenuous exercises, contact sports, jarring activities, excessive stretching, and lifting or pushing objects over 10 lb for at least 1 month or as advised by physician.	To prevent strain to pectoral muscle.
Explain the importance of breast massage three times a day for the first year after surgery as indicated. Inform patient that it takes 3–6 months for the reconstructed breast to appear natural in contour.	
Review the importance of monthly breast self-examination (BSE) of both breasts.	There is a three times greater risk of developing cancer in the other breast. Early detection can decrease the risk of mortality. Patient must make this a part of her routine, to note any changes in the way the remaining breast looks and feels. Instruct patient to watch for lumps, thickenings, redness, and swelling. If patient still menstruates, the best time to do BSE is 2–3 days after menstrual period ends, when the breast is least likely to be tender or swollen. If patient is menopausal, instruct patient to pick any day that is easy to remember to do it on a consistent basis.

Nursing Interventions	Rationales
Review care of affected arm, if appropriate.	

DISCHARGE PLANNING/CONTINUITY OF CARE

- Assure understanding and ability to carry out self-care at home.
- Assist in obtaining prescriptions, supplies, and a plan for refilling as needed.
- Arrange follow-up with physician for management after discharge.
- Refer to a home health agency if continued assistance with care is required.
- Refer to community agencies such as Reach for Recovery, ENCORE, or mastectomy support groups.

REFERENCES

Brunner, L. & Suddarth, D. (1992). *Textbook of medical-surgical nursing* (7th ed). Philadelphia, PA: Lippincott.

Mastectomy A Treatment For Breast Cancer (1990). Bethesda, MD: National Cancer Institute.

Suddarth, D. (1991). *The Lippincott manual of nursing practice*. Philadelphia, PA: Lippincott.

Swearingen, P. L. (199). *Manual of nursing therapeutics applying nursing diagnosis to medical disorders*. St. Louis, MO: Mosby.

MASTECTOMY

Gail Gaustad, RN, MS
Mercy Galicia, RN, BSN

Mastectomy is a surgical procedure done primarily for breast tumors. Treatment or surgical intervention is contigent on the tumor staging, which addresses tumor size, lymph node involvement, and distant mestastasis. Different types of mastectomies are performed based on the tumor staging: (1) partial mastectomy, also called lumpectomy, tylectomy, or segmental resection, is removal of the tumor mass and/or surrounding tissues; (2) subcutaneous mastectomy is the surgical treatment removing all underlying tissue skin, leaving the areola and nipple intact; (3) simple mastectomy is removal of the main breast structure and skin, leaving muscles and axillary nodes intact; (4) modified radical mastectomy is complete removal of breast, nipple, overlying skin, axillary nodes, and adjacent soft tissue; (5) radical mastectomy is complete removal of breast, nipple, overlying skin, pectoralis muscles, adjacent fat, fascia, and axillary lymph nodes; and (6) supraradical mastectomy is the same as a radical mastectomy plus removal of parasternal nodes.

ETIOLOGIES (INDICATIONS)

- Carcinoma
- Marked fibroadenomata

CLINICAL MANIFESTATIONS

- Single nontender firm to hard mass with ill-defined margins
- Skin and/or nipple retraction
- Axillary lymphadenopathy
- Breast enlargement
- Nipple discharge
- Redness
- Pain
- Fixation of mass to skin or chest wall

- Ulceration
- Supraclavicular lymphadenopathy
- Edema of arm
- Distant metastases: liver, bone, lung, brain

CLINICAL/DIAGNOSTIC FINDINGS

- Positive mammography
- Positive fine-needle biopsy
- Positive frozen section open biopsy
- Postive cytological exam of nipple discharge
- Increased sedimentation rate
- Increased serum alkaline phosphatase
- Hypercalcemia

OTHER PLANS OF CARE TO REFERENCE

- Basic Standards for Preoperative and Postoperative Care
- Pain Management: Patient-Controlled Analgesia

NURSING DIAGNOSIS: ANXIETY/FEAR

Related To
- Uncertainty of diagnosis or decisions about treatment protocol
- Effects of surgery on body image
- Loss of body part
- Feeling of altered femininity
- Anticipated postoperative pain and limitation
- Possible feeling of embarrassment about exposure of breast in perioperative period
- Unfamiliar environment
- Inadequate or lack of knowledge of surgical procedure
- Pre- and postoperative care

Defining Characteristics

Apprehension
Facial tension, accelerated speech and motor activity
Expressed concerns about actual/anticipated change in life
Difficulty verbalizing feelings
Sense of hopelessness
Inability to concentrate and relax
Crying and increased breathing

Patient Outcomes

Patient will
- acknowledge and discuss concerns.
- display a decrease in behavioral symptoms.
- relate lessened fear and anxiety after teaching to a level where informed decision making and on-going self-care are possible.

Nursing Interventions	Rationales
Determine level of understanding of surgical procedure.	
Assess for signs of coping that signal a readiness to learn.	Shock, disbelief, and confusion associated with diagnosis of cancer directly affect the patient's receptivity to teaching. Acknowledge that anxiety/fear may prevent effective coping.
Assess the amount of information the patient is able to take in.	Too many details or too much information can be overwhelming.
Provide information based on current needs of patient/significant other at a level they can understand. Reinforce the physician's explanation of surgery and review routine procedures, as needed.	

NURSING DIAGNOSIS: PAIN

Related To
- Surgical incision
- Trauma to tissue and nerves
- Dissection of muscle

Defining Characteristics

Care of pain in surgical site and arm and shoulder on operative side
Facial expression of pain
Guarded behavior
Lack of participation in patient care activities

Patient Outcomes

Patient will experience diminished pain, as evidenced by
- verbalization of decreased pain or relief of pain
- relaxed facial expression and body positioning
- increased participation in activities

Nursing Interventions	Rationales
Assess patient's level, location, intensity, and duration of pain prior to analgesic administration and reassess amount of relief obtained.	The amount of tissue, muscle, and lymphatic system removed can affect the amount of pain experienced. Damage of nerves in the axillary region may be more intolerable than surgical pain.
Provide patient with optimal pain relief with prescribed analgesic. Use preventive approach.	It maintains comfort level and allows patient to exercise arm and participate in care activities without pain hindering her efforts.
Explain phantom breast sensation, that is, sensations of "pins and needles," heaviness, numbness, discomfort, and sensation of both breasts being present most of the time.	Provides reassurance that these sensations are normal after breast surgery.
Provide diversionary activities as per patient's interest and preference.	

NURSING DIAGNOSIS: INEFFECTIVE BREATHING PATTERN

Related To reluctance to breathe deeply associated with chest wall incisional pain, effects of anesthesia, narcotics, restrictive dressings, fear, and anxiety

Defining Characteristics
Shallow, slow respirations
Diminished or absent breath sounds
Presence of adventitious breath sounds
Hyperventilation, dyspnea
Fear
Inability to cough

Patient Outcomes
Patient will maintain an effective breathing pattern, as evidenced by
- normal rate, rhythm, and depth of respirations
- clear breath sounds

Nursing Interventions	Rationales
Instruct and encourage to deep breathe and cough every 2 hr.	If breathing exercises are not done correctly, it can exhaust patient with minimal results.
Teach patient to support incision during pulmonary exercises.	To reduce pain and aid lung expansion.
Monitor vital signs and breath sounds every 4 hr until patient is ambulatory.	
Assess and relieve pain.	Pain interferes with breathing exercises.
Assess compression of chest dressing. Refer to surgeon if too restrictive.	
Ambulate patient as soon as allowed and tolerated. Support from the operated side. Explain that a sensation of feeling unbalanced is common initially, particularly if breast was large.	Allows good lung expansion and mobilizes secretions.

NURSING DIAGNOSIS: HIGH RISK FOR ALTERED TISSUE PERFUSION

Risk Factors
- Surgery
- Tension on surgical incision secondary to abduction of affected arm beyond 90° angle
- Persistent bleeding

Patient Outcomes
Patient will not develop bleeding, as evidenced by
- stable vital signs
- no undue, excessive bloody wound drainage

Nursing Interventions	Rationales
Monitor vital signs every 4 hr or per hospital standard.	Report hypotension, excessive drainage, edema, and lack of suction in drainage system.

Nursing Interventions	Rationales
Check dressing and drainage every 2 hr for initial 24 hr, every 4 hr first postoperative day, then every shift, unless abnormal drainage is observed.	Ensure suction and patency of the suction device by "charging" the device every 2–4 hr or as often as necessary. Pressure dressing is usually applied and reinforced if indicated.
Check for bleeding under axilla of operative side and in area on which patient is lying.	
Instruct to not abduct affected arm beyond 90° angle and to avoid excessive pressure to operative site.	Avoids tension to incision which can predispose bleeding.
Place needed items within easy reach.	Prevents excessive arm and shoulder extension.

NURSING DIAGNOSIS: HIGH RISK FOR IMPAIRED TISSUE INTEGRITY

Risk Factors
- Extensive axillary node dissection
- Obstruction of lymphatic flow associated with lymph node removal
- Infection
- Trauma to arm
- Lymphedema of affected arm

Patient Outcomes
Patient will not develop lymphedema in the affected arm, as evidenced by
- normal motor and sensory functions of operative arm
- absence of pain and swelling in affected arm

Nursing Interventions	Rationales
Assess and report signs of lymphedema: sensory and motor deficits, pain, sensation of heaviness, and swelling of operative arm. Measure affected arm daily at points 6 inches above/below elbow.	

Nursing Interventions	Rationales
Maintain patient in semi-Fowler's immediately postoperatively. Elevate operative arm on pillows, keeping elbow at heart level and hand higher than elbow.	Promotes gravity drainage of fluids.
Instruct patient to avoid prolonged abduction of arm and abduction beyond 90°.	Prevents pressure on axilla which can impede lymphatic flow and stress on the suture line.
Restrict use of operative arm for blood pressure measurement, venipuncture, and injections.	Decreases risk of infection, trauma, and lymphedema.
Promote passive, then active, exercises of hand, arm, and shoulder of affected arm as soon as indicated.	Stimulates circulation; promotes neuromuscular competence and prevents stasis.
Instruct and assist with mastectomy exercises. Encourage early initiation of finger flexion and extension, pronating and supinating forearms. Encourage patient to brush teeth and hair with affected arm as tolerated.	The purpose of postmastectomy exercises is to have complete range of motion of affected shoulder. This promotes venous return, reducing risk of lymphedema and preventing stiffness. Exercises are introduced gradually, increased in keeping with the ability of the healing tissue to withstand additional stresses. If skin grafting occurred or incision was closed with considerable tension, such exercises are limited and introduced gradually.
Emphasize the value of good posture.	Hunching favors affected arm and inhibits range-of-motion (ROM) effectiveness.

NURSING DIAGNOSIS: HIGH RISK FOR INFECTION

Risk Factors
- Surgical procedure
- Presence of drainage system
- Noncompliance to precautions of infection prevention
- Decreased resistance to infection
- Obesity

Patient Outcomes

Patient will remain free of wound infection, as evidenced by
- absence of redness, warmth, and inflammation of arm and/or wound area
- absence of foul-smelling wound drainage
- normal WBC
- normal wound culture

Nursing Interventions	Rationales
Monitor temperature every 4 hr or following hospital standards and report elevation.	Body temperature elevation is a strong indication of infection.
Use good hand-washing technique before and after patient care and encourage patient to do the same.	Minimizes patient's risk of nosocomial infection.
Restrict use of affected arm for blood pressure measurements, injections, and venipuncture.	

NURSING DIAGNOSIS: HIGH RISK FOR INEFFECTIVE INDIVIDUAL COPING

Risk Factors
- Diagnosis of cancer
- Perceived change in body image
- Lack of social support

Patient Outcomes

Patient will demonstrate the use of effective coping skills, as evidenced by
- verbalization of ability to cope with loss of a breast and diagnosis of cancer
- participation in treatment plan and self-care activities
- utilization of problem-solving techniques
- recognition and utilization of available support systems

Nursing Interventions	Rationales
Promote the development of a therapeutic relationship by maintaining continuity of caregivers.	May facilitate patient's verbalization of fears and concerns.

Nursing Interventions	Rationales
Include patient in planning of care, encourage maximum participation, and allow patient to make choices when appropriate.	Enables maintaining a sense of control.
Allow for anger and disbelief regarding diagnosis to surface. Allow patient to go through the grieving process.	Unaddressed feelings can inhibit effective coping.
Encourage to utilize support system to assist with coping, that is, family, friends, and clergy.	Involvement and presence of significant others may assist patient's coping.
Suggest appropriate support referrals: Reach to Recovery, American Cancer Society, mastectomy support groups, ENCORE (Encouragement, Normalcy, Counseling, Opportunity, Reaching Out Energies received—YWCA), and social services or pastoral care.	

NURSING DIAGNOSIS: BODY IMAGE DISTURBANCE

Related To loss of breast

Defining Characteristics
Missing breast
Verbalizes fear of rejection or reaction by others, negative feelings about body, feelings of helplessness, hopelessness, and powerlessness
Not looking at operated site
Preoccupation with loss of breast
Loss of social involvement
Nonparticipation in therapy plan and self-care

Patient Outcomes
Patient will demonstrate initial adaptation to loss of breast and integration of change in body image, as evidenced by
- acceptance of self
- maintenance of relationships with significant others
- participation in ADLs and therapy program
- active interest in personal appearance
- willingness to look at operative site
- willingness to participate in social activities

Nursing Interventions	Rationales
Assist patient with care; involve her in discussion that will provide further insights into coping skills and self-esteem.	To facilitate optimal adjustment, it is necessary to understand patient's coping skills.
Explain the normalcy of grieving the loss of a body part.	
Assess patient's support system and maintain contact with significant others as often as indicated.	
Maintain presence with patient during the first dressing change and encourage expression of feelings about appearance of the incision and change in body image. Reassure that the incision will look better each day.	
Review availability of adaptations, that is, breast reconstruction and prosthetic devices, as indicated.	
Provide temporary soft prosthesis as indicated.	Promotes social acceptance and allows patient to feel more comfortable about body image at discharge.

NURSING DIAGNOSIS: SELF-CARE DEFICIT

Related To impaired physical mobility associated with restricted arm movement, pain, fear of injury, and weakness

Defining Characteristics
Limited range of motion of affected arm
Self-bathing deficits
Self-dressing deficits
Feeling of hoplessness

Patient Outcome
Patient will perform self-care activities within physical limitations of the affected arm and postoperative activity restrictions.

Nursing Interventions	Rationales
Medicate for pain as needed, especially before activity.	Intense pain affects motor performance.
Position patient in alignment to prevent complications.	
Assist patient with personal hygiene tasks that require extension and abduction of arm on operative side. Encourage patient to gradually increase participation in self-care activities with affected arm.	
Include significant other in providing assistance with ADLs until patient can resume activities.	To provide support to the patient.

NURSING DIAGNOSIS: KNOWLEDGE DEFICIT REGARDING CARE AFTER DISCHARGE

Related To lack of exposure to information

Defining Characteristics
Inability to describe treatment plan
Inability to perform self-care skills
Verbalizes deficiency in knowledge or skill of follow-up information
Expresses inaccurate interpretation of information

Patient Outcomes
Patient will
- verbalize understanding of treatment after discharge.
- demonstrate necessary procedures correctly.
- relate what signs and symptoms are reportable and suggestive of complications.

Nursing Interventions	Rationales
Instruct about incisional care:	
1. Newly healed wound may have less sensation or possibly be more sensitive.	Related to severed nerves.
2. Suggest showers vs. tub baths and blotting incision dry.	Minimize exposure to infection.

Nursing Interventions	**Rationales**
3. Review signs and symptoms of infection: tenderness, redness, swelling, warmth of surgical area, and drainage. Notify physician.	If these are observed, put arm over head and "pump" fist to minimize swelling.
4. Massage healed incision gently with cocoa butter or vitamin E cream.	Promotes circulation, increases skin elasticity, and minimizes keloid formation.
Instruct on care of the drain if present at discharge.	
Review breast self-examination (BSE).	Essential to establish norm to recognize abnormality. Risk increases threefold for development of cancer in the other breast. Early detection can reduce the risk of mortality.
Instruct on care of the affected arm: 1. Avoid burns while cooking or smoking. 2. Avoid sunburns. 3. Have all injections, vaccinations, blood samples, and blood pressures done on the unaffected arm. 4. Use electric razor with a narrow head for underarm shaving to reduce the risk of injury. 5. Carry heavy packages or handbags on unaffected arm 6. Wash cuts promptly, treat with antibacterial medication, and cover with a sterile dressing; check often for signs of infection. 7. Never cut cuticles; use hand cream or lotion. 8. Wear watches or jewelry loosely, if at all, on operative arm.	Circulation of lymph is slowed related to removal of nodes and connecting vessels, thus increasing the risk of infection.

Nursing Interventions	Rationales
9. Wear protective gloves when gardening and when using strong detergent. 10. Use a thimble for sewing. 11. Avoid harsh chemicals and abrasive compounds. 12. Use insect repellant to avoid bites and stings. 13. Avoid elastic cuffs on blouses and night gowns.	

DISCHARGE PLANNING/CONTINUITY OF CARE

- Assure understanding and ability to carry out self-care at home.
- Assist in obtaining prescriptions and supplies and establishing a plan for refilling prescriptions as needed.
- Arrange follow-up with physician for management postdischarge.
- Refer to a home health agency if continued assistance with care is required.
- Refer to community agencies such as Reach for Recovery, ENCORE, or mastectomy support groups.
- Provide with information on where to obtain prosthetic breast devices and adaptive clothing.

REFERENCES

Guiliano, A. (1991). L. W. Way (Ed.), *The breast in current surgical diagnosis*. Norwalk, CT: Appleton & Lange.

After breast cancer—A guide to follow-up care (1990). Bethesda, MD: National Cancer Institute.

Mastectomy a treatment for breast cancer (1990). Bethesda, MD: National Cancer Institute.

Saleh, L. K. (1992). Practical points in the care of the patient post–breast surgery. *Journal of Post Anesthesia Nursing, 7*(4), 176–178.

Stein, P. & Zera, R. (1991). Breast cancer. *AORN Journal, 53*(4), 938–963.

Common Infectious Disease and Skin Conditions

▼

ACQUIRED IMMUNODEFICIENCY SYNDROME: OPPORTUNISTIC INFECTIONS, SECONDARY CANCERS AND NEUROLOGICAL DISEASE

LuAnn Greiner, RN, BSN

A healthy immune system is required in order for the body to defend itself against infection. Individuals with the human immunodeficiency virus (HIV) experience a depletion of T4 (CD4, T-helper) lymphocytes, which in turn predisposes them to opportunistic infections, secondary cancers, and neurological disease indicative of the progression of HIV to acquired immunodeficiency syndrome (AIDS), a chronic, life-threatening illness. Regardless of the particular AIDS-defining illness (Table 41.1) the individual presents with, the plan of care must incorporate the physical, psychosocial and cognitive manifestations of the development and progression of AIDS.

ETIOLOGIES

- Presence of the HIV
- Depletion of T4 (CD4, T-helper) lymphocytes leading to immunodeficiency predisposing to opportunistic infections, secondary cancers, and neurological disease

CLINICAL MANIFESTATIONS

- Nausea and vomiting
- Persistent diarrhea
- Persistent fever
- Anorexia
- Dysphagia
- Involuntary weight loss

- Night sweats
- Abdominal pain
- Peripheral neuropathy
- Headache
- Persistent cough
- Dyspnea on exertion
- Mental status changes
- Chest pain

- Fatigue
- Anemia
- Skin lesions/rash
- Vision changes
- Cytopenias
- Hypotension
- Dehydration
- Recurrent yeast infections

Table 41.1 • AIDS-Defining Illnesses

AIDS dementia
Bacterial infections (2 or more within 2 years)
Candidiasis (esophageal, pulmonary)
Coccidioidomycosis
Cryptococcal meningitis
Cryptosporidiosis
Cytomegalovirus (CMV)
Herpes simplex virus (HSV)
Herpes varicella-zoster virus (HZV)
Histoplasmosis
Invasive cervical cancer
Isosporiasis
Kaposi's sarcoma (KS)
Lymphoid interstitial pneumonia (LIP)
Mycobacterium avium complex (MAC)
Mycobacterium kansasii
Non-Hodgkin's lymphoma
Nonpulmonary tuberculosis
Pneumocystis carinii pneumonia (PCP)
Primary lymphoma of the brain
Pulmonary tuberculosis
Progressive multifocal leukoencephalopathy (PML)
Recurrent bacterial pneumonia (2 or more in 12-month period)
Salmonellosis
Toxoplasmosis
Wasting syndrome

Note: From Centers for Disease Control, January 1 1993.

CLINICAL/DIAGNOSTIC FINDINGS

- Total T4 lymphocyte count <200
- Abnormal chest x-ray consistent with pulmonary involvement
- Cultures (blood, wound, spinal fluid, stool, sputum) and/or tissue

biopsy positive for organisms indicative of opportunistic infection or
secondary cancer
- Central nervous system lesion on head magnetic resonance imaging
(MRI) indicative of opportunistic infection or tumor growth
- Abnormal ambulatory oxygen desaturation study consistent with
Pneumocystis carinii pneumonia (PCP)
- Ophthalmologic changes consistent with cytomegaloviral retinitis

OTHER PLANS OF CARE TO REFERENCE

- Pain Management: Patient-Controlled Analgesia
- Nutrition/Support: Total Parenteral Nutrition
- Long-Term Venous Access
- Lumbar Puncture
- Alterations in Conciousness
- Prevention and Care of Pressure Ulcers

NURSING DIAGNOSIS: HIGH RISK FOR SOCIAL ISOLATION

Risk Factors
- Activity intolerance associated with acute illness and progression of
disease
- Presence, and associated stigma, of a communicable disease
- Long-term hospitalization
- Financial instability
- Loss of established relationships
- Unemployment or underemployment
- Loss of usual means of transportation
- Homosexual or bisexual identity
- Relocation secondary to long-term care needs
- History of intravenous (IV) drug use and associated stigma
- Lack of adequate child care

Patient Outcomes
The patient will
- convey that feelings of isolation are validated by others.
- identify risk factors contributing to social isolation.
- identify and utilize resources available to reduce or eliminate risk
factors.

Nursing Interventions	Rationales
Assess for risk factors contributing to social isolation and feelings of loneliness.	
Validate the patient's feelings of social isolation and provide emotional support.	Validation of the subjective feeling of social isolation is imperative to collaboration with the patient in reducing or eliminating risk factors.
In collaboration with patient, identify existing support systems and their effectiveness.	
Reduce or eliminate risk factors contributing to social isolation: 1. Initiate physical therapy: muscle-strengthening exercises to promote maximum activity tolerance and sense of well-being. 2. Contact hospital social worker for assistance with financial concerns and establishment of community-based support. 3. Assist with referral to local AIDS service organization and/or local support groups available to persons with HIV/AIDS, if desired. 4. Identify and encourage participation in diversional activities that contribute to feelings of productivity and promote interaction with others. 5. Identify alternative means of transportation. 6. Assist with arrangements for provision of child care, if needed. 7. Provide supportive counseling to assist patient in exploring feelings associated with sexual identity, current illness, and presence of communicable disease. 8. Assist with referral to drug treatment program, if desired.	

Nursing Interventions	Rationales
Assist significant others in understanding the implications of chronic, life-threatening illness on one's self-image and identifying ways to provide support.	

NURSING DIAGNOSIS: PAIN

Related To
- Neuropathy
- Malignancy
- Immobility
- Diagnostic procedures
- Tissue ischemia
- Fear
- Anxiety

Defining Characteristics
Reports or demonstrates pain
Necessity of diagnostic tests/invasive procedures
Fear and anxiety associated with pain experience
Inability to concentrate
Insomnia

Patient Outcomes
The patient will
- convey that others validate the pain experience.
- identify the location and intensity of the pain.
- identify precipitating factors that increase the pain experience.
- identify side effects of pain-relieving measures and ways to manage them.
- attain optimal pain relief with improved comfort, rest, and mobility.

Nursing Interventions	Rationales
Assess subjective and objective data to illicit character and intensity of pain experience.	Complete information regarding the patient's pain experience will contribute to optimal pain relief measures.
Validate the patient's feeling of pain.	Validation of the pain experience will decrease associated fear and anxiety.

Nursing Interventions	Rationales
Identify aggravating factors which contribute to the pain experience, for example, fear of pain, activity, and oral intake.	
Identify measures currently used to relieve pain, including prescribed medications, recreational drug use, and nonpharmacological pain-relieving measures.	Discussion of current use of pain-relieving measures will illicit further information regarding the patient's pain experience and coping mechanisms.
Differentiate between chronic (greater than 6 months) and acute pain and administer analgesics accordingly.	Differentiation of chronic and acute pain will assist in identifying the most effective treatment modalities. Analgesics provide the most consistent pain relief when administered on a scheduled rather than an as-needed basis.
Instruct patient on management of common side effects of pain-relieving medications, specifically constipation, nausea, vomiting, and sedation.	Common side effects must be managed appropriately to maintain optimal pain relief.
Offer alternative pain-relieving therapies as indicated based on patient interest and ability to participate, for example, guided imagery, massage, music, and art therapy.	
Assess response to pain-relieving measures and consult with physician if optimal pain relief has not been achieved.	Multiple factors will influence the response to pain-relieving measures, necessitating ongoing evaluation and adjustment.

NURSING DIAGNOSIS: KNOWLEDGE DEFICIT—TREATMENT AND PROGRESSION

Related To
- New diagnosis
- Lack of exposure to information

Defining Characteristics
First admission to inpatient setting for AIDS-defining illness
Anxiety associated with progression of life-threatening illness

Inability of patient/significant other to verbalize understanding of diagnosis, treatment, and long-term therapies
Initiation of long-term IV therapies
Denial of presence or progression of disease

Patient Outcomes

The patient will
- verbalize understanding of diagnosis, treatment, and long-term therapies associated with acute/chronic illness.
- demonstrate correct technique for administration of IV therapies.
- perform proper infection control techniques and verbalize understanding of their role in prevention of disease transmission.
- define a plan for ongoing health care and identify and utilize available health care resources.

Nursing Interventions	Rationales
Assess for current knowledge of HIV infection and progression of disease and provide necessary information based on patient readiness to learn and physical and cognitive status.	Patients will present with extreme variations in the level of understanding of HIV infection and disease progression. Teaching will range from basic concepts of HIV infection to detailed information about specific AIDS-defining illness.
Instruct patient and significant other regarding specific presenting illness including signs and symptoms, treatment options, side effects of medications, and proper infection control techniques.	An understanding of the treatment plan is vital to quality of life and self-empowerment in the midst of chronic, life-threatening illness.
Utilize available resources, including written materials, videos, and consultation with HIV clinical nurse specialist, if available.	Written materials and videos will reinforce verbal instruction. The HIV clinical nurse specialists are experts in HIV education/management.
Contact home infusion services to provide instruction and coordination of supplies for home IV therapies, if applicable.	Short- or long-term home IV therapy will require detailed instruction and ongoing support after discharge.
If home IV therapy is indicated, instruct patient and/or significant other on care and maintenance of venous access devices.	Self-care activities promote independence. Meticulous IV line and site care decreases risk of phlebitis and line contamination.

Nursing Interventions	Rationales
Initiate referral to visiting nurse for reinforcement and monitoring of treatment plan, if indicated.	Patient and/or significant other will likely need ongoing nursing support and teaching following acute illness.
Initiate referral to local AIDS service organization (ASO).	Individuals who avail themselves of ASO services gain significant knowledge regarding disease process and treatment modalities.

NURSING DIAGNOSIS: HIGH RISK FOR INFECTION— NOSOCOMIAL

Risk Factors
- Weakened immune system related to presence of HIV
- Multiple invasive procedures
- Skin breakdown secondary to immobility and infection
- Bone marrow suppression as a side effect of immunosuppressive medications
- Long-term IV therapy/presence of venous access device

Patient Outcomes
The patient will
- identify risk factors for nosocomial infections.
- remain free of nosocomial infection throughout hospitalization.
- describe measures to maintain skin integrity.

Nursing Interventions	Rationales
Assess for risk factors associated with nosocomial infection: 1. baseline assessment of skin 2. baseline neutrophil count 3. use of bone marrow–suppressing agents 4. invasive procedures 5. indications for presence of long-term venous access device	
Monitor neutrophil count and initiate neutropenic precaustions if count drops below 500.	Transient neutropenia can occur secondary to the use of bone marrow–suppressing agents, further placing the patient at risk for nosocomial infection.

Nursing Interventions	Rationales
Adhere to universal precautions and body substance isolation at all times.	To reduce the risk of transmission of pathogens.
Follow strict aseptic technique when performing treatments and invasive procedures.	
Promote optimal skin integrity. 1. Perform site care to all venous lines every 72 hr. 2. Reposition immobilized patients every 2 hr. 3. Maintain adequate nutrition and fluid intake. 4. Follow strict aseptic technique with all dressing changes. 5. Maximize activity for patients restricted to bed. 6. Provide air mattress for bed, foam, or gel pad for chairs. 7. Assess skin thoroughly every 8 hr and prn. 8. Administer antidiarrheals as indicated. 9. If patient is incontinent of urine, provide perianal care every 2 hr and prn. Consider use of condom or indwelling catheter to prevent excoriation of skin. 10. Apply emollients to dry areas of skin.	The effects of immobility, the wasting syndrome and the altered nutritional status associated with AIDS, and the presence of excretions and secretions as the result of fevers, incontinence, and wound drainage each contribute to skin breakdown and, in turn, increased risk for nosocomial infection.
Instruct visitors on proper hand-washing techniques and other safety measures to prevent transmission of infections to which patient is susceptible, for example, upper respiratory infections and herpes simplex virus.	

Nursing Interventions	Rationales
Consult with physician to consider long-term venous access device if IV therapy is indicated for longer than 2 weeks.	The frequency with which short-term venous access devices must be changed and the patient's susceptibility to infection negate the use of these devices if IV therapy is indicated for longer than 2 weeks.

NURSING DIAGNOSIS: GRIEVING

Related To
- Loss of financial and physical independence
- Loss of social supports
- Changes in life-style secondary to progression of AIDS.

Defining Characteristics
Reports an actual or perceived loss
Anger
Depression
Withdrawal
Denial of need for assistance from others

Patient Outcomes
Patient will
- convey feelings of grief and loss.
- identify and utilize appropriate coping mechanisms for working through grief.
- identify and utilize available resources for counseling and support.

Nursing Interventions	Rationales
Establish a safe, trusting relationship that encourages expression of feelings.	
Provide supportive counseling that acknowledges patient's grief experience and associated feelings.	
Encourage to make choices in plan of care to increase feelings of control.	

Nursing Interventions	Rationales
Provide realistic, straightforward prognostic information when resolution of acute illness or progression of disease is not indicated.	
In collaboration with patient, identify effective coping mechanisms for working through grief.	
Identify and encourage participation in hospital and community-based support programs, for example, inpatient support group, local AIDS service organization.	

NURSING DIAGNOSIS: HIGH RISK FOR IMPAIRED PHYSICAL MOBILITY/SELF-CARE DEFICITS

Risk Factors
- Progressive, debilitating illness
- Visual, cognitive, and sensory impairments
- Malnutrition as a result of chronic diarrhea, wasting syndrome, and inability to maintain adequate oral intake
- Pain

Patient Outcomes
Patient will
- identify and utilize adaptive techniques to perform daily activities and optimize independence.
- identify and utilize community agencies to assist with self-care needs and ongoing support.

Nursing Interventions	Rationales
Obtain baseline and ongoing data of functional abilities and limitations using established functional assessment tools.	Early detection and ongoing monitoring of physical limitations allow initiation of therapies that promote optimal function and independence.

Nursing Interventions	Rationales
Identify factors which place patient at risk and institute interventions to minimize risks: 1. Monitor fluid losses and maintain adequate hydration. 2. Consult registered dietitian to assist in optimizing nutritional status. 3. Consult physical and occupational therapy for instruction on muscle-strengthening exercises and energy expenditure modifications. 4. Teach active and/or passive range-of-motion exercises as indicated. 5. Initiate pain-relieving measures and administer analgesics as prescribed to maximize activity tolerance.	Contributing factors must be identified and corrected to maximize activity tolerance.
Facilitate use of assistive devices as indicated.	
Initiate referral to a home care agency for functional assessment and initiation of ongoing physical and occupational therapies.	

NURSING DIAGNOSIS: HIGH RISK FOR INJURY

Risk Factors
- Weakness and fatigue
- Visual, cognitive, and sensory deficits
- Sedation associated with analgesics
- Hypotension associated with anemia, dehydration

Patient Outcomes
Patient will
- remain free from injury.
- identify potential hazards in the environment.
- describe general safety measures.
- obtain necessary adaptive equipment to promote safety.

Nursing Interventions	Rationales
Identify potential hazards in the hospital and home environment.	
Obtain baseline data regarding visual, cognitive, and sensory and physical limitations/deficits.	This information will direct the type of interventions and adaptive equipment needed.
Provide for orientation to the hospital environment.	
Initiate safety measures when patient is identified to be at risk for falls: 1. frequent reorientation 2. use of siderails 3. 24-hr sitter or attendant care 4. bed alarm 5. condom or indwelling catheter 6. close proximity to unit desk 7. assistance with activities 8. call light in reach at all times 9. use of soft wrist or chest restraint if other safety measures fail	
Discuss general safety measures in the home and provide necessary adaptive equipment.	
Initiate home care referral to perform functional assessment and initiate safety measures as indicated.	

DISCHARGE PLANNING/CONTINUITY OF CARE

- Initiate a discharge planning meeting that includes the patient, significant others, and representatives from all involved disciplines and referral agencies.
- Provide with necessary home care supplies and prescriptions and establish a plan for refilling prescriptions.
- Review and finalize home care plan, ensuring that adequate support services are available to the patient.
- Initiate referral to a home health care agency for ongoing nursing, therapy, and attendant care.

- Initiate referral to local AIDS service organization or other counseling agency for ongoing psychosocial support.
- Arrange for follow-up appointments with primary physician.
- Provide telephone numbers in case of questions or emergencies.
- Identify avenues for caregiver support and respite.

REFERENCES

Aranda-Naranjo, B. (1993). The effect of HIV on the family: Implications for care. *AIDS Patient Care, 7*(1), 27–29.

Bartlett, J. G. & Finkbeiner, A. K. (1991). *The guide to living with HIV Infection*. Baltimore, MD: Johns Hopkins University Press.

Kelly, F., & Holman, S. (1993). The new faces of AIDS. *American Journal of Nursing, 93*(2), 26–34.

Lewis, A. (Ed.). (1988). *Nursing care of the person with AIDS/ARC*. Rockville, MD: Aspen.

Wolfe, L. (1992). Grief, AIDS and the gay community. *AIDS Patient Care, 6*(4), 194–197.

▼

PREVENTION AND CARE OF PRESSURE ULCERS

Barbara King, RN, MS, CCRN, ANP
Susan Murray, RN, MS

Pressure ulcers are defined as an area of localized tissue damage caused by ischemia due to pressure. The most frequently identified pressure ulcer sites are over bony prominences, which include scapula, elbows, iliac crest, sacrum, trochanters, and heels.

ETIOLOGIES

- Intrinsic factors
  - compromised nutritional status
  - advanced age
  - elevated glucose levels
  - decreased circulation
  - decreased sensation
  - decreased immune status
  - decreased skin turgor
- Extrinsic factors
  - excessive pressure
  - excessive shearing
  - excessive friction
  - excessive moisture

CLINICAL MANIFESTATIONS

Stage I
- Nonblanchable erythema
- Epidermis intact

Stage II
- Loss of epidermis
- Painful
- Free of necrotic tissue

Stage III
- Loss of dermis to subcutaneous tissue
- Usually not painful
- May include
  - necrotic tissue
  - sinus tract formation/undermining (tunneling or track formation under the skin
  - exudate
  - infection

Stage IV
- Deep tissue destruction extending to fascia, muscle, or bone usually not painful
- May include
  - necrotic tissue
  - sinus tract formation/undermining
  - exudate
  - infection

CLINICAL/DIAGNOSTIC FINDINGS

- Altered nutritional state
  - hypoalbunemia
  - weight loss
  - hypocholesterolemia
  - decreased total lymphocyte count
  - negative nitrogen balance
  - protein deficiency
  - anemia
  - hyperglycemia
  - decreased serum transferrin
- Altered circulatory state
  - dehydration
  - low diastolic blood pressure
  - edema
  - decreased hematocrit/hemoglobin
- Infected pressure ulcers
  - elevated white blood cell (WBC) count
  - positive wound culture
  - osteomyelitis
  - fever

NURSING DIAGNOSIS: HIGH RISK FOR IMPAIRED SKIN INTEGRITY

Risk Factors
- Intrinsic factors: decreased serum albumin, obesity, emaciation, low diastolic blood pressure, peripheral neuropathy, elderly, poor skin

turgor, immunocompromised, hyperglycemia, medications, dehydration, edema
- Extrinsic factors: incontinence, diaphoresis, immobility, decreased activity, mechanical factors (shearing, friction, pressure), hypothermia

Patient Outcomes

Patient/caregiver will
- maintain intact skin.
- state necessary measures to reduce pressure/shearing/friction/moisture.
- state importance of adequate nutrition and fluid to maintain skin integrity.

Nursing Interventions	Rationales
Establish a position change schedule.	Frequency must be tailored to individual patient needs. The schedule should include major position changes and minor weight shifts at least every 2 hr.
Utilize pressure reduction/relief device in conjunction with position change schedule. (See Table 42.1)	Capillary closing pressure is 25–32 mmHg. Pressure-reducing devices lower pressure as compared to a standard hospital mattress or chair surface but do not reduce pressure below 32 mmHg. Therefore, the device must be used in conjunction with a turning schedule. Pressure relief devices (low air loss bed and air-fluidized bed) lower capillary closing pressure below 32 mmHg.
Assist with ambulation as tolerated.	
Utilize measures to decrease shearing and friction:	Shearing of skin layers occurs when patients slide down in bed.
1. Place head of bed less than 30° when not contraindicated.	
2. Use turning sheet, trapeze, lifts, and transfer boards.	Reduce surface cling and friction.
3. Use powder or cornstarch on surfaces contacting the skin.	Absorbs moisture; reduces friction.
4. Apply transparent dressing to high-risk areas.	Reduces surface friction.

Nursing Interventions	Rationales
Utilize measures to reduce excessive moisture: 1. Utilize pressure relief/reduction device which provides aeration (e.g., vented air mattress, low air loss beds, air-fluidized beds). 2. Apply moisture barrier creme to contacting skin. 3. Change gowns and linens when wet, as needed.	Excessive moisture and/or contact with urine or stool causes maceration and/or chemical erosion to the skin.
Monitor patient's nutritional and hydration status by assessing 1. intake and output 2. daily weight 3. calorie count 4. dietary consult 5. vital signs 6. BUN, creatine, cholesterol, albumin	Tissue hydration and positive nitrogen balance are critical for wound healing. Adequate fluid intake is necessary to maintain intact skin.
Provide education to patient/family/caregiver which includes 1. effects of and measures to decrease pressure/shearing/moisture/friction to the skin 2. Effects of medical problems on circulation and skin integrity 3. routine skin care and inspection of skin for signs of impending skin breakdown. 4. importance of adequate fluid and nutritional intake	

NURSING DIAGNOSIS: IMPAIRED SKIN INTEGRITY

Related To pressure

Defining Characteristics
Nonblanchable erythema
Disruption of skin surface and layers

Patient Outcomes
Patient will
- not develop further pressure ulcer formation.

- have adequate nutritional and fluid intake.
- verbalize signs and symptoms of infected wound.
- demonstrate activities and treatments which will promote wound healing.
- show signs of progressive wound healing.

Table 42.1 • Pressure-Reducing/Relieving Devices

Devices	Indications for Use
Waffle/egg crate foam mattress overlay: no pressure reduction/relief	Comfort only, does not provide pressure reduction/relief
Static air mattress: pressure reduction only	High-risk patient; presence of stage I or II pressure ulcer; presence of stage III or IV pressure ulcer and awaiting surgical consult
Low airloss bed: pressure relief provided	Limited mobility with one other factor: • Anasarca • Drainage and/or body fluids contained in pouching device • Presence of stage III or IV pressure ulcer • Postoperative myocutaneous flap • Pain management
Air-fluidized bed: pressure relief provided	Immobility with one other factor: • Drainage and/or body fluids not contained in pouching device. • Presence of stage III or IV pressure ulcer • Postoperative myocutaneous flap • Pain management • Hypothermia/hyperthermia

Nursing Interventions	Rationales
Identify stage of pressure ulcer.	See Clinical Manifestations.

Nursing Interventions	Rationales
Assess pressure ulcer for: 1. size 2. location 3. undermining/sinus formation 4. necrotic tissue 5. local infection (erythema, induration, purulent drainage, malodorous drainage, crepitus) 6. characteristics of exudate 7. pain to the wound and surrounding tissues	
Measure the depth or undermining of a pressure ulcer using the following technique: 1. With a gloved hand, insert a 6-inch cotton-tipped applicator into the deepest portion of the wound. 2. Grasp the fully inserted applicator with the thumb and forefinger at the point where the applicator meets the wound surface. 3. Carefully remove the applicator while maintaining the marking point. Measure from the tip of the applicator to the grasp point. This will indicate the wound depth.	Accurate measurement of wound size is necessary in order to evaluate the healing process.
Monitor patient for signs and symptoms of systemic infection, including 1. fever 2. leukocytosis 3. confusion 4. tachycardia 5. hypotension 6. malaise	

Nursing Interventions	Rationales
Monitor fluid and nutritional status: 1. intake and output 2. daily weight 3. calorie count 4. dietary consult 5. vital signs 6. BUN, creatinine cholesterol, albumin	
Institute measures to reduce pressure, shearing, friction, and moisture.	
Debride necrotic tissue, if present:	Presence of necrotic tissue hinders wound healing.
1. use of enzymatic debridement agents (Elase, Travase)	Enzymatic agents chemically break down necrotic tissue; ineffective unless moist environment is present.
2. physiological debridement using transparent dressings	Transparent dressings increase leukocyte migration and autolysis of necrotic tissue; cannot be used when clinical infection is present.
3. mechanical debridement with wet/dry gauze dressings	Wet/dry dressings provide nonselective debridement. Granulation tissue as well as necrotic tissue will be removed.
4. surgical consult for sharp debridement	Sharp debridement provides quick and effective removal of necrotic tissue.
Clean wound with appropriate cleanser at each dressing change. (See Table 42.2)	Wound cleansing promotes removal of wound debris and bacteria from wound surface.
Apply dressing as indicated by wound stage. Dressings may include gauze, hydrocolloid, hydrogels, calcium alginate, and transparent and polymeric foam. (See Table 42.3.)	Wound dressings absorb excess exudate, obliterate dead space, and keep the wound surface moist. Dead space hinders wound healing and predisposes the tissue to abscess formation. A moist wound surface enhances cellular migration and wound healing.

Nursing Interventions

Implement teaching plan which includes preventative measures, instructions in wound care, and signs and symptoms of infection.

Rationales

The patient/caregiver needs to be educated regarding the process of skin breakdown and preventative measures. Wound healing requires correct use of cleansing solution and dressing application.

DISCHARGE PLANNING/CONTINUITY OF CARE

- Observe patient/family/caregiver performing wound care.
- Provide with the necessary supplies and equipment prior to discharge and review plan for obtaining additional supplies.
- Arrange follow-up with local physician
- Consult a home health agency if continued nursing care or additional support services are needed.

Table 42.2 • Wound Cleansers

Cleanser	Use	Considerations
Normal saline	Cleanser recommended for all wounds	
Povidone-iodine	Effective in controlling bacterial growth in wounds	Inhibits and destroys macrophages and fibroblasts
Hydrogen peroxide	Provides mechanical cleansing via effervescent action	Destroys fibroblasts
Dankin's solution	Controls odor; is useful for staphylococcal and streptococcal infections; liquefies necrotic tissue	Destroys fibroblasts unless properly diluted
Acetic acid	Appropriate for *Pseudomonas* infections	Destroys fibroblasts when properly diluted

Table 42.3 • Wound Dressings

Dressing	Indications	Features
Gauze		
Impregnated • Aquaphor, Vaseline, Xerofoam	Most wound sites	Protects wounds
Not impregnated • Adaptic, Kling, Telfa	Most wound sites	Protects wounds
Transparent (film) Acuderm, OpSite, Tegaderm	Superficial abrasions, blisters, minor burns, donor sites, stage I or II pressure ulcers	Maintains physiological environment, provides bacterial barrier, transparent, conforms to wound, waterproof, provides autolytic debridement
Hydrogel Spenco, Vilgilon, Elastogel	Stage I, II, or III dermal ulcers, donor sites, second-degree burns, abrasions, blisters, lacerations	Maintains physiological environment when dressing is moist, relieves pain, translucent, provides debridement
Polymeric (foam) Epi-lock, Lyofoam, Allevyn	Stage I, II, or III pressure ulcers, dermal ulcers, donor sites, second-degree burns, abrasions, blisters, lacerations	Maintains physiological environment, reduces pain, provides autolytic debridement if dressing stays moist
Hydrocolloid • DuoDerm, Restore, Comfeel	Stage I, II, or III pressure ulcers, dermal ulcers, donor sites, second-degree burns, abrasion, blisters	Provides moist environment for wound healing, bacterial barrier, enhances autolytic debridement, waterproof, reduces pain
Calcium Alginate Kaltostat, Sorbsan	Moderate to heavy exudating wounds, control of minor bleeding, can be used in infected wounds, stage I, II, III, or IV pressure ulcers, venous stasis ulcers, diabetic ulcers, arterial ulcers, donor sites, dermal ulcers	Dressing absorbs exudate and forms a gel plug, creating a moist environment for wound healing, conforms to wound, provides autolytic debridement, painless to remove, provides hemostasis

Note: The dressing brands listed are only a sampling of the many products available. We do not endorse the use of any particular product.

REFERENCES

Braden, B. & Bergstrom N. (1989). Clinical utility of the Braden Scale for predicting pressure sore risk. *Decubitus, 2*(3), 44–51.

International Association of Enterostomal Therapy (IAET). (1989). Standards of care dermal wounds: pressure sores. IAET.

Krasner, D. (1990). *Chronic wound care—A clinical source book for health care professionals.* King of Prussia, PA: Health Management Publications.

Mertz, M. (1990). Intervention: Dressing effects on wound healing. In *New directions in wound healing.* ConvaTec, NJ: Squibb and Sons.

Pressure ulcers in adults: Prediction and prevention. (1992). Rockville, MD: U.S. Department of Health and Human Services, Public Health Service Agency for Health Care Policy and Research.

▼

INDEX

Note: Page numbers followed by t indicate tables;
numbers in italic indicate figures.

clinical manifestations, 209–210
defined, 209
discharge planning/continuity of
care, 216
indications, 209
infection with, 210–213
knowledge deficit, self-care
management, 213–214
laparoscopic, 209
pain with, in shoulder or neck
area, 215–216
open, 209
T-tube drainage with, 210–213
Cholecystitis, 209
Choledocholithotomy, 209
Cholelithiasis, 209
Circulation, impaired, signs of, with
breast reconstruction, 370
Circulatory system disease, signs of,
109
Clinical Laboratories Improvement
Act, 255
Cocoa butter, 389
Colitis, ulcerative, bowel resection for,
200
clinical/diagnostic findings, 201
Communication, verbal, impaired
laryngectomy and, 142–143
tracheostomy and, 177–179
Consciousness
altered, 273–278
airway clearance with, ineffective,
275–276
clinical/diagnostic findings, 274
clinical manifestations, 273–274
defined, 273
discharge planning/continuity of
care, 277
etiologies, 273
injury with, 276–277
intracranial adaptive capacity
with, decreased, 274–275
defined, 273
level of, assessment, with
craniotomy, 286
Continuity of care
acquired immunodeficiency
syndrome and, 405–406
altered consciousness and, 277
appendectomy and, 198–199
arteriography and, 78

bowel resection with ostomy and,
207–208
brain tumor and, 282
breast reconstruction and, 377
cardiac catheterization and, 86
cholecystectomy and, 216
corticosteroid therapy and, 250
craniotomy and, 288
diabetic patient discharged from
hospital and, 263
enteral nutrition and, 46
femoral-popliteal bypass and, 110
gastrectomy and, 221
hemodialysis and, 311
hysterectomy and, 349
insulin initiation and, 268
laryngectomy and, 148
lumbar puncture and, 294
mastectomy and, 390
nephrectomy and, 318
nephrostomy and, 326
Nissen fundoplication (hiatal
hernia repair) and, 225–226
pancreatic surgery (Whipple
procedure) and, 232
patient-controlled analgesia and,
66
peritoneal dialysis and, 334
pleural effusion and, 154
pneumonectomy and, 164
postoperative, 22, 94
prostatectomy and, 360
thoracotomy and, 191
thrombophlebitis/deep-vein
thrombosis and, 119–120
tracheostomy and, 181–182
venous access devices and, 34
ventral hernia repair and, 236
ventricular shunt and, 299
Contrast medium
allergy to, 75–76
with arteriogram, 71
diuretic effect, 83
Coping, ineffective
with brain tumor, 282
with gastrectomy, 220–221
with mastectomy, 380, 385–386
with pneumonectomy, 163
Coronary artery disease. *See* Artery,
coronary, disease of
Corticosteroid agents
complications with, 249

skin integrity with, impaired, 322–323

urinary elimination with, altered, 323–324

Nerve

facial (cranial nerve 7), surgical trauma to, swallowing and, impaired, 92

glossopharyngeal (cranial nerve 9), surgical trauma to, swallowing and, impaired, 92

hypoglossal (cranial nerve 12), surgical trauma to, swallowing and, impaired, 92

phrenic, referred pain of, 215

vagus (cranial nerve 10), surgical trauma to, swallowing and, impaired, 92

Neurological examination

with craniotomy, 286

postoperative, 91

preoperative, 91

with ventricular shunt, 299

Neutropenia, with acquired immunodeficiency syndrome, 400

Nicotine, adverse affects on healing, with breast reconstruction, 371

Nissen fundoplication (hiatal hernia repair), 222–226

defined, 222

gas-bloat syndrome with, 225

pain following, 224–225

Nitroglycerin

during cardiac catheterization, 81

for chest pain following cardiac catheterization, 85

Nonsteroidal anti-inflammatory agents, with venous access device implantation, 25

Norepinephrine, 251

Nutrition

altered

less than body requirements

enteral nutrition for, 37–41

with gastrectomy, 219–220

after laryngectomy, 139–141

with pancreatic surgery (Whipple procedure), 228–229

parenteral nutrition for, 48–52

with peritoneal dialysis, 332–333

with tracheostomy, 176–177

more than body requirements, with corticosteroid therapy, 245–246

enteral. *See* Enteral nutrition

parenteral. *See* Parenteral nutrition

O

Obesity, risk factor in cardiovascular disease, 109

Odor, ostomy, reduction of, 205

Osmotic agents, with craniotomy, 287

Osteoporosis, 243

Ostomy

appliance system for, 205, 206

care of, 204

wearing time, 207

care of, knowledge deficit, 205–207

complications with, 207

defined, 200

skin protection with, 206–207

types of, 203t

Oxygen

humidified, after laryngectomy, 137

with pneumonectomy, 158

Oxygen saturation measurement, after laryngectomy, 138

P

Pain

acquired immunodeficiency syndrome and, 397–398

appendectomy and, 196–197

appendicitis and, 196

bowel resection and, 201–203

breast reconstruction and, 367–368

sign of infection, 369

chest, following cardiac catheterization, nitroglycerin for, 85

chest tube and, 129

gastrectomy and, 218–219

headache, with lumbar puncture, 292

laryngectomy and, 141

lumbar puncture and, 292–293

mastectomy and, 380–381

Nissen fundoplication (hiatal hernia repair) and, 224–225

pancreatic surgery (Whipple procedure) and, 231–232

airway clearance with, ineffective, 169–171
altered nutrition—less than body requirements, 176–177
anxiety about respiratory distress, 167–169
clinical/diagnostic findings, 167
clinical manifestations, 166–167
cuffed, monitoring of, 172–173
defined, 166
discharge planning/continuity of care, 181–182
gas exchange with, impaired, 171–174
indications, 166
infection and, 174–176
insertion procedure, 168
knowledge deficit
  need for tracheostomy, 167–169
  self-care at home, 179–181
routine care procedure, 175–176, 180–181
suction procedure, 170–171
verbal communication with, impaired, 177–179
weaning from tube, 174
Traction, to urethral catheter, with prostatectomy, 356
Travase, 413
Trendelenburg position
  air emboli and, 53
  central venous catheter insertion and, 52
  vasovagal response to cardiac catheterization and, 83
Truss, 234
T tube. *See* Tube, T
Tube
  chest, 123–132
    anxiety with, 124–125
    clamping of, with pleural effusion, 152
    clinical/diagnostic findings, 124
    clinical manifestations, 123
    closed chest drainage system patency with, 126–128
    defined, 123
    discharge planning/continuity of care, 132
    impaired gas exchange/ineffective breathing pattern with, 125–128

indications for, 123
insertion procedure, 124–125
knowledge deficit—chest tube removal and home care, 131–132
pain with, 129
removal procedure, 131
stripping of, 127
with thoracotomy, 185
laryngectomy, 136
  care of, 145–146
  replacement, 138
  suctioning of, 135
  weaning from, 145
nasogastric
  with appendectomy, 197
  with bowel resection, 202
  after Nissen fundoplication (hiatal hernia repair), 224
nephrostomy. *See* Nephrostomy
T, with open cholecystectomy, 209
  dislodgment of, 212
  drainage color, 211
  infection with, 210–213
  obstruction, signs of, 211
  patency of, 211, 212
  removal of, 213
  self-care knowledge deficit, 213–216
tracheostomy, 136
  replacement, 138
  suctioning of, 135
  weaning from, 174
Tube feeding. *See* Enteral nutrition; Feeding tube
TURP (transurethral resection of prostate), 350, 358
Tylectomy, 378
Tylenol, 25

U

Ulcer, pressure, 407–416
  clinical/diagnostic findings, 408
  clinical manifestations, 407–408
  defined, 407
  discharge planning/continuity of care, 414
  etiologies, 407
  pressure-reducing/relieving devices for, 411t
  skin integrity with, impaired, 408–414